GRASSROOTS

GRASSROOTS

ORIGINAL PLAYS FROM ONTARIO COMMUNITY THEATRES

EDITED BY THEATRE ONTARIO

PLAYWRIGHTS CANADA PRESS

TORONTO · CANADA

Playwrights Canada Press
The Canadian Drama Publisher
215 Spadina Ave., Suite 230, Toronto, Ontario, Canada M5T 2C7
phone 416.703.0013 fax 416.408.3402
info@playwrightscanada.com • www.playwrightscanada.com

Playwrights Canada Press acknowledges the financial support of the Government of Canada through the Canada Book Fund and the Canada Council for the Arts, and the Province of Ontario through the Ontario Arts Council and the Ontario Media Development Corporation for our publishing activities.

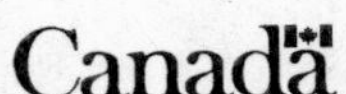

Canada Council for the Arts Conseil des Arts du Canada

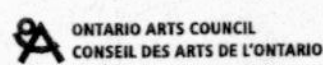

Cover image © iStockphoto.com / Jill Chen
Production Editor and Cover Design: Micheline Courtemanche

Library and Archives Canada Cataloguing in Publication

Grassroots : original plays from Ontario community theatres / edited by Theatre Ontario.

ISBN 978-0-88754-979-3

1. Canadian drama (English)--Ontario. 2. Canadian drama (English)--21st century. I. Theatre Ontario

PS8315.5.O5G73 2011 C812'.60809713 C2011-901760-1

First edition: May 2011
Printed and bound in Canada by AGMV Marquis, Montreal

Theatre Ontario is an umbrella organization
serving all practitioners of theatre in Ontario—professionals,
amateurs, educators, students, artists, technicians, directors,
producers, writers, and communities of all types.
In 2011, Theatre Ontario celebrates forty years of service to
Ontario. View our website at www.theatreontario.org
for a full range of services offered.

CONTENTS

INTRODUCTION
by Dennis Johnson iii

$38,000 FOR A FRIENDLY FACE
by Kristin Shepherd 1

HAMISH
by Michael Grant 83

NEVER SUCH INNOCENCE AGAIN
by J. Michael Fay 167

STAFF ROOM
by Joan Burrows 235

A YEAR IN EDNA'S KITCHEN
by Sandy Conrad 307

INTRODUCTION

Early in 2010, Theatre Ontario and Playwrights Canada Press published a call for submissions for a new anthology of plays. This would be the third collaboration between our two organizations. The first two books had been collections of one-act plays; this publication was to feature full-length plays originally produced by amateur community theatres in Ontario during the past decade. Thirty-eight submissions were received—each of them written by local playwrights rooted in the community where the play was produced.

Thirty-eight plays was definitely a surprise. And we discovered that number was only half of the world premieres produced by Ontario community theatres in that decade. Of the thirty-eight submissions there were sixteen comedies and seventeen dramas. The rest are a bit of both—everything from verse drama to murder mysteries to historical pageants to melodramas. Together, these plays gave me a picture of the world we live in and the issues at the heart of human experience—citizenship, death, old age, young love, family. Reading these thirty-eight plays was an amazing journey, but in each of them Ontario was present, emerging as a place that shares its thoughts, its hopes, and its fears and passions with similar places around the world.

The relationship between siblings and their dead or dying parent was just one such common theme. When a parent fades away, attention must be paid to certain changes. What is my place in the family? What will be my role when mother is gone? Who is my sister? Is she part of my future? Often photo albums, old letters, and even recipes force us to recall and restructure the past.

Sisterhood was connected to a wider theme—the family. A young urban professional, uprooted from her family, relocated to a new place, attempting to consolidate a new circle of friends—this is the stuff of love stories and comedy. A character who has lost his roots is in a storm of chaos, a life full of surprises both adventurous and funny. The unexpected is dramatic.

In many of the plays, the workplace emerged as the setting of choice. What better location for a murder mystery than a place where a police detective is completely ill at ease—an art gallery for example, or amongst a group of lawyers? The workplace is not a stable place. Jobs are under threat. Personal relationships interfere. Boredom creates subversive activity. Outsiders and newcomers feel out of place. Insecurity can be great fun for an author and an audience.

But secure roots can produce a different form of anxiety. A young person reared on the farm or emerging from years of idyllic summer-holiday routines can be suddenly faced with choices and changes forced upon him by the outside world. The city beckons. Farming methods change. New ideas make enemies. University can lift a young person into a new social level, rendering childhood friends obsolete. War challenges our principles and our patriotism. Marriage, especially for women, takes away independence—and dreams.

Most of these plays examine our roots (or lack of them) and how they affect our choices. Where do I belong? Urban or rural? This job or that one? There or here? Home or away? With this spouse or that one? Soldiering or protesting? These are plays about individuals who are exploring the changes that life forces upon them when values and events alter their world. The title *Grassroots* seemed to emerge inevitably from the content and concerns of these playwrights.

As a teacher reading these plays, I was acutely aware that publishing a script makes it available not just to a readership of theatre producers and directors. Teachers and students, as well, are constantly on the lookout for scenes and monologues useful for scene study, auditions, and classroom exploration. I know that the plays in this anthology will supply a wealth of useful material for schools and colleges, workshops and showcases.

What makes a play worthy of publication? Does it have to be produced by a professional company? Sometimes thoughtful and producible plays are overlooked in our culture. Thanks to Playwrights Canada Press, this initiative to publish an anthology of locally written plays will rescue a few of the worthies from a dusty filing cabinet. These exceptional plays will see future life on the stages of Ontario's theatres.

Dennis Johnson
Community Theatre Coordinator
Theatre Ontario

$38,000 FOR A FRIENDLY FACE

BY KRISTIN SHEPHERD

NOTES

The setting is a funeral home. Two sisters, strangers to each other for years, prepare for the funeral of their estranged and unloved mother. Their funeral director is a novice. Their florist is incompetent. The Last Supper Committee, whose frustration with each other reaches the boiling point, ending in a messy food fight, is catering the reception. Nobody (including the daughters) really knows or cares about the deceased. But somehow her funeral brings these vulnerable characters together and helps them carry on. In the end, it is stories that give life meaning—even if the facts get a bit mixed up. Out of tragedy comes comedy.

Kristin Shepherd, trained as a chiropractor, was an actor and community theatre board member for ten years before she turned her hand to writing a play for her theatre. The plays she was reading seemed to neglect life in a small town, and the lives of women over thirty. Kristin wanted to fill that void. "I think kindness is underrated, particularly kindness extended to difficult or unpleasant people. And although upper-case Kindness goes on through capital-P Philanthropy, lower-case kindness, the kind that shows up in sandwiches at funerals, makes the world go around every day."

Kristin credits June Keevil, the play's dramaturge and first director, with mentoring her through the lengthy process of rewriting. The play was first produced by the Gateway Theatre Guild in North Bay, Ontario, in 2005 and won the Samuel French Canadian Playwriting Contest in 2007.

$38,000 for a Friendly Face was first produced at Nipissing University Theatre, North Bay, Ontario, in May 2005. It was produced by Claire Powers and directed by June Keevil with the following cast, crew, and creative team:

Esther	Sally Macdonald
Marge	Nancy Van der Schee
Phyl (Phyllis)	Wendy Thoma
Matt	Bob Clout
Jane	Lorraine Conway
Annie	Kelly Maki
Alison	Kim Bean
Deliveries for Carmichael	Ashley Fricker, Helen Monette, Rick Lefebvre
Organist	Cathy Coleman

Stage Manager: Vicki Boyer
Assistant Stage Manager: Emily Miller
Set Designer: Dennis Geden
Costume Designer: Beth Jackson
Set Builder: Rob Ferron
Properties and Set Dressing: Nancy Davies
Lighting Design: Len Roy
Sound Design: Peter Nickle
Still Photography: Liz Lott
Scenic Painters: Nancy Davies, Claire Powers, Larry Lang
Makeup: Bunti Swanson
Hair: Jackie Larouche
Program / Graphic Design: Deb Sullivan
Front of House: Joyce Fell

CHARACTERS

MATT, new owner of the funeral home
JANE Bain, daughter of the deceased
ESTHER, head of the Last Supper Committee
MARGE, member of the Last Supper Committee
PHYL (Phyllis McLeary), member of the Last Supper Committee
ALISON, flower delivery person
ANNIE Bain, daughter of the deceased
Various delivery people (seven), who may be played on stage or off

SETTING

The play takes place at the back of the funeral home, with the makeshift kitchen on one side and the chapel on the other. The bathroom is downstage of the kitchen and the back hallway is downstage of the chapel.

ACT ONE

SCENE ONE

At the lectern, in the chapel. The delivery people can be played on stage or off.

Enter DELIVERY ONE.

MATT *(earnest, eager to help, and not particularly confident)* Yes. Thanks. It goes in the front. If you turn right at the end of the hall, then it's, let's see, the first door on your left.

Exit DELIVERY ONE.

Enter DELIVERY TWO.

DELIVERY TWO Carmichael?

MATT Hello. Yes, that goes in the front kitchen. If you go to the end of the hall and turn left it's the second door. *(Exit* DELIVERY TWO.*)* They're double. Double doors.

Enter DELIVERY THREE.

Are you with Carmichael or Bain?

DELIVERY THREE Carmichael.

MATT These go in the front chapel. Just go to the end of this hall, and turn right. The first door on your left is the chapel. *(Exit* DELIVERY THREE.*)* It has an oak pedestal, about this high, *(He indicates.)* just to the right of the door.

Exit DELIVERY THREE.

Enter DELIVERY FOUR.

In the front, I think. If you follow her, you'll be all right.

Exit DELIVERY FOUR.

Enter JANE, *who is ill at ease and awkward.*

In the front, just down the hall, turn… I'm sorry, what have you brought?

JANE Nothing. Why?

MATT You're here for Carmichael?

JANE No. Bain.

Enter DELIVERY FIVE.

DELIVERY FIVE Carmichael.

MATT *(to* DELIVERY FIVE*)* Oh. Just down the hall. Turn right at the end. Look for the…

Exit DELIVERY FIVE.

JANE I'm Jane. My mother is… *(She indicates "somewhere around here.")*

MATT Of course, Miss Bain. We spoke last night. Come with me.

Exit MATT *and* JANE.

SCENE TWO

In the kitchen.

Enter ESTHER, *dressed formally. Her hair has a ridiculously tight curl and she is wearing too much makeup. She puts a box of groceries on the counter and posts a menu for the day—sandwiches, squares, punch. She then exits to the bathroom to fix her hair and check her makeup.*

Enter MARGE, *whistling or humming. She reads the menu and stops whistling. She tears down the menu and leaves.*

Enter ESTHER, *who begins unpacking the groceries.*

Enter PHYL, *dressed in black.*

The women unpack the groceries and begin preparations throughout these scenes.

PHYL *(looking strangely at* ESTHER*)* Hi, Esther. Great hair.

ESTHER Thank you.

PHYL You know, there are boys out there on skateboards, practising goodness-knows-what on those cement steps. They're going to kill themselves, not to mention their total lack of respect for the people trying to get inside. Imagine trying to dodge sharp, flying weapons—really, aren't they, when your heart is bursting with grief. Bursting.

ESTHER I've got ham, tuna, and egg, on white and brown—well, sixty per cent whole wheat. I worked like a demon last night. Marge is bringing her date squares and the pineapple-carrot Jell-O.

PHYL Those squares are fabulous. So small, so perfect for the mourners. Nothing so big you'd choke on it.

ESTHER I told her to start cutting them smaller. They go further that way. No one'll take three. They'll take two, no matter how big, but they feel like pigs taking three.

PHYL Pigs, Esther? These people have lost loved ones.

ESTHER Well, they haven't lost their appetites, have they? And we do have a budget to keep in mind.

PHYL Are you all right today, Esther? You're not getting that chest cold, are you?

ESTHER No, I feel fine.

PHYL So did Susan's mother, and then, wham, it was pneumonia, and you know what happened then.

ESTHER I feel fine, Phyl. Do I not look fine?

PHYL You look very colourful. *(She pauses, seeing ESTHER's reaction.)* Like spring, I suppose.

ESTHER Good. That's what I was aiming for.

PHYL It's October.

ESTHER I know.

PHYL You never wear makeup.

ESTHER I know. I just thought, it's fall, and a bit of makeup makes sense in the fall, when you're paler. As a rule.

PHYL Well, as long as you're all right.

Enter MARGE with grocery bags.

MARGE Gorgeous day out there. What's with the hair, Esther?

PHYL Hi, Marge. It's a spring look she's aiming at.

MARGE Well, it's… stunning. And your makeup is… stunning.

ESTHER Thank you.

MARGE *(with an edge)* And Phyl, my friend, you look radiant again today.

PHYL Don't start, Marge.

MARGE Colour is good, Phyl.

PHYL It doesn't seem fair to the deceased.

ESTHER The deceased don't care.

PHYL Or to the loved ones. Imagine that burden of loss. The heaviness. The sheer…

MARGE We don't have to harp on it.

PHYL Would you rather we were tap dancing, Marge? Or skateboarding down cement steps with no helmets on? Last Supper Committee. That's the name.

MARGE God, they look fantastic out there. Don't you wish you could try it?

PHYL No, I don't, and I'm not sure what God has to do with it one way or another.

ESTHER Well, there are only three of us this morning, hardly enough to call us a committee. We'll have to work like fiends to get enough ready.

PHYL Things'll be different back here. No dishwasher, no ovens, no sinks. How'll we do this without a sink?

ESTHER We'll just do it, that's how. Carmichael is at four in the main chapel. It's being catered in the kitchen.

PHYL Catered? That sounds fancy.

ESTHER Beef stew, mashed potatoes, mixed vegetables—good luck keeping those from drying out for one hundred and eighty people. Anyway, Matt asked if I'd do the Bain food back here. We have a sink in the bathroom. We have cutlery that doesn't match. It'll be a smaller event. Nothing wrong with sandwiches and squares.

MARGE Who's doing the Carmichael food?

ESTHER Helen.

MARGE / PHYL Oh / Ah.

ESTHER He needed a caterer. It's just business.

PHYL / MARGE Just business. / Of course. / That's right. / Absolutely. / Oh yeah.

ESTHER I am completely organized.

PHYL Is it a 2:00 p.m. funeral?

ESTHER Two p.m., but not a funeral. Just a visitation, so we'll need the food for 2:00. And we don't know the numbers, so I'm prepared for forty. We'll make do if more show up.

PHYL Two p.m. is the best time. Gives you a chance to wake up, get your feet under you, but not so late in the day that you're too tired for your grief.

ESTHER / MARGE
Mmm.

PHYL And a visitation is a good choice. Of course, some need the full funeral, the reality of the casket, and that walk down the aisle…

MARGE Phyl…

ESTHER I should say something about the casket for this one.

Enter ALISON while ESTHER is speaking. ALISON is surly by nature.

PHYL What? What is it?

ALISON Flowers. *(No one hears her.)*

ESTHER It's just that…

PHYL Is it oak? I love oak. Oak is so dignified. Even if it's just veneer.

MARGE Phyl, for God's sake.

PHYL What? And do you really need to take the Lord's name in vain, here? Is it not oak, then?

ESTHER No, it isn't oak. That isn't it.

PHYL Is it maple? It wouldn't be mahogany.

MARGE Don't encourage her, Esther.

ESTHER Forget the casket, then.

PHYL We'll see it soon enough, I suppose.

MARGE We'll all see it soon enough.

ESTHER I made up the menu.

PHYL Where? *(The board is blank.)*

ESTHER Marge, that's you, isn't it?

MARGE I'm going to die if I have to eat crustless sandwiches one more time.

ESTHER Crusts are too messy.

PHYL You'd hardly want to choke on crusts while you're saying your final goodbyes.

ESTHER Crumbs all over the place.

MARGE I like the crusts.

PHYL Needing the Heimlich manoeuvre when you're so inconsolable that you're doubled over already.

ESTHER I'd spend my entire life vacuuming.

MARGE I like the crusts.

ALISON Flowers.

ESTHER / PHYL / MARGE
What?

ALISON Flower delivery. For Bain.

ESTHER Mrs. Bain is no longer with us, thank you very much, but you can bring them in here. You're two hours late.

ALISON Whatever.

Exit ALISON.

ESTHER She's a treat.

PHYL She looks a little pale.

MARGE I thought a salmon soufflé.

ESTHER Well, that's daft.

PHYL You know, Marge, last time you wanted a lobster mousse, and the time before last, for Susan's funeral, you wanted something else…

ESTHER It was asparagus and goat-cheese frittatas, for sixty-four guests. And even if you could do warm frittatas for sixty-four, which you cannot, asparagus and goat cheese, Marge? What were you thinking? Even if it tasted good, and that's hard to imagine, we'd be stuck with festering leftovers, and we have exactly no money for that.

MARGE *(firmly)* I thought a salmon soufflé.

ESTHER Marge, you have date squares.

MARGE No, actually, I don't.

ESTHER It says on my list that you have date squares and your Jell-O mould.

MARGE No mould.

ESTHER Pineapple-carrot. Look. It's number three on my list.

PHYL Your squares are so perfect, Marge. They're so small.

ESTHER Organization, Marge. I don't know what you're doing with this salmon thing…

MARGE Susan loved asparagus, that's all, and I like salmon.

PHYL Susan was such a wonderful cook.

MARGE She was a terrible cook.

PHYL What a thing to say!

ESTHER If we don't get a grip on things here, Matt'll never make it.

MARGE You're very devoted for a volunteer.

PHYL Not to mention that other thing.

ESTHER Thank you so much for not mentioning that other thing, Phyl. I am devoted to no one. I just hate to see him bungle this before he even gets it off the ground.

PHYL If you say so.

ESTHER I say so. Listen, I don't want to be picky about this, but we can't afford your soufflé, Marge.

MARGE I made it last night. With my own ingredients. No charge.

ESTHER *(offended)* I see. Well. I suppose we can make room on the menu. As long as nothing else changes. There's no time to make Jell-O now, of course, so that's a change of plans, but I may be able to find some date squares downtown. If I get a minute.

PHYL Sheila dropped off a vegetable tray this morning. I have it with me.

ESTHER Good, that's good. With her dip?

PHYL Two cups of ranch. I love that dip.

ESTHER Two cups, that'll be tight.

MARGE I also brought jalapeno pie.

ESTHER Jalapeno pie? That sounds hot!

MARGE It's October. Hot is good.

ESTHER You know, Marge, I have four-and-a-half scrapbooks of inexpensive and delicious snack foods to choose from. There's no reason to go out of your way to burn their tongues off.

MARGE Come on, Esther! Are you not completely sick of ordinary funerals?

ESTHER What? Would you prefer salmon funerals? A jalapeno funeral?

MARGE Yes, I would, as a matter of fact.

ESTHER This is completely ridiculous! And Matt is counting on me to… Phyl? Help me out here.

PHYL Well, people do need comforting food when they're grieving, Marge. I don't know how comforting the jalapeno would be in a dark time.

ESTHER Jesus Murphy, a dark time. Listen, Marge. If this costs us a penny…

MARGE Not a penny.

PHYL And who is Jesus Murphy, I'd like to know.

ESTHER Or if people laugh, or they're offended…

MARGE They won't be. They'll be thrilled to see something other than egg salad and tuna.

ESTHER Well my sandwiches are already made. Egg salad and tuna and ham. I spent hours on them last night, and I'm taking the crusts off. No discussion.

MARGE So we'll do both.

ESTHER I will not let this be a disaster.

MARGE My soufflé'll bring the house down.

PHYL I don't know. It sounds airy. Light.

ESTHER I can just imagine Helen…

PHYL A bit flaky, almost.

MARGE Helen'll be envious. There's no way she could do soufflés for one hundred and eighty.

ESTHER I'll have to reorganize everything. I want the sandwiches and squares up front.

MARGE Okay.

ESTHER I'm flexible.

MARGE You're going to hurt yourself, you're so flexible.

PHYL Do you remember Fran's last summer? Her husband brought in those mincemeat pies.

ESTHER No one ate them.

PHYL Mincemeat is more a Christmas thing. He didn't know any better. The grief! The agony!

ESTHER I may be too flexible.

MARGE I don't think so.

ESTHER I go with the flow.

MARGE You certainly do.

Enter ALISON.

ALISON Flowers.

MARGE What's your name?

ALISON Alison.

MARGE What's your favourite food, Alison?

ESTHER What are you doing, Marge? Why does that matter?

ALISON I don't like food.

ESTHER Good.

MARGE Well, if you did like food, what would you like?

ESTHER Marge.

ALISON Breakfast, maybe.

ESTHER Marge, it's a funeral.

MARGE It isn't a funeral, it's a visitation. What kind of breakfast?

ESTHER I'll take the flowers. You can think about breakfast while you bring in the rest. It might be faster if you bring in more than three at a time.

ALISON There are no more.

ESTHER What?

ALISON This is it.

ESTHER We have three flowers for the funeral?

PHYL Thank goodness it's not a funeral.

ESTHER Thundering mother of God. Three flowers?

PHYL Thundering what, Esther?

ESTHER I ordered three dozen. Did you make this mistake?

MARGE Esther, I saw buckets of flowers on the way in.

ESTHER Those are for Carmichael. There isn't one arrangement for Bain yet. Not one.

PHYL Oh, no. That isn't good.

MARGE It's early. There'll be flowers.

ALISON Cream of wheat, maybe.

ESTHER Mother of God, I don't believe it.

MARGE Do you spice it up at all?

PHYL That's Mary, Esther, and yes, she is the mother of God.

ALISON Why?

MARGE We're trying something new.

ALISON My brother used to put those stupid cinnamon hearts in mine.

ESTHER That is absurd.

MARGE I like it.

PHYL This is going to be some funeral.

MARGE It's not a funeral.

ESTHER Jesus Murphy.

PHYL Esther.

ESTHER Jesus Murphy.

ALISON Whatever.

SCENE THREE

In the chapel, which has seen better days.

MATT ushers JANE into the chapel. During the scene he rearranges the empty vases in an attempt to make the file boxes look more elegant/funereal.

MATT Here we are, Miss Bain.

JANE *(trying, at first, to find out how much MATT knows about her mother)* Thank you for taking care of things. My mother was... Well, you probably knew her.

MATT No, I didn't, really.

JANE Well, she was... It's important to me that her funeral is as... because she was so...

MATT Of course it will be. Although you understand there won't be an actual funeral for your mother.

JANE Yes, yes, you said that.

MATT She may have discussed it with you.

JANE We didn't... actually... get around to that.

MATT Some people don't like to burden their children.

JANE stares at him.

She chose a very simple event, really, and she didn't specify much about the details. Probably leaving that up to us to discuss together.

JANE All right then. I'm ready.

MATT These events really are more for the living than the not-living. The beyond-living. Unless, of course, we consider the question of an afterlife, in which case she's still... alive, but in a different... living... arrangement.

JANE Oh God!

MATT What?

JANE Still alive? Jesus.

MATT No, no. Don't even... I was on the wrong... Let's talk about our Celebration of Life. We'll put your pictures up—you brought pictures?

JANE A couple, but I don't think... they aren't exactly...

MATT Good, and perhaps, later, we'll discuss some stories, ones you'd like to share with friends at the celebration.

JANE *(horrified)* Friends?

MATT When will your family be joining us?

JANE Our family is… very, very small.

MATT How small?

JANE Extremely small.

MATT I see.

JANE You know, this place is so dark, it's a bit claustrophobic. I wonder if we could go… I mean, at some point… My mother… I really need to see that she's… permanently… settled in here. *(quietly)* Dead.

MATT Oh. Well, of course she is.

JANE So, she's here somewhere.

MATT She's right here. This is our Sunshine Chapel. This is where we'll be celebrating this afternoon.

JANE says nothing. She is not comforted by this room.

The Sunshine Chapel is perfectly suited, I think, to an intimate event.

JANE Intimate?

MATT Intimate. Less… impersonal. More… personal. Of course, if we need more room for the guests we can open that wall up into the hall. It's a retractable wall. It's new.

JANE So she'll be in here?

MATT She is here. Right over there. *(MATT points to two small boxes.)*

JANE Where?

MATT Right there.

JANE By the boxes?

MATT That's her casket. *(He sees JANE's reaction.)* Maybe I should open up that wall right now.

JANE Those are file boxes.

MATT It was her casket of choice, Miss Bain. She wanted something simple, something understated, something less ornate.

JANE My mother is in there?

MATT Yes, she is. She said the smaller interim resting place would suit her more than adequately.

JANE There are two boxes.

MATT Pardon?

JANE Why are there two boxes?

MATT I thought we might get to that. Tough to avoid it, really.

JANE Where is my mother, exactly? Which one is she in?

MATT It's a delicate situation. She's… she's in both.

JANE She's in both boxes?

MATT Both caskets, yes.

JANE I don't understand.

MATT Actually, for the most part, she's in the one on the left.

JANE Jesus!

MATT The smaller one.

JANE Jesus.

MATT It's just her hip in the other one.

JANE I'm going to throw up.

MATT Her right hip. The titanium. It doesn't cremate. She wanted a separate casket for it. A kind of co-casket. A matching casket.

JANE Matching caskets?

MATT Would you like some time with her?

JANE To do what?

MATT Well, I thought…

JANE Do you mean alone with her? With the boxes?

MATT The caskets, yes. You said you wanted to see that she was… permanently… settled in.

JANE *(urgently looking for an exit)* I don't think so.

MATT I'm sorry. Is there no one we can call for you?

JANE No. I'm fine.

MATT Anyone.

JANE There is no one.

ANNIE *(from offstage)* Janie?

MATT Who's that?

ANNIE Janie?

MATT There's someone calling your name.

JANE There is not.

Enter ANNIE *with a takeout coffee cup.*

ANNIE Janie! Hey, bit of a miracle finding you back here. There's some kind of huge party being set up out front.

MATT Hello.

ANNIE Hello back.

ANNIE *places her coffee cup on one of the coffins.* MATT *picks it up.*

MATT I'm Matt Watson, funeral director here.

ANNIE Annie Bain.

MATT Jane's…?

JANE / ANNIE No relation. / Sister.

MATT *(not understanding)* Oh, I see. All right, then. Why don't I check on the flowers? They're late.

JANE I hate flowers.

ANNIE Bit gloomy back here. 'Course it suits the occasion. Not to mention the star of the occasion. Do you have an ashtray?

MATT No, actually, there's no smoking in the building. Why don't I—

ANNIE *(interrupting)* It's a bit late for the second-hand to be hurting anyone in here, don't you think? *(*JANE *grabs her arm.)* Ow!

JANE Stop it.

MATT Good, then. Right.

Exit MATT.

ANNIE Let go of my cigarettes. Hey, it's good to see you. I'm not staying.

JANE You're what?

ANNIE Not staying.

JANE But you're here.

ANNIE Passing through.

JANE You're four hours from home.

ANNIE I needed some milk. What time's the funeral?

JANE She didn't want a funeral. It's a visitation. A gathering of friends.

ANNIE *(incredulously)* Friends?

JANE I know. You're not staying?

ANNIE Nope.

JANE You drove four hours to say hello?

ANNIE I needed two per cent.

JANE Two per cent.

ANNIE For the cottage.

JANE What cottage?

ANNIE Peter's cottage.

JANE Who's Peter?

ANNIE Just a guy.

JANE You're missing this... for a guy?

ANNIE I'll be heartbroken to miss the whole visitation thing, but yeah.

JANE Is he important, this guy?

ANNIE Don't know. I'll let you know if it turns into something.

JANE How old is he?

ANNIE He's sixty-two—or three, I guess.

JANE A toddler.

ANNIE You're still so quick to say the shittiest thing you can think of.

JANE Well, what can I say? I'm happy for you. Again.

ANNIE Anyway, she said to change the subject, I need the milk, and there's a Mac's on the main drag. They have good two per cent there. Hey. Where is the belle of the ball? The witch of the west.

JANE Keep your voice down.

ANNIE Is she freshening up somewhere?

JANE She's over there.

ANNIE Where?

JANE There.

ANNIE By the file boxes?

JANE Sort of.

ANNIE What do you mean, sort of?

JANE She's inside. I hope she's inside.

ANNIE She's smaller than I remember. But that's the thing about gravity, right? You just keep shrinking.

JANE Except there are two of her, now.

ANNIE How long's it been since you've heard from her? *(JANE doesn't answer.)* Not long enough, I guess. You know, if gravity still works after you're dead, they'll need to move her to a pizza box soon.

JANE God, I hope she's in there.

ANNIE Then we'll read about it at the checkout at Loblaws: "Unpleasant Dead Woman Found in Manilla Envelope."

JANE It's a casket.

ANNIE A manilla casket.

JANE It's her interim resting place.

ANNIE Manilla interim resting place.

JANE You're such an ass.

ANNIE And you're a fart sniffer. What's in the other box? Did she take a friend with her?

JANE No. It's all her.

ANNIE In both boxes?

JANE Yeah.

ANNIE What a freak.

JANE Why could she not pick one box? Then you'd know she was dead, wouldn't you, you'd know she was all in one place and done with.

ANNIE Half for you, half for… whoever else wants her. Maybe half of her'll be easier to live with. Especially dead.

JANE It isn't half. She's mostly in the one on the left. It's her hip in the one on the right.

ANNIE Holy shit. *(She begins to laugh.)*

JANE It's titanium. Leave it to her to start multiplying just when she's supposed to go away for good.

ANNIE *(with false sincerity)* You seem bothered by it, Janie.

JANE What I'm bothered by is you, Annie. *(pause)* I didn't mean that. So, did you take the weekend off?

ANNIE I took the foreseeable future off.

JANE You mean you quit?

ANNIE Yeah.

JANE Again.

ANNIE Yeah.

JANE Well, why change, right?

ANNIE It was Crappy Tire. Don't get your holier-than-thou going. Besides, I have other possibilities.

JANE *(sarcastically)* Yeah? What kind of possibilities?

ANNIE It's nothing. Forget it. Right, Mom?

JANE Quiet.

ANNIE Jane, Jane, Jane. I don't think you can hear much once you're in the ashtray.

JANE Jesus, Annie. Stop talking like that.

ANNIE What? It is basically an ashtray, isn't it? Or two ashtrays.

JANE You're such a jerk. *(Pause, indicates that she didn't mean that, either.)* Of course, there'll be no one here.

ANNIE I know.

JANE You should stay.

ANNIE I'll stay for coffee if you'd like, despite the fact that you don't seem to have changed since forever. We can do root canals on each other, stick forks in each others' eyes if you'd like. But I am not staying for any fond farewell with the cardboard boxes. I need milk. Excuse me.

Exit ANNIE.

SCENE FOUR

In the kitchen.

ALISON You can't make me stay.

ESTHER No, I can't. But I can call Rose's Roses and ask who was responsible for bringing three flowers.

ALISON Go ahead and call them. See if I care.

ESTHER You could be fired for a thing like that. A funeral with three flowers.

ALISON I said go ahead and call. You'd be doing me a favour.

PHYL Do you remember what Rose did for Gillian's? That huge wreath, all yellow roses.

MARGE She had lousy taste in men, that Gillian.

PHYL I don't think there was a dry eye in front of that wreath.

ALISON Most people think that three dozen roses stuffed in a wire form means you're gifted.

ESTHER She'll be sold out for Carmichael by now. My God, I won't be able to find dandelions for these people.

PHYL My gosh.

ALISON It's a stupid place to work. I was going to quit anyway.

PHYL Quit and do what?

ALISON Maybe start my own place.

ESTHER You've certainly got the personality for it.

ALISON You know, this is also a stupid place.

MARGE No it isn't. Esther's a little tense today, that's all.

PHYL A little dressed up. She might have a fever.

ESTHER I do not have a fever. And what do you mean by a little dressed up?

PHYL Do you want me to feel your forehead, Esther?

ESTHER No, Phyl, I do not. For God's sake.

PHYL No need to drag God into this.

MARGE Why don't you help us out, Alison? We're short today, and I could use your help with the cilantro.

ESTHER Cilantro?!

MARGE It's a garnish, Esther, it's nothing. *(to ALISON)* And you can tell us all about quitting, and cream of wheat, with the hearts. What do you say?

ESTHER Marge, we are not doing porridge.

MARGE Are you from around here, Alison?

ALISON Mason.

MARGE But you live here now?

ALISON I do.

PHYL Married?

ALISON doesn't respond.

MARGE No need to tell us everything right off the bat. Here, scissors are better for that.

As soon as ALISON *finishes cutting the cilantro, she'll begin cutting flowers out of the paper in which she brought the flowers, and whatever paper she can find after that. Her cutting will go on through most of Act One.*

ESTHER Three flowers.

MARGE Esther, people will bring more.

ESTHER But the daughter'll be here by now. It'll look like nobody loves anyone in there.

MARGE Esther?

ESTHER Yes, Marge.

MARGE Leave it alone, all right?

ESTHER Leave it alone, she says.

PHYL I love these little sandwiches.

MARGE Who was she, Mrs. Bain? Was she that short woman with the little dog on Main West?

PHYL It's a cairn terrier, that dog. I think it's diabetic.

ESTHER No, that's Nora Stewart. She moved into town with her dog after her husband… You know. What an idiot.

PHYL He was a good man!

MARGE Phyl, he set fire to your brother's barn. He was crazy.

ESTHER He was a little off, Phyl. Mrs. Bain lived on Ferguson, right by the piano teacher's place.

MARGE Which one?

ESTHER You know that little bungalow with the yellow carport?

PHYL Why a carport on that corner and not a garage, I don't know. Pretty risky.

ESTHER Exactly. The north wind'll bury a car in there, but she was a Southerner. Must not have known any better.

MARGE Southerner from where?

ESTHER The City.

MARGE / PHYL Ahhh / Ohh.

MARGE How old was she?

ESTHER Mid-sixties, maybe. There's a daughter from out of town.

PHYL Her husband?

ESTHER Matt says no husband.

PHYL Poor thing. Church?

ESTHER None.

PHYL Southerner. No church. No husband.

MARGE *(sarcastically)* How did she survive?

ESTHER Never at bingo. I'd have seen her at the door.

PHYL Legion?

ESTHER No. What about the pool?

MARGE I never saw her.

PHYL How can nobody know her? How long did she live here?

ESTHER Ten years anyway, Matt said.

PHYL She couldn't have spent all that time alone.

ESTHER She came through the store often enough. She wasn't nice. Cold, standoffish. Some people have a way.

PHYL Were you friendly back?

ESTHER Not especially.

ALISON Surprise.

ESTHER It's hard to be friendly to rude people. *(to ALISON)* Here. Cut this tag off for me. Please.

PHYL What did she buy?

ESTHER She liked that trail mix, the kind with the dried cranberries. That's the most expensive mix in stock, except at Christmas. And Earl Grey tea. And imported shortbread. Who'd buy cookies that have been around long enough to be shipped from overseas, I don't know, and pay through the teeth for them.

PHYL Imported shortbread.

ESTHER I'm not on cash very often, I don't remember what else.

PHYL How did she die?

ESTHER I don't know.

PHYL Someone must know.

ESTHER Matt'll know. He's not saying.

PHYL Maybe it was an aneurysm.

ESTHER Matt didn't say.

PHYL Barb's aunt had an aneurysm. Happened like that. She smacked her head against the shower wall, broke five tiles—smashed them to pieces the size of loonies—and never made it out of the tub.

ALISON Gross.

MARGE Phyl, does it ever occur to you that you might be kind of obsessed with all of this?

ESTHER Marge.

PHYL I don't know what you're talking about. I am not obsessed. Who made her funeral arrangements?

ESTHER She did. Last winter.

PHYL Some people know their time is near. It gives them time to prepare for the end. That's lucky.

MARGE Like winning the 6/49.

ESTHER Mrs. Bain was perfect that way. Came in early, made her choices. Paid in full.

PHYL Paid in full?

ESTHER Now that's lucky. Phyl, is that it for the squares?

PHYL Paid in full? I thought she didn't have much money.

ESTHER That cranberry trail mix? She had money. I'll have to cut them in half again. We'll spread them out.

PHYL You know, I do know one little thing about the deceased.

ESTHER What's that?

PHYL From the library. I suppose confidentiality doesn't matter so much now that she's gone to her peaceful resting ground. Well, and now that I'm leaving.

MARGE Not yet, you're not.

PHYL Actually, I am.

MARGE You have a year left.

PHYL No.

MARGE Phyl? What are you talking about?

PHYL It's nothing.

ESTHER What about Mrs. Bain?

PHYL Bronwyn, her name was Bronwyn Bain!

ESTHER I thought you didn't know her.

MARGE You never mentioned knowing her.

PHYL She was a patron at the library. And we had a kind of… well, a kind of relationship, I suppose. Not a friendship, really, but a… an understanding. Perhaps.

ESTHER What the heck does that mean? An understanding?

MARGE A relationship of some kind?

ESTHER Perhaps?

PHYL She didn't give a hoot about what anyone thought. As though she didn't need another soul in this world.

ESTHER As though she was better than the rest of us.

PHYL Maybe. That's what the others thought. But she was so fierce about it. I'd like to be fierce.

MARGE What was this understanding?

ESTHER This relationship of some kind?

ALISON Perhaps.

ESTHER *(snapping)* Alison, we can't get a word in edgewise.

ALISON Excuse me for breathing.

MARGE Honey, she's joking. Aren't you, Esther?

ESTHER Yes, I'm joking. What relationship?

PHYL Mrs. Bain—Bronwyn—died with $377 outstanding in overdue fines.

ESTHER Three hundred and seventy-seven dollars? How many books did she take out?

PHYL Only two at a time. It was more the number of times she took books out. Two books each time. Thirty-four times. Sixty-eight books in total.

MARGE You can't do that. Ray tries to do that 'cause he can't be bothered to look under the bed for his old books, but they won't give him any new ones till he brings them back. It's the only exercise he gets, reaching under the bed.

ESTHER And Matt! I find his books lying all over the place here. He'd owe millions if it weren't for me. I know the rules. You have to pay, or no more books.

PHYL And there was our relationship, I guess. She'd come in without her books, and bring two new ones to the counter. Always to me, as far as I know. I'd explain the overdue policy and she'd thank me, with this grim mouth and one eyebrow hiked way up. I can't even do that thing with one eyebrow. And I just did it, checked two more out.

ALISON I'll bet you can catch a bit of hell for that.

PHYL Yes, you can.

ESTHER She probably had a nice little library at home by the end.

MARGE What kind of trouble did they give you, Phyl?

PHYL They called it an unexpected disappointment, an unfortunate ending to a career. They moved my retirement date up.

ALISON They canned you?

PHYL No, they didn't fire me, exactly.

MARGE When are you finished?

PHYL Yesterday. At three.

MARGE Oh, Phyl.

ESTHER Phyl.

PHYL You know, I went on checking out books to Mrs. Bain, even after I'd been reprimanded. Seven more times. Fourteen books.

ALISON That is great.

ESTHER What?

PHYL Do you think so?

ESTHER What that is is complete disregard for your own rules.

MARGE Oh, Phyl.

ESTHER I smell onions. It's not right to have onions at a funeral.

MARGE It isn't a funeral. Don't worry about it, Esther.

ESTHER Don't worry about it, she says.

MARGE Jalapenos and onions. They're fantastic for you.

PHYL I wonder what a woman like that would choose for her own funeral service?

ESTHER I'm going to say one more thing about Mrs. Bain.

MARGE My God, did everyone know her?

PHYL What about her?

ESTHER I'm just going to say it and then we'll leave it, I don't want to discuss it at all. And I don't want any strange looks in front of the family or friends.

PHYL It's open casket, isn't it? I love open casket.

ALISON That's morbid.

PHYL I'll be here for this one.

ESTHER You're here for every one.

MARGE I may stay for this one, too.

ESTHER / PHYL What?

MARGE Is there something wrong with that?

ESTHER No.

PHYL No.

ESTHER I might as well tell you, then. It isn't open casket.

MARGE Good.

PHYL That's a shame. Rachel had open casket. She looked fantastic, except, you know, I never saw Rachel's mouth closed while she was alive—you know how she loved to talk—so it was a little unnatural, I thought, seeing her in that casket, with her lips pressed together.

ESTHER Well, there's no more mouth for Mrs. Bain, open or closed.

MARGE God Almighty.

ALISON Shit.

PHYL There's no need... No more mouth? What do you mean, no more mouth?

ESTHER She was cremated.

PHYL Before the service? Susan did that, too. They put her in that gorgeous red dress of hers, that washable silk she bought for their thirtieth—do you remember it, Esther? She looked so happy in it—and then they cremated her, dress and all.

MARGE Don't start, Phyl.

PHYL Red pumps and all.

MARGE Here we go.

PHYL Mouth and all.

ALISON Gross.

ESTHER Here's the thing. She's in two boxes.

PHYL / MARGE What?

ESTHER Mrs. Bain. She's in two little caskets.

PHYL Two caskets?

ALISON Holy shit.

MARGE It's about time.

PHYL What do you mean, about time?

ESTHER Not a word more, now. We're done with it.

ALISON Maybe one is full of books.

ESTHER We will not discuss it. Let's get to work.

PHYL I hope they weren't cremated. That'd be illegal, burning library books. Two boxes? I've never heard of that.

ESTHER Let's just leave it alone.

PHYL Was she a huge woman?

MARGE This is good.

ESTHER I said no discussion.

PHYL Maybe some people just turn into more ash than others. My Uncle Lanny needed an extra-large urn. He was a gem of a man, but he was dense.

ESTHER Enough! God Almighty.

PHYL No need to toss the Almighty around, Esther. Two caskets!

This conversation fades out.

SCENE FIVE

In the chapel. JANE *is sorting through pictures.*

Enter MATT, *with a lamp and a purse. From time to time he shifts the two caskets in an attempt to make them look like one entity.*

MATT Excuse me, Miss Bain. I thought I'd just add a little light. So it won't feel so claustrophobic. So gloomy. Because this should really be a happy occasion. *(*JANE *does not look happy.)* Well, a time of contemplation and reflection, certainly, but with some… happy… *(He plugs in the lamp, turns it on.)* under… tones. How are the pictures coming?

JANE They're fine.

MATT Why don't we have a look together?

JANE No.

MATT I can do that, if you like.

JANE No, they're no good, they're… overexposed. Besides, there'll be nobody… I like your purse.

MATT Actually, it isn't mine.

JANE It's a great colour on you.

MATT It's your mother's.

JANE No, I don't think so.

MATT It is. I thought you might…

JANE All right, all right, that's enough. Maybe it is hers.

MATT It is. She asked me to find it at her house after her… passing.

JANE Did she say anything…

MATT Anything…?

JANE Anything, oh, I don't know, at all, about anything.

MATT She said she'd leave the final financial arrangements. For today's… events here.

JANE Oh, okay.

MATT But that's not… I thought you might like something personal. There are a few things inside.

JANE *(staring, horrified, at the purse)* Sure. That's just great.

MATT I have some thoughts on your mother's celebration.

JANE Oh.

MATT I mentioned earlier that we might have family and friends share stories. Memories, if you will, of your mother's life. They say that sharing helps everyone in times of grief.

JANE Do they say that?

MATT If we can get your stories first, I'll be able to write a warmer, and perhaps a more meaningful, obituary for this afternoon's guests.

JANE Guests?

MATT If you're uncomfortable, speaking in front of people, you could both share a few stories with me, and I could relate them to the others. Whatever makes you comfortable.

JANE Mr.…

MATT Watson. They say that sharing grief helps to…

JANE My sister's gone. To get milk. Two per cent. She might not be back.

MATT She'll be back in time for the visitation.

JANE No…

MATT She can share then if she'd like. Or not. There's no pressure around this.

JANE Well, it's interesting that you say that, because it feels like an awful lot of pressure. Here. *(She hands him the pictures.)*

MATT You know, I think these will be just… *(He looks through the pictures, holding them up. The father's head is cut out of each picture.)* Well, isn't that something.

JANE The holes are my dad. My mother was very good with scissors.

MATT Remarkable.

JANE She was extremely crafty.

MATT What I meant was…

JANE She could cut just about anything. With scissors, with an X-acto knife. Steak knife, potato peeler, she could really cut.

MATT They say time is a great healer.

JANE Who says that?

MATT What?

JANE Who says that about time?

MATT *(pause)* They do.

JANE *(angrily)* Well that's really good to know, isn't it, because they must know what they're talking about. I'm sorry. It was nice outside this morning.

MATT October is a good month.

JANE Yeah.

MATT The colours.

JANE Yeah.

MATT There are fewer crimes committed in October, on average.

JANE Crimes?

MATT Yes, I think people are just happier in the cooler weather. Even the criminals.

JANE Are you worried I'm a criminal?

MATT No!

JANE Well, who are the criminals?

MATT I'm sorry, I've got that wrong. Wrong direction altogether.

JANE I can't figure out what's happening here. With all of this. I don't know what to do.

MATT Well, let's look for one good thing, one comforting thing, for instance, something…

JANE Comforting? You know, if I wanted comfort, I'd go home.

MATT I suppose so.

JANE I mean, what's comfortable about this? Would you be here if you were looking for comfort?

MATT I… I haven't thought about that. Maybe I haven't got that right, that part.

JANE I think my mother might stay put, but wouldn't the rest of us just go home?

MATT Yes, I suppose so.

JANE Unless, of course, home is no good either. Then there isn't much of a choice.

MATT No. You're right.

JANE So, I'll stay.

MATT Yes.

JANE That's excellent advice.

MATT Well.

JANE Thanks for your help.

MATT That's… that's what I'm here for.

SCENE SIX

In the kitchen.

ESTHER My mother used to say that the secret to a great marriage was shift work. Decades and decades of shift work.

PHYL My mother said it was frying onions. Have onions frying when he came in the door at night.

ALISON Unbelievable.

PHYL She had a cast-iron frying pan that weighed more than she did.

ESTHER Marriage is ridiculous. A waste of valuable time.

MARGE So sentimental, our Esther.

PHYL What about you, Alison?

ESTHER Are you married?

ALISON doesn't respond.

MARGE You don't have to answer that.

PHYL Kids?

MARGE No need to answer that, either.

ESTHER And what are you, Marge? Her lawyer?

ALISON *(to PHYL)* Are you married?

PHYL Well…

ESTHER Phyl's husband…

PHYL Yes, I am married.

ESTHER *(interrupting)* That's enough of that. Coffee time. It's a miracle we ever get any food done for these things.

MARGE But we do.

ESTHER Alison, there's a kettle behind you. Right there. You owe me a few favours, I'd say.

ALISON I do not owe you favours.

ESTHER Three favours, in fact. Or maybe three dozen. Come on. Help me with the coffee. After that you can go home.

ALISON *(She grabs the kettle.)* This is such a sick way to spend a morning.

ESTHER Alison?

ALISON I'm coming.

ESTHER Phyl, Marge, you two keep working. We're behind by my watch.

MARGE We're always behind by your watch.

ESTHER And I'm always right. We'll be back.

Exit ESTHER and ALISON.

MARGE *(sitting, tired)* God, she's a tyrant.

PHYL Gosh. Would you like a sandwich, Marge?

MARGE No. No sandwiches, thanks.

PHYL What, are you done with sandwiches?

MARGE Yes, I am. I am done with tiny sandwiches and I am bored to death with Jell-O salads.

PHYL *(pause)* It's a gorgeous day out. I'll bet Ray's doing leaves today.

MARGE He is.

PHYL And when does Julie's gang arrive?

MARGE Tomorrow.

PHYL He'll be excited, then. *(pause)* Two caskets. That's a new one. Do you mind if I have a sandwich? I like the triangles. Maybe a chocolate-coconut square, too.

MARGE Knock yourself out.

PHYL *(pause)* Two caskets. Would she have her body in one and all her worldly possessions in the other, do you think?

MARGE I can't stand the way we cut those squares into such small bits.

PHYL Or maybe some parts of herself in one and some in the other.

MARGE So small you can hardly taste them.

PHYL I'd put my thin parts in one and my fat parts in the other.

MARGE So small you can hardly breathe.

PHYL Except for that plantar wart on my left foot. I'd give that a box of its own.

MARGE And what is it with Jell-O? Someone gets sick again, and dies, and we break out the Jell-O mould.

PHYL You know plantar warts, they last forever. They'll have to bury it alive. So that's three boxes for me.

MARGE You know, we watch someone die and then we make Jell-O. And then, right away, someone else gets sick and dies and we make Jell-O again.

PHYL 'Course, that third box would be a pretty small one, with just the wart. Those roots go way in, though. They'd take up a bit of room. *(pause)* Marge?

MARGE What if making the Jell-O is what makes the next person get sick and die? Maybe then we should stop making Jell-O. We should stop cutting the crusts off the goddamned sandwiches.

PHYL Three boxes.

MARGE We should…

PHYL Me, my fat, and my wart.

MARGE I saw that bozo at the clinic on Thursday.

PHYL Don't.

MARGE I was supposed to go a year this time, but I've been tired.

PHYL You need more naps. You don't take naps.

MARGE It's funny. You're tired, and you can never know, anymore, whether it's back again or whether you just need to get to bed earlier.

PHYL You need sleep. And you need to eat.

MARGE I want to talk to you about something.

PHYL That's what you need. A snack and a nap.

MARGE In case it's more—

PHYL *(cutting her off)* Be quiet.

MARGE Phyl.

PHYL No. You be quiet. You were fine last time, right? You've been swimming. You're fine.

MARGE Phyl, I don't feel right.

PHYL Stop it.

MARGE Listen.

PHYL No. I don't want to hear that. If you set your mind to it, you'll be all right. You told me that. I have to leave.

MARGE For God's sake, Phyl.

PHYL Do not bring God into this. I have to leave.

MARGE Please stay.

PHYL This is not hard. You're fine. I'll just go downtown, right now, and get the date squares, and we'll cut them up when I get back. We'll cut them up into smaller squares. Everything'll be fine. *(Exit* PHYL.*)*

MARGE Phyl?

SCENE SEVEN

In the bathroom. ALISON *is filling the kettle.*

ESTHER Fill it with cold, right up to the top. I'll make a cup for Matt. That's enough water.

ALISON You said to the top.

ESTHER That's close enough.

ALISON You're not easy to get along with.

ESTHER Well, thank God for you being Miss Congeniality, then. I'm wearing too much makeup.

ALISON You got that right.

ESTHER I knew it. It's ridiculous.

ALISON Don't take it all off. Just do this with your fingers. Not like that. Don't rub. Blend. Like this. Here. I'll do it. *(ALISON changes ESTHER's makeup.)*

ESTHER I wanted to look like spring.

ALISON You look like a crackhead.

ESTHER Watch my eyes. Are your hands clean? The last thing I need is infected eyes.

ALISON Like you don't look totally infected with all that makeup on. Stay still. Who's Matt?

ESTHER Well, he's… He owns this place. Can you lighten up a touch with your blending? I'm going to lose an eye.

ALISON You might look better with one eye.

ESTHER He was a cop here until last year. Not tough enough, but… Anyway, the OPP moved in a few years ago and just took right over. And then, at a town-council meeting two years ago, there was a vote, and they just let Matt go. The mayor, Phyl's fathead cousin-in-law-and-no-fault-of-Phyl's, said he was sorry, but they couldn't justify paying $38,000 for a friendly face, with the OPP only a phone call away.

ALISON So.

ESTHER *(ESTHER looks for cups, paper towels, etc., under the sink.)* So. With one bad vote and a majority this big, *(holds her finger and thumb up, indicating a narrow margin)* Matt's career was over. It was a stupid decision. So, we just scraped him off the floor—that took a bit of doing—and he took over here when Al Stinson retired in May.

ALISON What do you mean it took a bit of doing?

ESTHER Well, how would you feel if you were fired, basically, by your own town council? So, I help out here a bit with the Last Suppers.

ALISON Why do you help?

ESTHER Well, it's the decent thing to do. To help your neighbour.

ALISON Is he your neighbour?

ESTHER *(raising her voice)* No, I don't mean the neighbour that lives beside you.

ALISON You mean the one that doesn't?

ESTHER Yes. I mean the one that doesn't.

ALISON You don't have to yell. I can hear you.

ESTHER You're so... You bring three flowers. You think your neighbour is the person who lives beside you. He was never my neighbour.

ALISON All right. Shit.

ESTHER He was my husband.

ALISON What?

ESTHER You heard me.

ALISON Shit.

ESTHER My hair looks foolish.

ALISON Wait. *(ALISON takes ESTHER's hands and does her hair.)* Don't touch it, you'll make it worse.

ESTHER I don't know what happened. It started with small things. His pauses. The way he considered everything to death. He didn't boil an egg without thinking about it for an hour. I could see myself sitting at that kitchen table during those pauses, going nowhere together for another forty years and then dying, and not even knowing I was dead for a while, 'cause there wouldn't be any difference. Then all of it—the blue bows on the wallpaper in the kitchen—and I picked that wallpaper—the sound of the neighbour's basset hound barking every time I turned the outside lights on—I just wanted to kick that dog in the head. I wanted to scream all the time. And one day it happened.

ALISON You kicked the dog.

ESTHER No, I didn't kick the dog! You don't kick dogs. I just blew. I told him I had to leave. His face looked so small. He has a small head, and it looked smaller than ever right then. I took a suitcase to this one-bedroom above the Mike's Mart on Stanley. Everything in that place, even the toaster, was greasy on your fingers. And the cigarette smoke...

Three days after I left, he called and asked would I like to go for coffee. I said, "I won't come back," and he said, "I know, it's just coffee." So, we met at the Tim's downtown. He was waiting at one of those tables for four in that corner by the bathrooms. With a coffee for me. Medium, just milk. Same thing the next day. We've had coffee almost every morning since. Six years.

ALISON Really?

ESTHER After a year or so, I asked him who in their right mind would ask me out three days after I'd done that? I mean, was he not hurt, or angry? And he said, oh, sure, he was all of that. But you can only be angry for so long, he said.

ALISON No way.

ESTHER How can a man like that survive without neighbours, without someone's help?

ALISON *(reaching for the cups)* Gimme those.

ESTHER So, I know I'm difficult to get along with.

ALISON I've met worse. Not many, but I've met worse.

SCENE EIGHT

In the chapel.

Enter ANNIE.

ANNIE Four-fifty for a litre of two per cent, I can't believe it. Now that is whacked!

JANE No one's going to come to this thing.

ANNIE She's a closed box, Janie. In fact, of course, she's two closed boxes. I need a smoke.

JANE No, you do not. Listen, Matt, the funeral guy, he wants stories for this… this not-funeral thing. Warm, funny stories.

ANNIE You know, maybe Mom didn't make it to the warm phase of her life. Maybe if she'd lived into her eighties she'd have become funny. Not likely. Forgiving. Not likely.

JANE He said we should look through her purse.

ANNIE Jesus, is that her purse? She probably had her hands on that.

JANE He said we'd like it because it's something personal.

ANNIE Her fingerprints'll be all over it.

JANE You know, she is multiplying. She's in three places, now.

ANNIE On the other hand, maybe there'll be cash in there.

ANNIE *takes the purse.*

JANE Don't touch it.

ANNIE Or smokes. *(She reaches in.)* Or Kleenex. Ooo, that's personal. *(finding a cellphone)* Hey.

JANE A cellphone.

ANNIE She must have lost my number. And yours.

JANE Do you think her voice is in there somewhere?

ANNIE That's creepy. Do you want it?

JANE No.

JANE puts the phone in the bag.

ANNIE Look, it's a little key. Looks like a key to a diary. Or a very small heart.

JANE What else?

ANNIE Paper. Two sheets. They'll be notes saying, "Gosh, you two were the best."

JANE *(taking the papers)* It's weird to see her writing.

ANNIE Or receipts for two caskets and a funeral with no guests.

JANE It might be private or something.

ANNIE What do you think, Mom? Do you mind? Woop, still not talking to us. Go ahead.

JANE *(She puts her glasses on.)* "Coffee cream. Two Ida Reds."

ANNIE When did you get the glasses?

JANE Last year.

ANNIE You look like her.

JANE No, I don't. "Toothpaste."

ANNIE Tough to get a really personal picture of her life from toothpaste.

JANE Then "library."

ANNIE Library what?

JANE It just says "library."

ANNIE Hey. Here's a lipstick. Same colour as always. Looks just like yours.

JANE Does not.

ANNIE Look, it's the same colour.

JANE Mine isn't as dark.

ANNIE Maybe you're losing your colour vision, too.

JANE Or maybe you're demented. This is a totally different colour.

ANNIE Okay, stink bomb.

JANE Bloodsucker fish. Do you remember anything about her?

ANNIE I remember that winter coat, you know, the black one, from the…

JANE The one with the hood and the hairy arms…

ANNIE Yeah, and she'd do it up and she'd look just like that, you know that song…

ANNIE begins to laugh.

To the tune of "Itsy Bitsy Spider," JANE sings "Extremely Small Tarantula Climbed Up The Bedroom Wall." JANE is deadly serious throughout the singing. ANNIE joins in, less seriously.

JANE And she'd pull on her hood to flatten the…

ANNIE But she looked even worse then.

JANE Which made you laugh.

ANNIE Which made her mad.

JANE She hated kids' songs. Why would you hate kids' songs?

ANNIE Who cares? It was four million years ago.

JANE I loved that song.

ANNIE So, that's good, right? Is that the kind of story your funeral director is looking for?

JANE You're a jerk.

ANNIE Of course I am. And you're a snotlicker. Give me the other paper.

JANE passes the second note to ANNIE.

JANE What?

ANNIE "Daisies." Three of them. Look. I love daisies. What's that beside them?

JANE *(taking the paper)* I hate flowers.

ANNIE You do not.

JANE They stink. "October third. October tenth."

JANE freezes.

ANNIE *(taking the paper back)* "October seventeenth." One daisy for each. That's just last week, the seventeenth. Which day?

JANE I don't know. Who cares?

ANNIE It was Sunday.

JANE It might be some other year, for all we know. Jeez, you know, I left my… I left something in the car.

JANE gets up to leave.

ANNIE Last Sunday, the seventeenth. That was the day I quit. So, they're all Sundays, right? The third, the tenth, the seventeenth.

JANE I don't know, and so what, anyway? It doesn't tell us anything.

ANNIE Maybe she was going to church. Not likely.

JANE Let's get a coffee. Or lunch. Or dinner.

JANE grabs the note back and crumples it.

ANNIE Wait. Don't throw it out. You were the one who mentioned the purse, for Christ's sake.

JANE Take it, then.

JANE throws it back at ANNIE.

ANNIE And why daisies, do you think? Maybe she knew she'd be pushing them up soon.

JANE You are disgusting.

ANNIE She used to call Gran on Sundays, remember? They'd yack for an hour, the two of them. Sundays at ten. She said it was better than church.

JANE *(stopping in her tracks)* What?

ANNIE I don't know what that'd have to do with daisies, though. Mom said it took her a year after Gran died to stop picking up the phone on Sundays.

JANE I don't remember that.

ANNIE Will it take us years to stop calling? Woop, guess we're over that part already, aren't we, Mom?

JANE Be quiet.

ANNIE Quiet yourself. If she'd called me once in the last ten years, I'd keep my voice down.

JANE Please, just shut up. She's right there.

ANNIE All right, all right. Something warm, all right.

JANE Just shut up!

ANNIE Responsible sister has nervous breakdown at mother's funeral. Younger sister, jerk, apologizes.

JANE Shut up!

ANNIE It's okay, Janie. It's okay.

SCENE NINE

At the lectern.

Enter DELIVERY SIX.

DELIVERY SIX Carmichael.

MATT Thank you. That looks great. If you'll just…

ESTHER That way. Turn left. *(Exit* DELIVERY SIX.*)* Carmichael looks huge.

MATT Bigger than we thought, but it seems to be running well.

ESTHER It's hard to keep food hot as the numbers go up.

MATT Helen seems to think it'll be all right. *(He sees* ESTHER*'s reaction.)* 'Course what does she know? No. Have you seen any flowers for Bain?

ESTHER Not yet.

MATT How are things in the back?

ESTHER Tip-top. We're almost ready to go. It was nothing. I could have done both. Easily.

MATT Well. I'll get back to the front, then. I'll be with the Carmichaels if anyone needs me.

ESTHER I won't need you. Everything is fine back there.

MATT You look different today, Esther. Did you do something with your hair?

ESTHER No, just the same old thing. You know, Matt, I've been thinking of cutting back on Dutchies. They can't be good for you. Do you even like Dutchies?

MATT I do. I like them.

ESTHER But those crullers, they're terrible. That saturated fat, you know…

MATT I like the crullers.

ESTHER Well, that's good. And they taste good, I know, I just thought…

MATT Of course, if you want to cut back…

ESTHER No, I don't want to cut back, I just meant… I was thinking of something different.

MATT We can go every other day, if you like.

ESTHER No, no.

MATT Or every third day.

ESTHER No. I love the crullers. I eat them at home sometimes, you know, while I'm at home. Sometimes I eat two. And then a Dutchie. I was just thinking about… arteries and things.

MATT Arteries?

ESTHER Yes, and cholesterol. Bad habits.

MATT You think it's a bad habit?

ESTHER No, not the Dutchies. Not Tim's. I don't mean that. It's more about the arteries.

MATT I haven't thought much about arteries. What about arteries?

ESTHER It's nothing. It's not about that. Forget I said anything. We've got work to do.

MATT Yes, we do, I suppose, but if you…

ESTHER Right.

MATT I'd be happy to hear about your arteries.

ESTHER Oh, never mind.

Exit ESTHER.

MATT What did I say?

Exit MATT.

SCENE TEN

In the kitchen.

ALISON I'm gonna leave now. This is kind of a loser way to spend the day, putting out sandwiches for dead people.

MARGE You're right.

ALISON Got a busy day ahead. No offence.

MARGE None taken.

ALISON But, you know, I did tell Esther I'd stay. Make the porridge. Apparently she wants the porridge, yeah. How strange is that? Shit. I'll stay for a couple of minutes. This sucks.

Enter ESTHER.

ESTHER Well, things are looking great in here. And our timing is perfect. Everybody happy? Marge?

Enter PHYL. She is a wreck.

PHYL I have date squares.

ESTHER Phyl, you are a saint.

PHYL I have cream of wheat.

ESTHER Oh, for God's sake.

PHYL No hearts. So I got stars.

ALISON I'll take those.

ESTHER Phyl, why are you helping Marge make ridiculous food?

PHYL Do you think they had enough time with us?

ESTHER What? Who?

PHYL The ones who died. Bronwyn Bain. I can't help wondering. About whether she had enough time to say everything she wanted to say. About whether she finally had all the books she wanted. About whether she can actually rest in peace. I didn't have enough time with my mom. How could you ever have enough time? For the last few years she didn't even know us, my brother and me. She thought I was her sister, Gracie. She thought I was poisoning her food. We'd go to the manor, my brother and I, I'd bring a banana loaf or some brownies, which she wouldn't eat. He'd pull out his guitar and we'd sing, *(singing)* "All of me"—it was her favourite song. And this huge smile would crack her face open, and she'd limp along with us. There wasn't a person in that room who could carry a tune. Tone deaf, every one of us.

ESTHER Phyl? *(PHYL doesn't answer.)* My mom loved the *Lone Ranger* song.

All but PHYL sing it, all keeping an eye on PHYL.

I think she had a thing for him. A good, reliable guy on a horse. You know. She hummed it, too, whenever she didn't want to hear what we were telling her. You'd say, "Mom, I think it's time you gave up driving." After that time she wiped out the mailboxes by her place. And she'd start humming. *(She hums a bit.)*

MARGE My mom's was "Softly and Tenderly." *(By Will L. Thompson. She sings a few bars. ESTHER joins in.)* "Softly and tenderly Jesus is calling. Calling for you and for me." It was her dad's favourite song. That was my Gump. He'd cry when you sang that to him—after his stroke, anyway. He was an awful man before the stroke, but he softened up after.

PHYL He was not awful.

MARGE *(angrily)* Yes, he was, Phyl. Anyway, after his stroke, I'd say don't cry, Gump. You can't afford to lose the weight. 'Cause he'd lost so much weight, then. After, when we carried him out of the church, it was as though we were carrying air, he was so light. How does someone disappear like that?

ALISON My mom doesn't sing.

ESTHER That can't be right. Everyone sings. Even Phyl sings in the car. I sound great in the car. I sound like Ella Fitzgerald.

ALISON *(angrily)* I said she doesn't sing. She never sings. What's wrong with that?

ESTHER Nothing wrong with that. No. That's good. That's fine. Okay, then. Phyl, bring me the date squares. I think we're going to be all right this afternoon.

PHYL You know, there's this man who hangs around in periodicals at the library. He's this huge, hulking troll of a man. He looks like something from under a bridge in a fairy tale.

MARGE Phyl, if this is another story about mahogany caskets and bursting with grief, I'm going to scream.

PHYL His hair just pours down, black as black, from the top of his head down to his elbows. No one goes near him. He reads this small paperback—he brings it with him to the library—why would you do that?—and it looks really small because his hands are so big, each finger is like a sausage. He stands, facing the window in periodicals, and just reads his paperback. I try to get closer, sometimes, to see the title, but I swear there's a kind of invisible wall around him. All I can think of when I see him is that there is no way I breastfed my son long enough. Every time Aiden has a cold—and he's twenty-six for God's sake—I'm positive it's because I didn't breastfeed him long enough. Someone should have breastfed that man longer. Someone should still be breastfeeding that man. I could be this Bain woman. Buried in pieces. *(pause)* I miss being kissed.

MARGE I love being kissed.

PHYL You don't deserve to be kissed.

MARGE Oh, yes I do.

ESTHER *(quietly, almost to herself)* I miss being kissed. *(seeing the others' reactions)* What's wrong with that?

PHYL If I could be anything today, I'd be kissed.

MARGE I'd be kissed in the water. In the deep end, kissing my Ray.

PHYL If I could be anything, I'd be Franklin the Turtle.

ALISON Franklin the Turtle?

ESTHER It's a long story. Don't get her started. I'd be a nun.

PHYL You would not!

ESTHER Really, I would be. Married to God.

MARGE With his hands on my face, and the sound of his voice right here.

PHYL We do not need to hear about his hands on your face, Marge. What is the point of hearing that? And you, *(to* ESTHER*)* how can you even joke about being a nun, with all your profanity, throwing God and Jesus Murphy around like they were crumbs off a bad loaf of bread.

ESTHER Well, why not? If you can be Franklin, why can't I be a nun? And if God is the Great Organizer—and he would be, wouldn't he, Phyl?—then I'd be married to someone just like me. That'd be great. We'd run the town. And God's got everything figured out, already, right? So I wouldn't have to wait for him to think. He'd know the difference between heart disease and lunch, for God's sake. There'd be no having to get your words right. With men, you know, it's so much… I think you have an effect on the man you're with, and maybe it isn't always good. And I wonder, if I was "married to God," well, maybe God could handle me without being adversely affected. If you know what I mean.

PHYL If I could pick two things, I'd be Franklin the Turtle on the first day and a real nun, married to God, on the second. Can we pick two? I'm picking two. I want to be a nun who was a nun right from the start, though. No Jim.

MARGE Phyl, you don't mean that. You loved Jim. Don't leave him out.

PHYL Don't you tell me who to leave out or what it is I mean. You tell me one thing.

ESTHER Okay, Alison, now you tell me who's sounding a little tense now? A little overdressed, whatever that means.

PHYL Did you not say that you could make yourself healthy? And I thought you were crazy. But here you are. And you're fine. So you were right and I was wrong.

MARGE Phyl…

PHYL So just stop with all that business before, about wanting to talk to me about anything else.

MARGE I think it's back.

PHYL Don't say that.

MARGE Please listen to me.

PHYL Do not say that. And don't tell me I can't be a nun who never knew my Jim.

ESTHER Phyl…

PHYL If you can throw everything away, so can I.

MARGE I'm not throwing anything away.

ESTHER Phyl, Marge. Come on, now. Both of you, stop it.

MARGE You… you are as stubborn as Jim was.

PHYL Don't you mention Jim.

MARGE He was a stubborn man.

PHYL You have no right to say anything about him…

MARGE He was stubborn and he was hard on Aiden from the time that boy learned to walk.

ESTHER Marge, what are you…

PHYL What are you doing?

MARGE He wasn't perfect.

PHYL Why are you saying this…?

MARGE He drank too much.

PHYL No. Stop.

ESTHER Marge.

PHYL You're being cruel!

MARGE He drank till he couldn't see straight, some nights with Ray.

PHYL I'm leaving. I can't do this.

MARGE Don't leave. Stay. I'm trying to tell you something.

PHYL I don't want to hear what you're saying.

MARGE Please stay.

PHYL I will not stay. How dare you talk about my husband like that? You are horrible. Do you hear me? You ass… bag… head. *(She throws food.)* You are an awful human being!

MARGE Yes, I am.

ESTHER Marge! Phyl!

MARGE *(throwing food)* I am awful!

PHYL and MARGE continue to throw food during the following lines.

ESTHER Pull yourselves together!

PHYL How dare you!

MARGE Listen to me!

ESTHER Stop it, for God's sake! Please, you two!

PHYL How dare you say these…

MARGE I am awful!

ESTHER Stop shouting! You're making a mess of everything!

PHYL You, you're… you…

MARGE We're all awful, aren't we?! I'm cruel, you're right, and you're stuck. You're so stuck, you haven't changed your clothes since Jim died.

PHYL Don't!

MARGE And Esther, well… And what happens to all of that? We get sick and die or we get hit by a bus and die, who knows, and all of a sudden people are eating Jell-O salads with coconut—who came up with dessicated coconut, I'd like to know—and going on about how we were so selfless and kind and perfect till you could choke on it! We do it here every week, we make these goddamned sandwiches with white bread on one side and brown on the other, with pink cream cheese in the middle—what the hell is that all about? We do it to our friends and our mothers and our husbands. I don't want the crusts cut off when I'm dead! Can you hear me?! I want it all there. Good, bad, and ugly. Three caskets. Breastfeed that! Inject that into your veins! Radiate yourself with it. For God's sake, Phyl, do you not miss the awful things about Jim?

PHYL I loved my husband. He was a saint. And I've had more than I can take of you. If this is friendship, these things you're saying, I don't want it! *(She turns to leave.)*

MARGE You know what, Phyl? The last thing I need today is the sight of your self-righteous fat ass stomping away in front of me. And if you don't want this friendship, I can certainly do without.

Exit MARGE.

PHYL I can't believe this! I can't believe it!

Exit PHYL.

ESTHER *and* ALISON *survey the mess.*

ESTHER You cannot just blow up and leave. You can't just create disasters wherever you go. Are you listening to me? You can't!

Exit ESTHER.

ALISON I'm sorry.

Enter ESTHER.

ESTHER The day is ruined, isn't it! Look at this. Matt is going to… And of course Helen'll just sweep in and… And those two! Do you see what they've done to each other? Can they not hear each other, for Christ's sake? You can't just blow up and leave! *(Exit* ESTHER.*)*

ALISON I'm sorry.

Curtain.

ACT TWO

SCENE ONE

In the chapel.

Enter MATT *with a remote and a lamp, which he plugs in.*

MATT Well, Anne. You're back.

ANNIE I am.

MATT There. Look. *(He clicks the remote, and the pictures, with heads missing, begin to flash.)* I think they look just fine, don't you?

ANNIE They're certainly… big.

MATT Yes, well. They say that if you live a large life, your ending won't be so…

ANNIE So what? So small?

MATT I'm sorry, I've got that wrong.

ANNIE Can we help you with something, Matt?

MATT Yes, well, I was wondering whether you'd like any help with the retrospective. Your stories.

ANNIE They're just pouring out of us now.

MATT Good. That's wonderful. And I'm sure you won't be the only ones sharing.

ANNIE Why, do you have stories?

MATT About your mother?

ANNIE Right.

MATT Well, no. I didn't know her at all, except for our one meeting here, but her friends, your friends… Well, I suppose we'll just do what we can. Why don't I check on the flowers.

JANE Do you not think that flowers are completely pointless?

MATT Well, if you need me at all, just call.

Exit MATT, *after turning the slides off.*

JANE Annie, we haven't seen each other in two years.

ANNIE People drift. I've been busy.

JANE You live four blocks away.

ANNIE It's five blocks.

JANE Four and a half. *(pause)* I miss you.

ANNIE I've been busy. Mixing paint. Painting.

JANE And you hate it.

ANNIE I hate mixing. Not painting.

Pause.

JANE You mean painting-painting?

ANNIE Yes, I mean painting. Janie, do not say anything. Please, for the love of God, do not say anything except "good for you," 'cause if you do, if you say anything shitty, I'll leave this second and I will never forgive you. Say "Good for you, Annie."

JANE nods.

Say it.

JANE Good for you, Annie.

ANNIE Peter is an interview.

JANE What do you mean, Peter is an interview?

ANNIE It's nothing.

JANE It doesn't sound like nothing.

ANNIE He has a gallery. He saw something he liked on an old website.

JANE Which one?

ANNIE Downtown Iris.

JANE That woman.

ANNIE Yeah.

JANE On Queen Street.

ANNIE Just say "Good for you, Annie."

JANE That was good.

ANNIE So, I'm taking him some new stuff, just to show him.

JANE New stuff?

ANNIE It stinks, maybe, and it's been, like, seven thousand years since I've…

JANE Good for you, Annie.

ANNIE Jesus, and I was shitty even when I was good, I don't know what I'm doing.

JANE Annie. Good for you.

ANNIE I don't want any calls from you saying, "How'd it go?" Just leave it, all right?

JANE All right.

ANNIE I'll stay for the purse. Then I gotta go.

JANE I don't want to do the purse.

ANNIE Chicken liver.

JANE I hate being here. I hate all of this.

ANNIE Two sisters, one middle-aged and miserable, one much younger, much more fun to be with, brought together, at last, by hating all of this.

Enter MATT with another lamp. During this scene he plugs it in and turns it on.

MATT Excuse me. I said before that I didn't know your mother.

JANE Yeah.

MATT That I only spoke with her that once when she came in to make final arrangements.

JANE Yeah.

MATT That's all true.

ANNIE It's good of you to confirm that, Matt.

MATT Yes.

ANNIE Sometimes it's good to hear things more than once.

MATT So, I didn't really know her friends. But maybe you do. Know some friends we might call for this afternoon. Because I'm not having much luck in that direction.

JANE Oh.

ANNIE Well.

JANE We should tell you something.

Enter ESTHER. She's a mess, covered with flour, curls not what they were.

ESTHER Excuse me.

MATT Esther.

ESTHER I'm sorry to interrupt. The kitchen is… We were making sandwiches and… I had it completely organized. Everything is going to be… Would you like a coffee? It's not hot, but it's… it's cold. I could make more.

MATT I'd love one.

ESTHER Here. It's cold.

MATT I like it cold.

ESTHER I'll bring you another one later, a hot one.

MATT Are you all right, Esther?

ESTHER Tip. Top. Everything is just fine. Excuse me.

Exit ESTHER.

MATT Esther and I are… We've known each other for twenty-one years. On Wednesday, it'll be twenty-one years. I don't think she would care to hear that. Her hair looks different today. She's a very interesting woman. Just this morning, she mentioned arteries, which is a completely new area of interest, as far as I know.

It could be that she's also interested in capillaries. There's a lot to think about there, with blood vessels.

Exit MATT.

ANNIE Far too young for me, but I like him. Come on, let's finish the purse. *(She picks up the purse.)*

JANE *(reaches for the purse)* I'm going to say it one more time. I don't want to do the purse. Can you hear that? It's brutal, touching her things. It's none of our business.

ANNIE Janie. *(She grabs the purse back and begins to look through it.)* Lighten up, will you, for once in your life. I'm trying to do the right thing. It's the first time in twenty years, don't get in my way.

JANE Leave it.

ANNIE Jane, back off, will you? Christ, is it any wonder we don't get together, ever? Stop telling me what I should do, what I shouldn't do. I'm doing the purse. End of story. *(pause)* You know, maybe the daisies on the paper meant something. Loves me, loves me not, and all of that.

JANE Enough with the daisies, will you? They're irrelevant, Annie. You're such a… you're unbelievable.

ANNIE I know what I am, thanks very much. Okay, forget it. No more daisies. You were the one who showed me the purse. The daisies, woops, forget I said that, were in the purse. Take it easy.

JANE Don't tell me to take it easy.

ANNIE Look. Tweezers. Or will tweezers piss you off, too? They're good ones, too. Do you want them? I'll take them.

JANE *(upset)* Why? Why would she carry tweezers in her purse?

ANNIE Maybe she liked plucking her eyebrows while she was out shopping.

JANE Tweezers, Jesus.

ANNIE Some eyeliner. I've got a kind of Joan Crawford thing going in my head, now.

JANE Oh, that's nice.

ANNIE *(bringing a small case from the purse)* Some kind of case. Locked.

JANE Just as well.

ANNIE The whole purse should be locked. Hey. I'll bet that's what that little key's for. Where's the key?

JANE I don't know.

ANNIE *(finds the key)* Look, it fits.

JANE What is it?

ANNIE It's a picture, and confetti or something.

JANE What are these little bits?

ANNIE *(looking at the picture)* It's us. Look.

JANE You and me?

ANNIE And her.

JANE I don't remember that.

ANNIE It's your first communion. I remember the crown thing.

JANE *(remembering)* She made those dresses.

ANNIE Yours is blue.

JANE And yours is purple. Why did you always get purple?

ANNIE I dunno. 'Cause you always got blue. They had that matching embroidery or something across the front.

JANE Look at her. She's smiling. God. She looks so happy.

ANNIE It's weird, seeing her happy. They were flowers, weren't they, across the front?

JANE Yeah.

ANNIE It must have taken her forever to do those. These daisies, do you think…

JANE Leave them. Leave them alone.

ANNIE Do you think there's any chance—you know, do you think there's any chance she thought about us in the last while, before she died?

JANE No. I don't. She didn't.

ANNIE How do you know that? I could be wrong. Maybe I've been wrong. How can we…

JANE Stop it, Annie.

ANNIE Show me the other stuff.

JANE No.

ANNIE I want to see it.

JANE I don't want to.

ANNIE Come on, Janie. Show me the bits. What are they?

JANE Don't.

ANNIE What?

JANE Leave it!

ANNIE Show me.

JANE This is sick.

ANNIE grabs the bits.

ANNIE What is it?

JANE No.

ANNIE Oh my God.

JANE I have to go.

ANNIE It's Dad's heads.

JANE Don't say that.

ANNIE Dad's heads. I'm sure that's him. It is. It's Dad. He looks good.

JANE Jesus!

ANNIE Hey, Dad.

JANE We ought to be in an institution of some kind, don't you think? For looking at any of this. For coming here at all.

ANNIE What do you mean?

JANE Can we not just bury her, Annie? She left. She went away, she stayed away. End of story. Didn't write, didn't call, didn't return calls. What do you want? I don't know if she was cracked in the head or just didn't care. At all. So the key here, the little key here, is just to put her away somewhere, completely, every piece of her, in the ground, and get the hell out of here.

Gone. Over. Done with. Dad's heads, Annie? God, she must have been crazy.

ANNIE I don't think so.

JANE I need to go.

ANNIE Maybe she just left and couldn't come back.

JANE I've got to go. I'm sorry.

ANNIE Maybe she just left and then she couldn't figure out how to make it better.

JANE I'll see you later.

ANNIE Do you not wish you could fix any of this?

JANE No, I can't fix it. I tried and tried and tried.

ANNIE What if we could? You know what? I am a jerk. You're right. And I'm a coward, and yes, I wish that I could… that I could love a man for more than six weeks at a time. I wish that we could see each other without it blowing up every time. I wish you were nicer to be with, and you know what, Janie? You're not. I wish I'd had the basic courage to stop mixing paint five minutes after I had the job. I mixed paint for seven years, for Christ's sake. Jesus. I could end up in there, I know it. A couple of pathetic pizza boxes in an empty funeral home. Can't do that, Janie. I have to try something else. And what if I'm wrong about her, what if I've been wrong? Tell me. Tell me, for fuck's sake. *(JANE doesn't respond.)* Jesus.

Exit ANNIE to the bathroom.

Enter MATT.

MATT How are you doing with the purse?

JANE It's a great purse. Lots of compartments. It's strange to think that when we were leaving messages, she was off to the library and the grocery store. For Ida Reds. Getting her lipstick right, plucking her eyebrows. And just not returning calls. For years.

Then there's gravity. These boxes'll just get heavier and heavier. And they'll multiply. There'll be seven or eight of them before you know it and she will never be gone.

(JANE laughs.) Maybe I'm cracked. *(to MATT)* Nice day outside. Not many crimes being committed. *(to herself)* Not many.

SCENE TWO

In the bathroom. PHYL *is a mess, covered in food-fight debris.*

ALISON *is nearby—close enough to hear the conversation.*

ANNIE Wrong fucking door. I need a smoke.

PHYL Oh, that's lovely language.

ANNIE Go to hell.

PHYL You go to hell.

ANNIE And my hair is a disaster. Do you have a cigarette?

PHYL You go to hell.

ANNIE Thank you for your generosity.

PHYL You'll die of cancer smoking those.

ANNIE Why is my hair such a disaster?

PHYL It's the humidity. That's October for you.

ANNIE It was October yesterday and my hair was fine.

PHYL Maybe you're wrong. Maybe your hair was a disaster yesterday, too.

ANNIE You're a sick woman.

PHYL Yes I am. Have you got any clips, or bobby pins?

ANNIE Do I look like I have hair clips?

PHYL *(taking* ANNIE*'s hair)* Here, hold still. I'll try not to get too close. Wouldn't want you catching anything.

ANNIE Some hairdresser.

PHYL I thought of being a hairdresser once.

ANNIE Me too. Then I wanted to be a marine biologist. Everyone wants to be a marine biologist at one point. I need a cigarette so badly.

PHYL Two years ago I was Franklin the Turtle.

ANNIE I do not care about that.

PHYL The library held a children's day during the March break, and fifty-three children showed up to meet Franklin. But the costume that arrived on the bus from Ottawa that morning didn't fit Sylvia, my supervisor, who was supposed to be Franklin. And that costume has to fit just right or you can't see out of Franklin's mouth. *(to* ANNIE*)* Give me your finger. *(She uses* ANNIE*'s finger to hold some hair in place.)* So, with no notice whatsoever, I had to be Franklin.

You should have seen the kids' faces. It was the way they looked at me. Or at Franklin. I mean, I know they weren't looking at me, but they looked… they made me feel as though I had never once in my life made a mistake. Can you imagine that?

ANNIE Never making a mistake?

PHYL No. I mean having someone look at you as though you've never made a mistake. When they looked at me like that, I felt safe.

ANNIE Who are you?

PHYL I was safe for six months. I'm Phyllis. I'm a librarian. No, that's wrong. I was a librarian. You know, people come, and go. You can't seem to count on anything. They fire you, or not fire you, exactly, but let you go, which is worse…

ANNIE Bastards.

PHYL They are bastards. It's a horrible word, but it's true. They get sick and they die, don't they? They die, without giving you a chance to have any real time with them…

ANNIE Bastards.

PHYL So you do everything you can to stay away from it all, but you can't leave it, can you?

ANNIE Oh, sure you can.

PHYL No, you can't. You can try, and it might feel like it's working for a while, but you can't just be married to God. Were you ever a nun?

ANNIE No.

PHYL You know, if I could be anything today, I'd be looking out my kitchen window, with everything all right. But I can't do that.

ANNIE But you can leave. We can leave. I'm leaving.

PHYL No, you can't leave. You know why? Because if you leave the part that you can't stand, the part that shoots through you like some kind of bursting aneurysm myocardial stroke thing—if you leave that part, you're leaving Jim altogether.

ANNIE Well, I can leave Jim, whoever Jim is. I can leave anyone.

PHYL No, you can't. It'll be fifteen months on Wednesday. You can't leave these awful numbers—fifteen months, his birthday coming up on the twenty-ninth, we would have been married twenty-eight years, he died eleven days after his cough was looked at. *(pause)* They called it a galloping cancer, like it was something at a bastard fall fair. You know, he came home after that first appointment with the specialist and he was sitting in the car, in the driveway, for I don't know how long. I could see him out the kitchen window. I was making potato salad, a new one, with an oil dressing, instead of mayonnaise. Black olives. When he pulled in, I was peeling the potatoes. I should have known. I watched him while they boiled, and then while they cooled, and he didn't look up once to see me. I kept chopping and chopping the olives, waiting for him. They were in the smallest pieces by the time I finally made myself go out there. He kept his hands on the wheel while he told me. Both hands on the wheel. And then, right away, he got out of the car, and put up the hood, and showed me how to check the oil. He laughed, watching me do it. I was so mad at him. I thought, he should be taking this seriously, shouldn't he? But you know, who am I to say how we should be? How we should do it. Who am I to say for the others?

ANNIE What others?

PHYL Marge. The Last Supper Committee. We were in the other room, making food for the funeral this afternoon.

ANNIE It's not a funeral.

PHYL What's the difference?

ANNIE I dunno.

PHYL Are you the daughter?

ANNIE One of them.

PHYL And you're leaving?

ANNIE nods.

For good?

ANNIE nods.

You have to stay.

ANNIE I'd be completely cracked to stay. You wouldn't understand.

PHYL I don't have to understand. You have to stay.

ANNIE You just said you can't tell the others how to do it.

PHYL You're right, you're absolutely right. Do what you want, then, be your own marine biologist.

ANNIE I tried to stay. I did, but I keep making mistakes.

PHYL That doesn't matter.

ANNIE Yes, it does.

PHYL No, it doesn't. Think of Franklin. What matters is looking at each other as though we've never made mistakes. That's what matters. Give me your other hand. *(She puts it in place, holding some hair.)* You shouldn't chew those nails. And you know, if you stopped smoking, you wouldn't be so nervous to begin with.

SCENE THREE

In the chapel.

JANE I have a story.

MATT That's good to hear. It'll make you feel better.

JANE I'm tired. I need some air.

Pause.

MATT That's a good story.

JANE *(to the casket)* Are you listening? This would have been a lot easier if you'd written a letter, instead.

SCENE FOUR

ESTHER and MATT with coffee at the lectern. ESTHER is stunned.

Enter DELIVERY SEVEN.

DELIVERY SEVEN
Carmichael.

MATT stares at him/her for a moment, but says nothing.

ESTHER That way.

Exit DELIVERY SEVEN.

Carmichael.

MATT You have something on your blouse.

ESTHER Oh.

MATT And in your hair. There.

ESTHER It's nothing.

MATT And here. Smells like salmon.

ESTHER Thanks.

MATT Did you have a good morning back there?

ESTHER Not tip-top.

MATT Esther? Have any flower arrangements come through the kitchen?

ESTHER Well, no.

MATT How is the food looking?

ESTHER It could be better.

MATT Esther, did any of your friends in the kitchen know Mrs. Bain?

ESTHER Not really.

MATT I wonder if the Last Supper women might stay for the visitation. Just in case we need to fill the place up a bit.

ESTHER They've all… There was this… I don't know if there's anyone left. Well, in fact, I do know. There's no one left. Unless Alison stayed, but she didn't want to be here in the first place, so she'll be gone, too. I've made a mess… Are there any guests yet?

MATT No.

ESTHER Just the daughter?

MATT There were two daughters. They may have gone.

ESTHER Well, this just can't be. We'll have to get moving, find some more people, some more sandwiches. Marge and Phyl are… There's no time… and the food is all over… I don't know what to do.

MATT Esther? Thanks for the coffee.

ESTHER The coffee, Matt? The coffee? There's no time for that. You should see the kitchen. Coffee, for God's sake!

MATT It's all I can do. I've written a three-line obituary, I called about the flowers—I don't know what's going on there. And I don't know if anyone is coming this afternoon.

ESTHER So, think of something else.

MATT I've done everything I know how, Esther. The one good thing I can think of now is to thank you for the coffee.

ESTHER When everything is gone to hell. Blown to smithereens.

MATT Yes.

ESTHER When people have said horrible things.

MATT Yes.

ESTHER And nothing can possibly work out.

MATT One good thing.

ESTHER Thank you for coffee.

MATT Yes.

Pause.

ESTHER Matt? Would you like to try coffee with lunch tomorrow?

MATT At Tim's?

ESTHER Or dinner. At my place.

MATT That's a kind offer. I'd like to think about it, if you don't mind.

ESTHER Fair enough. It was a thought that crossed my mind. Just now. It doesn't matter one way or another. I just thought I'm a bit tired of Dutchies. And muffins.

MATT Is it the arteries?

ESTHER Not really, no.

MATT I'd like to think about it.

ESTHER And Timbits. I'm tired of Timbits.

MATT nods his head.

Pause.

Okay, then. Thank you for thinking about it.

Exit ESTHER.

MATT Okay, then.

Enter ALISON, with her coat on.

Are you with Carmichael?

ALISON I brought flowers for Bain.

MATT Good. How many arrangements?

Pause.

ALISON Three.

MATT Well, that's a start.

ALISON Have you ever met someone who didn't get any flowers when she died?

MATT Well…

ALISON What if someone was such a total loser that no one showed up for the funeral? What would you do then? Would you just leave her here and go home?

MATT No. I'd stay.

ALISON Even if you were the only one?

MATT Yes.

ALISON Bullshit, and you didn't even know her?

MATT Yes.

ALISON Why? Why would you stay?

MATT Because you have to help, where you can, with the family, if there is one, and their stories…

ALISON What if there are only bad stories?

MATT There's no such thing as only bad stories. Stories are made up. So, you tell the good stories.

ALISON So, you just make them up?

MATT I don't know what you do. We had a funeral here last week. A man showed up and told a story about the deceased taking his driver's exam. There was something about opening the sunroof every time it started to rain. *(MATT laughs.)* And the driver's ed guy getting soaked. Turned out this guy telling the story, he had the wrong funeral altogether. Came to Thursday's funeral on Friday. But it was good to laugh. So, I just know that good stories are better. Did you know Mrs. Bain?

ALISON Only what I heard this morning, in the kitchen. Was she alone when she died?

Pause.

MATT Yes, she was. It was a stroke. A neighbour found her a few days later. There were fliers piling up at the front door.

ALISON She has a kid here?

MATT I hope so. Will you stay?

ALISON I've been trying to leave all morning.

MATT Bit like her dying all over again if no one's here for her. I suppose they cooked up a storm back there this morning.

ALISON You could say that, yeah.

MATT Thank you for the flowers.

Pause.

ALISON We should thank Esther, I think.

MATT I will.

ALISON We hit it off right from the start. She's great.

MATT Yes, she is.

ALISON She's pretty hot, don't you think?

MATT I haven't thought about that. For a long time.

ALISON Maybe you should. I gotta go.

Exit ALISON.

SCENE FIVE

MARGE sits on a chair in a back hallway of the funeral hall. She is covered with flour.

Enter ESTHER.

ESTHER I need your help.

MARGE It's been a long day, Esther. I don't need company.

ESTHER Fine, then. You want to throw away a perfectly fine friendship, you go to it. But Matt asked me to do this event, and that's what I'm going to do. The Bain visitation is spread all over the place in there.

MARGE She is completely obsessed with all of this, with heart attacks and strokes and aneurysms, and broken tiles the size of loonies. And her clothes, for God's sake, she's like a vulture. Doesn't it feel like she's flying in circles over your head? I can't stand it.

ESTHER Jim died with about three minutes' notice—of course she's different. She's bleak and black and she's taken ownership of Jesus all of a sudden That's the way it is. But you don't say those things to her face, for God's sake. And to say those things about Jim… I don't know what the hell you were doing.

MARGE Well, what the hell is she doing, turning these people into saints? Into something so perfect that they couldn't have been here at all? I hate that. Can't you see what's happening?

ESTHER You don't want to be sick again, that's what I see happening. You don't want to join Mrs. Bain or Susan or Jim or your mother or my mother. No one wants to join that lineup.

MARGE That isn't what I'm saying.

ESTHER So, while you're figuring out what it is that you do want to say, stop being mean to Phyl. She doesn't need it. She'll come out of it soon enough. Throw some food at me if it'll make you feel better.

MARGE Oh, for God's sake. I hate this food.

ESTHER It's your food, Marge, smell it. Here, throw some salmon. *(She picks something off her sweater/out of her hair.)* Throw some cilantro, Marge. It's just a garnish. Come on. Where are the eggs? Where are they?

MARGE I'll crack one over your head.

ESTHER Crack two. Come on.

ESTHER takes MARGE by the arm and pulls her toward the kitchen.

MARGE Esther…

ESTHER What do you want? Jalapenos? Is that what you want?

MARGE Yes, I want jalapenos. That's exactly what I want. *(pause)* Thank you for asking. What do you want?

ESTHER I want… I want lunch. Lunch or dinner. Either one. I'm flexible.

MARGE Esther?

ESTHER What?

MARGE You're so flexible it hurts.

SCENE SIX

ALISON enters the chapel with the three flowers and her scissors. She looks around the room and leaves.

SCENE SEVEN

PHYL is in the kitchen, sitting. Enter MARGE.

PHYL I forgot my purse.

MARGE I'm sorry.

PHYL I didn't think it would happen. Even while it was happening, I thought, this isn't happening. But it was.

MARGE It was awful. I…

PHYL At three, she handed me my purse. She handed it to me, and just stood there until I left the library. I don't even know if I can borrow books anymore. Do you know what they said to me?

MARGE What did they say?

PHYL It won't go on my official record, as if that matters, but they said they'd lost confidence in me, in my ability to do the right thing. They said someone had to put a stop to it.

MARGE I'm sorry, Phyl. And I'm sorry about what I said.

PHYL Don't.

MARGE I wasn't trying to be cruel. I was trying to tell you something…

PHYL Do not tell me anything. Please.

MARGE All right. Will you try this?

MARGE hands PHYL a colourful scarf.

PHYL I don't like it.

MARGE For five minutes.

PHYL It's too much.

MARGE Just put it in your pocket. For two minutes.

PHYL I'll look like an over-the-hill skateboarder, with no helmet. I'll crack my head open, my brains'll spill out. There'll be no one to help…

MARGE Phyl, it's a scarf. It's a bit of colour.

PHYL People should be more careful with colour. They have no idea what can happen. *(pause)* You're never afraid.

MARGE Of course I'm afraid. Do you think I'm a dim-wit? Some days I can hardly breathe.

PHYL I wish I could help.

MARGE You can.

PHYL I said I wish. It wasn't an offer.

MARGE I want to teach you how to swim.

PHYL Swimmers die in the water, Marge. One big gulp and it's all over.

MARGE Everybody dies, Phyl. Me, you. *(Enter ESTHER.)* Everybody dies. You should learn to float before you die.

PHYL I don't want to die in the water.

ESTHER Oh, for God's sake.

MARGE Please, Phyl.

PHYL I'll think about it.

ESTHER Don't mind me. I'll just sweep up around you while you plan your death by drowning, you two.

ESTHER begins to sweep.

Enter ALISON.

ALISON I was fired this morning. So basically, I can't go home today. It's too hard on my mom. *(She begins to leave, and comes back.)* I try to do good things, but they get turned around. So now I'm just trying to keep my mouth shut. *(She begins to leave, and comes back.)* I'm also pregnant, which isn't good. *(pause)* There's no guy. Well, there was sperm, you know how it is, but… I was so stupid. You know, this Mrs. Bain, she's doing all right. If someone took me, right now, and put me in some boxes, piece by piece, I wouldn't take up much room, you know, which would be good, and, I'd stop breathing, after a while, which would kinda be a relief, at this point. What do you think?

ESTHER Well, Alison…

Exit ALISON *to the chapel.*

Marge! Phyl! Help out, for Christ's sake. Speak up.

MARGE Poor kid.

PHYL Holy mackerel.

ESTHER We have to do something.

Enter ALISON.

ALISON I don't know my mother's favourite song. Maybe if she was dead I'd know it. My brother's dead, though. He was skiing at Lake Louise. Anyway, he was killed in an avalanche, day after Christmas. I have this dream, sometimes, and in it, I was with him, holding his hand while it happened. So he wouldn't be alone. Maybe it would have been more like going to sleep, then. I could say, shhhh, and he could just close his eyes. "Twinkle, Twinkle, Little Star." Billy's song. Maybe it wasn't his favourite, but it was the one he sang with me. *(She sings a few lines of a rap version, with actions.)*

Pause.

ESTHER That's a fantastic song. *(pause)* Isn't that a fantastic song?

PHYL I thought it was more of a children's song.

ALISON No it isn't.

ESTHER Cripes.

MARGE Alison. Sing it again. We'll do it with you.

PHYL I can't sing.

MARGE Yes you can. You can sing.

ALISON Up above the world so high…

They sing a few lines, imitating ALISON's rap singing and actions. ALISON struggles toward the end, and they trail off.

MARGE It'll be all right, Alison.

ALISON You can't say that. How do you know?

ESTHER Because I'm older. I'm smarter. Well, maybe not smarter. I'm more organized.

ALISON That's bullshit.

ESTHER You're right. I don't mean that.

MARGE We'll stay here until it is all right.

ALISON How? What can you do?

PHYL We'll do our best, which is what we're all doing, all the time.

MARGE Look at me. We'll do our best.

ESTHER See? See? That's right. That's what I meant. We'll do our best. Jesus, God, this is going to kill me, this job.

SCENE EIGHT

In the chapel.

Enter MATT, who sits, looking at the new flowers made by ALISON.

Enter ANNIE.

ANNIE Hey. *(seeing the flowers)* Wow.

MATT Hey.

ANNIE Have I missed it? The funeral thing, the…?

MATT Celebration of Life. You haven't missed it.

ANNIE Where's Janie?

MATT I don't know.

ANNIE Did she leave?

MATT I hope not.

ANNIE I hope not, too, her being the only child and all. *(MATT looks uncomfortable.)* Just messing with you, Matt.

Enter JANE.

Hey.

JANE You stayed.

ANNIE Thank that hairdresser in the bathroom.

JANE I shouldn't have come.

ANNIE We could make a run for it right now if you want, Janie.

MATT Well, then. I'll tell the others we're almost ready.

ANNIE There are others?

MATT There's Esther.

Exit MATT.

JANE I have to tell you something.

ANNIE What's that?

JANE It's something bad.

ANNIE You know what, Janie? Whatever it is, let's just say "Good for you," okay? Can we just forget all the bad stuff, for now, and just say "Good for you"? Can we do that?

JANE I have to tell you.

Enter the women from the kitchen and MATT. The women have plates of poorly reassembled food and a bowl of punch. MATT uses a remote to turn on the headless pictures, which provide a continuous slide show during the service. The Last Supper women see the pictures for the first time during MATT's welcome.

MATT Here we are. Welcome, everyone. Welcome to Mrs. Bronwyn Bain's farewell. We're a little late starting, but I wanted to make sure we could all make it. This is good. We have chosen to bid her farewell by sharing our thoughts and memories together. To tell a story or two over a glass of punch. Feel free to enjoy sandwiches and... *(He notices the mess assembled on the plates.)* a few other snacks while we chat. Who would like to start? *(The women have passed the plates around.)* Jane, Annie, when you've had a bite, I wonder whether you'd begin by sharing with us some of the memories you discussed this morning.

ANNIE Oh my God, this is hot! Oh, God. Oh, shit. Is there water?

PHYL Have some punch.

MARGE It's jalapeno pie.

ESTHER I knew it was too hot.

ANNIE It's fantastic!

PHYL Try a bit of porridge.

ANNIE Oh my God!

PHYL It'll cool your mouth.

ESTHER Or a square. There are squares. Have two.

PHYL Have three.

ESTHER Have two.

PHYL *(to MARGE)* She's a marine biologist.

ANNIE It's so hot!

MARGE Jalapenos. They're fantastic for you.

ESTHER Would you like a little sandwich? Have some ham.

ANNIE Thank you.

PHYL There are carrots. And ranch dip. Here.

JANE No. Thanks.

ESTHER No crusts on those sandwiches. *(They all drink and eat. A prolonged silence.)*

MATT Jane? Annie?

Pause.

JANE I don't know what to say. I don't have any… My mother…

Pause.

ESTHER *(desperately)* Your mother was a great snacker. Yes, I remember how much she loved that trail mix with the dried cranberries in it. She had excellent taste. In snacks. *(pause)* And Phyl, you knew her from the library, didn't you?

PHYL Yes. Your mother loved books.

ANNIE She did love books.

PHYL She collected books.

JANE I didn't know that.

PHYL Yes, she did. We had a kind of relationship at the library.

ALISON / MARGE

Perhaps.

ANNIE Perhaps what?

PHYL Perhaps we have all kinds of stories about your mother. She had a carport, of course, which is unusual in the north. *(No one speaks.)* In fact, she had a bit of an interest in carports.

JANE What do you mean? Do you mean architecturally?

PHYL Yes, architecturally… and in other ways.

JANE What ways?

PHYL Well… environmentally. *(pause)* They only have two walls, you know, so they use fewer… walls.

ANNIE I think I can picture that.

JANE Did no one know her?

ANNIE Sure they knew her. They're telling us they knew her. Aren't you?

Pause.

MARGE Your mother wasn't an easy woman.

ANNIE No, she wasn't.

MARGE She made people uncomfortable. She wasn't friendly.

ESTHER Marge.

JANE You're right. She wasn't friendly.

MARGE She alienated people at the checkout when she got her groceries.

ANNIE See, they did know her.

MARGE Let me tell you about what she did at the library.

ESTHER Marge? Marge, don't tell all the stories. Let the rest of us have a chance.

ANNIE I'd like to hear more.

Pause.

MARGE She used to go to the library, without her books, and…

ESTHER Marge. Let… let someone else get a word in.

Another silence.

ALISON I knew her.

ESTHER What?

ALISON I knew her.

PHYL / MARGE / ESTHER / MATT
You did? / What?

ALISON A little bit, yeah. I was with her when she died.

ALL You were? / What?

ALISON Yes. I was on one of my morning walks, with Aiden, my son—he had a cold. I don't think I breastfed him long enough. Anyway, I was taking him for a walk and I saw her place, on Ferguson. The one with the carport. There were fliers piled up in the mailbox, and some underneath, on the front step. I thought I'd pick them up. Then I heard the radio, so I knocked a couple of times, and tried the front door. It was open, so I said hello. She answered, your mom, from her bedroom. She was sitting up with pillows propped behind her, reading a paperback. I didn't look closely enough to see the title. She said she'd been too tired to clean up the mail for a few days. I made us some tea.

ANNIE She did drink tea.

ALISON And we talked. She showed me lots of pictures, from scrapbooks she'd made. Some of you two, as kids. One of her, floating in a pool.

JANE We never had a pool.

ALISON Maybe it was from a vacation. I don't remember. She said she loved floating in the deep end. And then there was a funny one of her in a turtle costume.

JANE A turtle costume?

ANNIE What is it with these turtles?

PHYL How do you know about her turtle costume?

ESTHER Mrs. Bain's turtle costume?

ALISON She also said how much her friends meant to her. And she could be unfriendly at times, but her friends were there for her. She said the Last Supper Committee changed her life. *(to JANE and ANNIE)* And she wished she'd been able to see her kids again.

ANNIE That's incredible.

ESTHER Absolutely incredible.

ALISON And then we sang a few songs with Aiden, and drank our tea. Earl Grey tea, I think it was.

JANE Earl Grey.

ALISON We had some shortbread.

ANNIE She loved shortbread.

ALISON It was imported. Looked expensive.

ESTHER She loved that shortbread.

ALISON Then I put Aiden on the bed, and I took her cup to the kitchen. When I came back her eyes were closed, and her hands were resting on the pictures on her lap. She hadn't even taken her glasses off.

ANNIE We saw her glasses today.

PHYL She died then?

ALISON Just as peaceful as that. She just went to sleep. I held her hand for a while, and then I called Mr. Watson.

JANE So.

ANNIE Wow.

MATT Well.

ANNIE I'm glad you were there. All of you.

ESTHER Well. Us, too.

PHYL What are friends for?

Pause.

ESTHER Alison, what songs did Mrs. Bain sing with Aiden?

ALISON What?

ESTHER You mentioned singing songs with Aiden.

ALISON Right. "All of Me."

PHYL I love that song.

JANE It's a strange choice for Mom.

ALISON Maybe we didn't sing that one. Maybe it was playing when we got there. But we sang that *Lone Ranger* song.

JANE The 1812 Overture.

ANNIE She'd love that.

ALISON "Softly and Tenderly." It's a hymn, I think.

MARGE It is. It's a hymn.

ALISON And "Twinkle, Twinkle, Little Star."

JANE Twinkle, Twinkle? I don't think so.

PHYL *(to MARGE or ESTHER, in order to distract JANE and ANNIE)* I think she may have taken a book out on the Lone Ranger.

ANNIE She wasn't into kids' songs.

ALISON *(angrily)* It is not a kids' song. And she sang it all the time. With her friends. *(She begins to sing it, and the Last Supper women join in.)*

Pause.

ANNIE That is great.

Pause.

JANE *(cracking up slightly)* It's a beautiful song. Thank you. For the flowers, which are... and your stories. I don't know how much you, I mean if you really knew...

Pause.

MATT So, if that's all, from everyone, perhaps we'll gather up our...

ANNIE Wait. I have a story. About my mother. If we have time. My sister Jane and I were going through some picture bits. My mother made us these dresses when Jane had her first communion. I was seven, I think. The other girls all wore white dresses. That's what you did, for first communion. But our dresses were blue and purple. We looked like crayons in a bag of marshmallows. We were gorgeous. And all over them she embroidered white daisies with green leaves. She did it by hand. She loved her daisies. In the picture, she looked really happy with us. I have it, if you'd like to see it. She probably wouldn't mind me showing it to her friends.

MATT We'd love to see it.

MARGE I'd love to see her.

PHYL Me too.

ESTHER Me too. Eat up, please. We have all this food. Have a sandwich, Marge.

MARGE Is there any porridge left?

PHYL I love these squares.

ALISON passes trays of food, humming.

Exit MATT, exit ALISON and ESTHER to the bathroom, MARGE and PHYL to the kitchen.

SCENE NINE

ESTHER and ALISON in the bathroom.

ESTHER Did you rehearse all of that, or does it just come out all by itself? *(Exit ESTHER to the kitchen.)*

MARGE and PHYL in the kitchen.

PHYL Just so I'm clear about this, Alison wasn't actually with Bronwyn when she died.

MARGE No, Phyl. She wasn't.

PHYL It sounded real.

MARGE Architectural interest in carports? That was good, Phyl.

PHYL I'm doing my best, Marge.

MARGE Whatever it takes, Phyl.

Exit PHYL.

SCENE TEN

JANE and ANNIE in the chapel.

ANNIE God, it's hard to believe, with the turtle and everything, but she had so much right: the glasses, the tea, the unpleasant part. And I can picture it, Mom changing a bit, given enough time. I mean, look at her carrying that picture in her purse. And Dad's heads. Maybe she was warming up.

JANE Thanks for coming, Annie.

ANNIE Do you think she was telling the truth, that woman? Do you think Mom said all that stuff?

JANE Yes I do. *(She's lying.)*

ANNIE Do you have time for a coffee, Janie? Or two per cent? Or a forty of vodka? God, my mouth is still burning.

JANE You won't be late for your meeting with the guy?

ANNIE No. I'll be there. You know, I was hoping we might go over a few things for the interview. I'm looking for a way to make seven years of mixing paint sound like a success story.

JANE It'll be all right.

ANNIE Thanks, Janie. For all of it.

JANE I'll meet you outside in a minute, okay?

ANNIE You all right?

Enter MATT, who begins to clean up.

JANE Yeah. *(ANNIE begins to leave.)* Annie?

ANNIE Yeah?

JANE I don't think they knew her.

ANNIE Yes, they did.

JANE I don't think they knew her. I don't think she had friends.

ANNIE Please don't say that.

JANE Your story about the dresses was great.

ANNIE I think they probably knew her.

JANE I have another daisy story.

ANNIE I'm pretty sure they were right.

JANE October third was a Sunday. I was having a bad day, which is not that unusual anymore. I don't know why and I don't know what's happened to my life but, you know, who cares. The point is that on October third I was having a bad day. So, I just didn't answer the phone when it rang. I didn't pick it up. And there was no message. On October tenth, which was also a Sunday, it rang again. At ten. I don't know how you know, but it rang four or five times and I thought, pick it up. It's her. Pick it up. And there was no message. But I knew. Last Sunday, I left the house at 9:30, just to be sure I wouldn't be there, because I had a feeling. And there was a message this time, but it was nothing. Just a few seconds of nothing, and then someone hanging up. That was October seventeenth. Three daisies.

ANNIE Janie.

JANE So, there's my story.

Exit JANE to the back hallway of the funeral hall.

MATT Are you all right?

ANNIE No, I'm not. All this time, she's… She talks about why I should be here, and the whole time, she's… No, I'm not all right.

Exit ANNIE. She goes to the bathroom and sits/stands in front of the mirror.

SCENE ELEVEN

In the kitchen.

MARGE *(to ALISON)* Thank you for your… memories of Mrs. Bain in there.

ESTHER Not that yours weren't completely heartwarming, Marge, but I think Alison's timing was good. You know, before you got into the petty theft part of Mrs. Bain's life.

MARGE I'd like to ask you three a favour. When my time comes, I'd like you to make my last supper. I want big sandwiches, Esther. Any filling you want, but I want the crusts left on.

ESTHER Marge, not to make a point of it, but every time they take one of those sandwiches, they're taking four of the triangles. Four each. We could feed them asparagus and goat cheese for that kind of money.

MARGE I want the sandwiches.

ESTHER Marge…

MARGE Phyl, you can make your squares.

PHYL You don't like my squares.

MARGE I've changed my mind. You can make whatever you like, for as long as you need to.

PHYL Have you changed your mind about the swimming lessons?

MARGE No, I have not. Will you let me teach you?

PHYL It's pretty risky.

MARGE I'd also like jalapeno pie. You start with an oven-proof dish. A layer of sliced, pickled jalapenos. You can get them at the Valumart but they're cheaper in the huge jars at Costco, Esther. Half a big brick of old cheese grated over the jalapenos. Five eggs whisked and poured over top. Bake it at three twenty-five for fifty minutes. Let it cool for a bit before you cut it.

ESTHER People'll drop like flies eating it.

PHYL It'll burn holes in their throats.

ESTHER It'll be great business for Matt.

MARGE And about my service. I don't want, "She was kind."

PHYL You were not always kind.

ESTHER You were also stubborn.

PHYL You were too colourful. It was dangerous.

ESTHER You were no good with authority. You never stuck to the schedule.

PHYL You were too ready to give up on your friends.

ESTHER You should have told your friends when their hair and makeup made them look like crack addicts.

ALISON You were kind to strangers.

ESTHER What?

ALISON She was.

ESTHER Marge doesn't want good things. She wants bad stories and three caskets.

ALISON You can't just have bad stories. That'd be pathetic. I'm not cooking for it unless we have both.

PHYL *(to MARGE)* I hope it's a long way off, your death.

ALISON It'll be years.

ESTHER How do you know? Oh, let me guess, because you're going to be by her side with tea when she goes, right?

MARGE *(to PHYL)* I hope so, too.

PHYL We'll do your lunch. If we're still here, 'cause you never know what might happen. I may drown before you go. Esther may be killed by one of those skateboarders.

ALISON We'll do your lunch.

MARGE Thank you.

SCENE TWELVE

In the back hallway.

JANE This is so stupid. *(into the cellphone)* Mom? Hi. I miss your… I'm sorry for all the time we missed, and I'm sorry I didn't pick up when you called.

SCENE THIRTEEN

In the chapel with MATT and ESTHER, who's just come in from the kitchen.

MATT That was quite a funeral.

MATT / ESTHER Not-funeral.

MATT Thank you for bringing the Last Supper women.

ESTHER It was nothing. It was no Carmichael.

MATT I don't think Carmichael could possibly be this good. *(pause)* I didn't see the salmon.

ESTHER It didn't make it out here. There might be a bit left in the back.

MATT I'd love some.

ESTHER I'll get you a plate.

MATT I mean tomorrow, with coffee.

ESTHER Where?

MATT At your apartment. If you want to, still. I thought we might talk about blood vessels. And other things.

ESTHER Well, I…

MATT Just lunch, if you don't mind. They say you shouldn't drink coffee after lunch. I don't know whether that's a cholesterol thing, or an arterial thing, or something else altogether.

ESTHER Good. That's good.

Exit ESTHER *to the kitchen. Exit* MATT.

SCENE FOURTEEN

In the kitchen with MARGE, PHYL, *and* ALISON *cleaning up. They're humming. Enter* ESTHER.

ALISON I don't have a job.

ESTHER Neither does Phyl and she's all right.

PHYL I'm all right.

ALISON I'm really good with flowers, but not so good with the people part.

ESTHER Aaahh, you're all right.

ALISON *(to* PHYL, *after a pause)* I thought you and I could open a flower shop together. Both out of work, and me with a kid to take care of.

PHYL I don't know.

MARGE Phyl.

ESTHER Phyl likes flowers.

PHYL I also like books, but I'm not opening a library.

MARGE You could use a bit of colour.

ALISON I'm good at it. I really am.

MARGE *(to* PHYL*)* You could work the counter.

ALISON You'd take good care of people. I know you would.

PHYL I like the people.

ALISON So will you think about it? Please?

PHYL Yes, I will.

ALISON Thank you.

ESTHER Jesus, Mary, and Joseph. Incredible.

MARGE I knew it'd be a good day.

SCENE FIFTEEN

In the chapel.

Enter JANE. *She collects six flowers, puts three flowers on one casket.*

Enter ANNIE.

ANNIE She looks good with flowers in her hair.

JANE That's her hip.

ANNIE That's okay.

JANE No, it's not.

ANNIE Look at me.

JANE I should have picked up the phone.

ANNIE No mistakes, Janie. It's a Franklin thing, a turtle thing, I'll tell you about it later. It's okay.

They put three more flowers on the other casket.

She's probably all excited after the celebration.

JANE Do you think she can hear us?

ANNIE I don't know why not. Hey, Ma, what's up? What's that? Oh, Janie's okay, don't worry, just a little messed up after the funeral. Oh, you're right, after the Celebration of Life. You were listening.

JANE *(stiffly, and without enthusiasm)* Hi, Mom.

ANNIE *(to the casket)* Hey, those were good stories today. You have some good friends, Mom. Yes you do. What's that? Some two per cent? Sure, we happen to have some out in the car, don't we, Janie? Hey, Mom, tell her to brighten up, will you?

JANE I'm trying. I am. *(She tries to smile. It looks ridiculous.)*

ANNIE Come on, Mom, I'll help you up. *(She picks up the boxes and they begin their exit.)* Look at you twirling! That's pretty good, what with the hip and all.

JANE Wait. Wait a second. I think we should leave her hip here.

ANNIE That's kinda gross, Janie.

JANE I think we got that multiplying… gravity thing all wrong. I don't think she wants the titanium anymore.

ANNIE But she wanted both, she said she did.

JANE People change. You said that.

ANNIE Yes, I did. *(She puts down one box.)* Okay. If that's what you want, both of you, I'm good with it. What do you think, Mom? Yeah? Hey. Good for you, Mom. Janie, say good for you. *(pause)* You said you would. Say good for you.

JANE Good for you.

ANNIE Now say good for us, Janie. Just say it.

JANE *(unsure of herself)* Good for us.

ANNIE Not bad, for your first try. It'll do. *(She lifts the one remaining box higher.)*

During the following lines, JANE and ANNIE begin their exit. Their conversation fades.

Mom, slow down, for God's sake, we can't keep up. Oh, she'll be all right, she's a little choked up, that's all. You could have choked on some of that food, I'll tell you, I don't know what they were doing with that. Maybe we'll hit the party up front for some decent food. Hey! Maybe they'd like the hip, too! There's an idea.

JANE Stop. That's awful.

ANNIE Why? I'll bet they've only got one measly casket up there so far. Big honkin' funeral and only one casket, what's that about? It was a good day, wasn't it, Janie? It was. It was, it was a good day.

Closes with the Last Supper women singing in the kitchen, MATT at the front desk, ANNIE and JANE leaving the chapel.

The end.

HAMISH

BY MICHAEL GRANT

NOTES

Michael Grant started writing *Hamish* when he and his wife, Sherry, adopted their first son, Brendan, a boy with no Scottish blood who was about to be raised in a world of Highland culture. Michael started examining his own roots and it led him to this hilarious story about a workaholic Canadian whose wife has forced him to take a vacation in the land of his ancestors, all so she can tell him that she is pregnant. Neither of them bargained for an encounter with the ghost of his great-great-great-great-grandfather and the antics of the locals.

Hamish originally premiered in 2007 at the Elmira Theatre Company and was entered in that year's Western Ontario Drama League Festival. In 2008, the Kincardine Theatre Guild mounted a second production of the play, billing *Hamish* as "A Scottish Play" to appeal to Kincardine's local heritage in Bruce County. Elmira, where the play originated, is famously rooted in Mennonite and German culture, but this play clearly spoke to all audiences. It is not about Scotland; it is about family everywhere.

Michael Grant was born and raised in Listowel, Ontario, and graduated from the Humber College theatre program, where he was first exposed to playwriting workshops. After several years of working in professional theatre, he settled down in Elmira where his first efforts in playwriting were short family plays for the Elmira Maple Syrup Festival. Since *Hamish*, he has written two other plays and adopted two other children. Michael's latest play, *Bare Bear Bones* is being produced by Elmira Theatre Company in 2012.

Hamish premiered at the Elmira Theatre Company Inc. on January 31, 2007, with the following cast and crew:

Tomas	Gerry Kraft
Gordon	David Laverty
Kelli	Greta Dearing
Hamish	Andrew Frey
Shelby	Dan Pitman
Annette	Deb Deckert

Producer: Deb Deckert
Director: Michael Grant
Stage Manager: Joe Brenner
Assistant Stage Managers: Kathy Fahey and Christine Wagner
Set Design: Paul Dietrich and Phil Dietrich
Lighting Design: Gord Grose
Sound: Phil Read
Props: Cathy Read-Wilson, Linda Bruder
Set Dressing: Sue Rose and Deb Deckert
Costumes: Cassandra Grant
Hair & Makeup: Danielle Deckert
Play Polisher: Brian Coatsworth

CHARACTERS

TOMAS
GORDON
KELLI
HAMISH
SHELBY
ANNETTE
ANNIS

ACT ONE

SCENE ONE

The set consists of a croft set in the Scottish Highlands. It should be immediately obvious that the building is several hundred years old, yet well maintained. It consists of a stone fireplace downstage right with a sofa and coffee table and possibly a chair and side table around it. Upstage right has an exit to a bedroom. On the upstage wall is the main entrance into the cottage and one or two windows. The upstage left side should hold a small kitchenette with a sink and table and chairs. There is an exit to the pantry downstage left beside the stove. As the curtain rises, the set is empty and dimly lit. We should hear a single bagpipe playing softly in the distance. It is night and moonlight streams through the windows.

TOMAS enters. He is the proprietor of the cottage. He is a rather elderly man but still has a spring in his step. He is whistling "Scotland the Brave."

TOMAS *(burdened with luggage)* Here ye go then, better late than never! Mr. Grant, your home away from home.

GORDON *(Also carrying luggage. He is a handsome man in his thirties.)* Thanks again for sticking around. We didn't know how to get a hold of you when our flight was delayed.

TOMAS Ye're not ma first guests to be delayed. Bless the man who put a pub at the airport! Besides, it's the least I could do considering the direct descendant of the grand Hamish Grant is returning to his homeland! Aye, 'tis a proud day, sir.

GORDON Now, Tomas, remember…

TOMAS I am sorry about the car ride. The Highlands weren't meant for cars. I mean with all the hills and glens ye cannae be travelling the way of the crow. It can take a wee bitty time.

GORDON That's hardly your fault.

TOMAS Aye, but I think your wifey was a wee bitty surprised.

GORDON I beg your pardon?

KELLI enters quickly, she is a pretty lady in her thirties. She is in an obvious hurry.

KELLI *(as she enters quickly)* Excuse me, excuse me. Nice place, Tomas, just lovely.

She immediately exits to the bedroom.

Pause, both men watch the doorway.

(re-entering) Ah, pardon me. That's the bedroom.

TOMAS Aye, 'tis. I hope it fits your fancy.

KELLI *(trying to hold her composure)* Yes, yes, I'm sure it'll be just fine.

TOMAS Splendid.

KELLI But what I'm really curious to know is, where is the… *(searching for the word)* ah… ah…

TOMAS Loo?

KELLI Yes, the ah, loo.

TOMAS *(indicating the door beside the stove)* It's out that way.

KELLI Behind the stove?

TOMAS Aye, and through the pantry.

KELLI *(under her breath as she goes)* No wonder they went to the New World, they couldn't find a bathroom in the old one.

She exits.

TOMAS *(to GORDON)* There's a natural spring just outside there. Besides, it helped to keep the plumbing close together. Ye've got to remember, when your great-great-great-great-grandda lived here there was nae plumbing. We added it thirty years back. We didnae want to go ripping apart the auld place so we just installed it all on that side.

GORDON Smart thinking.

TOMAS Aye, it happens to me every now and then, regardless of what the missus might say.

GORDON *(admiring the cottage)* It is a beautiful little place, Tomas, all the stone and woodwork.

TOMAS Aye, she may be old but she's solid. *(bangs on the wall, some dust falls from the rafters)* They dinnae build them like this anymore.

GORDON No, I guess not.

TOMAS Your great-great-great-great-grandda built this himself. He chaved awa' over it in the spring and summer to get it done so his missus and the lads would have a roof over their heads come winter, 'cause there's nothing colder then a Highland winter.

GORDON You should try my boss's office sometime.

TOMAS What ye be saying?

GORDON Oh nothing. I know all about the cold winters, we come from Canada. You know, hockey, snowmobiles, igloos…

TOMAS Aye, but ye should be proud of what your great-grandda did here. It wasnae an easy task, ye know, building this here hoose in one year on top of everything else he did for this little community. Look here now, we have a portrait of him over the fireplace. Look at him, such confidence and strength. He was a grand man. *(pauses for an emotional moment, fighting back tears he blows his nose)* Ach, but what am I telling ye for, ye know all about it.

GORDON Well, actually, no.

TOMAS Beg your pardon?

GORDON I don't know much about my history. I suppose that's why Kelli booked this trip. So I could learn.

TOMAS But you know about Hamish Grant?

GORDON Sorry, not a thing. My folks died when I was a baby and my great-uncle and aunt raised me.

TOMAS *(touches a portrait of St. Andrew, we assume for strength)* They must have told ye about the clan, your history.

GORDON No, they were from my mother's side and didn't know much of my father's family.

TOMAS returns to the picture, pulls it away from the wall to reveal a flask taped to the back. He thinks better of it, returns the picture.

TOMAS But you must have a relative on your father's side to teach you, a grandda, uncle…?

GORDON Nope, I'm the only one.

TOMAS Good heavens! Ye really are daft now, aren't ye? Lad, your family has one of the richest histories in all of the Highlands. I have ma work cut out for me, don't I?

GORDON No, really, Tomas, it's not necessary. I'm just looking for some quiet relaxation.

TOMAS Awa wi' ye! We can't have ye leaving here as daft and blind as when ye arrived. You're the last of the line. You have to know!

GORDON I appreciate the offer, really I do, but it's not…

TOMAS *(realizing)* My God! Ye're the last Hamish Grant. It's sad to see such a grand family tradition lost.

GORDON What tradition?

TOMAS *(disgusted)* They named ye Gordon.

GORDON Yeah?

TOMAS Ye have nae other relatives?

GORDON That's right.

TOMAS Nae brothers?

GORDON I was an orphan, singular.

TOMAS Sad.

GORDON *(frustrated)* What?

TOMAS Your name.

GORDON What about my name?

TOMAS Since anyone can remember, yer line of the Clan Grant always named their first son Hamish in honour of the man who built this and protected this land. Your name's Gordon. That means sometime after your family went to the New World they lost the tradition. *(sits, disappointed)* 'Tis sad to think how mere miles can crumble simple family values.

GORDON I hate to say it but the tradition hasn't crumbled. Gordon is my middle name. First name's Hamish!

TOMAS *(lifting his leg)* Here, pull the other one.

GORDON Look, it's on my driver's licence.

He shows it to TOMAS.

TOMAS Nice photo!

GORDON Look at the name. *(sarcastic)* The tradition lives.

TOMAS Why do ye call yourself Gordon?

GORDON When my parents died, I went to live with my great-uncle and aunt. They never liked the name Hamish so they just called me by my middle name, Gordon.

TOMAS Ye should have protested!

GORDON How could I, I wasn't even four years old. It's kind of hard to build a protest sign when you can't spell.

TOMAS Ach, it's nae right.

GORDON They thought it was best. Hamish wasn't too popular of a name when I was growing up.

TOMAS The name Hamish is a thing to be proud of.

GORDON I suppose. But I think they were afraid that the other kids would pick on me. So they used Gordon instead.

TOMAS Get picked on because your name is Hamish Grant?

GORDON Yeah.

TOMAS Did it help?

GORDON Hell no. They changed my name to protect me and then dressed me like a dork. Yeah, big help! I looked like the interior of a '73 Chrysler Cordoba until I graduated. It was pathetic.

KELLI *(re-entering)* What's pathetic?

GORDON Oh, nothing, dear, I was just telling Tomas about my past.

KELLI What's pathetic about your past, hon?

TOMAS I reckon ye two met after graduation.

KELLI That's right. My brother introduced us.

GORDON We work at the same firm.

KELLI That's right, and sixteen months later we were married. *(She hugs* GORDON.*)* Think, honey, that was five years ago this very weekend.

GORDON *(unhappy to be here)* And half a world away. *(They kiss.)*

TOMAS That's ma cue. When the lasses start getting frisky, 'tis time for me to run. It's a philosophy that kept me happily single for years.

GORDON I thought you were married.

TOMAS Aye.

KELLI What happened?

TOMAS She ran faster.

KELLI You're not going anywhere. You just sit right down there and relax. I'm going to go unpack. You fill Gordon in on all the local sights. I told you, I plan on seeing as much as I can in the next two weeks.

TOMAS I guess I could stay a wee bitty longer. If I time it right, when I get home, the old cheetah might be asleep. *(pause as* TOMAS *begins an obviously rehearsed shtick)* Dry… dry… Quite dry… It does seem a wee dry in here, don't ye think, Hamish?

KELLI Hamish? I haven't heard you called that since our wedding.

GORDON It's a long story, Kel. I'm sorry, Tomas, can I get you a glass of water?

Pause.

TOMAS *(grabbing* GORDON *by the arm)* Are ye sure ye've got Scottish blood in those veins?

GORDON What?

KELLI I think you'll find a bottle of Scotch in the small black bag, Gord. It's in the bedroom.

TOMAS *(patting* GORDON *on the head)* Now there'd be a smart lassie.

GORDON Huh? *(realizing)* Oh yeah, of course, the Scotch. I'll get you a glass.

TOMAS *(shoving him to the bedroom)* Ye get the bottle, I'll get the glasses.

KELLI *(as she is picking up the luggage)* It's so beautiful up here. It's just like I imagined it. All the hills, the cottage, even the air. It smells so… clean.

TOMAS *(as he spit-shines the glasses using a tea towel)* Wait till old MacGregor over there starts his fertilizing. It'll knock ye over. The only time he spreads it thicker is closing time at the pub.

KELLI Really?

TOMAS Ach, aye get a few drinks into him and he'll tell ye the way of the world. Hell, he had half of us believing the world was turning flat again. But you should be all right. It's past spreading time. *(pause)* In the fields that is. The pub is due in about an hour.

KELLI It is beautiful though. Just like a movie.

TOMAS Aye, our guests always expect to see Braveheart charging over the hill at any moment.

KELLI I can even hear bagpipes.

TOMAS gives her a quick look.

GORDON *(entering)* Yeah, I hear them, too.

TOMAS *(quickly)* Oh that, 'tis naught.

KELLI Is there a, what do you call it, a ceilidh?

TOMAS No, 'tis… *(searching)*

GORDON Well, it's a little late for a parade.

TOMAS No, 'tis someone practising.

KELLI Who, a neighbour?

TOMAS Aye, probably the MacGregor boy.

GORDON Kind of late to be practising, don't you think?

TOMAS No, no. Not for him. He's a wee bit of a nighthawk if you know what I mean. Play all night if they let him.

KELLI Really?

TOMAS Ach aye, it's naught to worry about. You'll soon get used to it. You won't even notice him.

KELLI I hope not. I love the sound. I'll listen for them every night.

TOMAS I dare say ye won't be disappointed, ma lady.

KELLI I'm going to get unpacked and get out of these clothes.

GORDON Would you like a hand, dear?

KELLI No, I'll be fine. You sit and learn about the area. I told you, I want to see it all.

She exits.

TOMAS *(intently examining the bottle of Scotch)* So, what would you like to know, lad?

GORDON *(deep in thought)* Pardon?

TOMAS *(intently examining the bottle but does not open it)* Huh?

GORDON Pardon?

TOMAS Huh?

GORDON Pardon?

TOMAS About the area. What do ye want to know?

GORDON Oh, I don't know. Where's the nearest telephone or maybe a fax machine?

TOMAS Huh?

GORDON *(takes the bottle from him and sets it on the table)* Email! You must have email! You have a website. You must have the Internet.

TOMAS *(picking the bottle back up)* Sorry, no. Ma laddie takes care of that Internet stuff. He stays in Inverness. I cannae be bothered with that computer nonsense.

GORDON Damn!

TOMAS We have a telephone up at the hoose.

GORDON Well, that's better than nothing.

TOMAS Nae really.

GORDON What do you mean?

TOMAS It's nae better than nothing.

GORDON *(confused)* Huh?

TOMAS It's nae better than nothing. 'Tis nothing.

GORDON What?

TOMAS Nothing. I pick up the receiver and nothing. Dead.

GORDON Your phone is dead?

TOMAS Aye.

GORDON When will it be fixed?

TOMAS When I call the service.

GORDON When you call them? You mean you haven't called them!

TOMAS How the hell am I suppose to call them? My phone's dead!

GORDON *(pause)* Ahh, yes. *(takes the Scotch from him)* I give up.

TOMAS *(following him, focused on the bottle)* It's a hell of a predicament when ye think about it.

GORDON How long's it been dead?

TOMAS Since October.

GORDON Last October?!

TOMAS Aye. I imagine the bastards will want ma first-born with a side of chips to fix the damned thing.

GORDON How in the world do you conduct business without a telephone? You're on the Internet for crying out loud. *(sets the bottle on the table)*

TOMAS *(picks up the bottle and offers it to* GORDON *to open)* I told ye, ma laddie takes care of the Internet stuff. He takes the bookings and everything and then every Saturday morning he rings the MacGregors over there, and I get all the information I need. He does the rest.

GORDON *(doesn't take the bottle)* But, my God, how do you live without a telephone?

TOMAS *(thinking)* You would think quietly, wouldn't ye? But no.

GORDON No?

TOMAS Hell no! When we had a telephone the old roadrunner would speak to her sisters in Glasgow three times a week. Now that she dinnae have them to speak to… *(pause)* Have ya ever felt your ears go numb?

GORDON Oh, she can't be all that bad.

TOMAS Can't be all that bad? Lad, it took her a week and a half to figure out that the phone was dead!

GORDON This is just great!

TOMAS What are you complaining about? Ye havenae even met her yet. I'm married to her. *(offers the bottle)*

GORDON *(taking the bottle)* What?

TOMAS *(crosses and sits alone on the sofa)* Listen, Hamish, things work a wee bitty different up here. 'Tis a much quieter and simpler lifestyle than ye got in your big cities. We take the time to stop and smell the heather. It's nae that hustle and bustle way ye live. Always racing from one place t'other not really gettin' anywhere and never stopping to enjoy yersel along the way.

GORDON *(sets the bottle on the table and crosses to the sofa)* So, what you're telling me is that I'm stuck here in the Scottish Highlands with no chance of contacting the outside world.

TOMAS *(extends his hand expecting a glass of Scotch, there is none)* I could be wrong, but I'm sensing that ye don't want to be here.

GORDON Really! Am I that transparent! *(pause)* I'm sorry, Tomas, it's just that I was working on a huge case back home and I'm anxious that it goes all right.

TOMAS Is there no one else that can deal with it?

GORDON I guess, it's just…

TOMAS *(picks up the bottle and offers it again to GORDON)* Then let it be, lad. If ye're thinking about work, how do ye expect to enjoy your vacation?

GORDON I don't.

TOMAS Ye don't? This is the trip of a lifetime! Ye've come home to your family's croft. It's a chance to relive the past.

GORDON I don't know anything about my past.

TOMAS *(shoving the bottle into GORDON's chest)* Then take the time to learn.

GORDON *(sets the bottle down on the table)* I'm not interested in my family's past. It's history. It doesn't affect me now. It's irrelevant.

TOMAS Irrelevant!?

GORDON I'm sorry, Tomas. It's just… I don't know. I don't even know why Kelli booked this trip. I guess she thought I needed a vacation.

TOMAS *(following with the bottle and a glass)* I cannae say I disagree.

GORDON Maybe it's the jet lag, I don't know.

TOMAS 'Tis fine, Hamish, get some rest. I think ye'll see things different in the morning.

Disappointed, TOMAS sets the unopened bottle on the table, kisses his fingers, and touches it.

Nothing clears the mind like the crisp morning air of the Highlands.

KELLI enters. She is now wearing a sweater and pyjama pants.

KELLI I sure hope that's true.

GORDON Honey, there you are. How's the unpacking going? Let me help.

KELLI It can wait. I'm on vacation. I didn't travel halfway around the world just so I could race in there and unpack. I was beginning to feel like my mother. I just want to put my feet up and relax. *(sits on the sofa)*

TOMAS Now there's a lass who knows how to enjoy her vacation. Are ye taking notes, lad? *(hopeful)* Now quine can I get ye a wee dram?

KELLI No, no thank you, Tomas, I'm fine for the moment.

TOMAS all but collapses with disappointment and frustration.

GORDON Are you sure, honey?

KELLI No, really, I'm fine. Now, Gordon, what have you learned about the area?

GORDON Well, not much. I'm afraid that I was telling Tomas how I really didn't want to…

TOMAS *(quickly)* Lets see now, I told the lad about hiking the Monroe over by Mac Dougall's Ridge.

GORDON Huh?

TOMAS Aye, 'tis the best view of the area. I also told him about the tours of the loch. What else, Hamish?

GORDON Well, ahh…

TOMAS Ach aye, I forgot. The Gathering.

KELLI The what?

GORDON The what?

TOMAS The Gathering… of the clan. You mean the two of ye don't know anything about it? That's why I thought ye were here, for the Gathering.

KELLI I'm sorry, we have no idea what you're talking about.

TOMAS By heavens! Ye two travelled all the way from Canada to be here without knowing this weekend is the annual Gathering of the Clan Grant.

GORDON What the hell's a Gathering?

TOMAS Ye'll know soon enough, lad. I intend to make sure of it personally. But for now I should be going, let ye two settle in.

KELLI Oh, Tomas, do you have to?

TOMAS I think it best, ye manny here could use some rest. Besides, the old gabbing gazelle should be asleep by now. That means some quiet time with my pretty little lady.

KELLI You're not having an affair?!

TOMAS If ye count drooling over the weather girl on the telly an affair, then aye. Now, you'll find all the linen you need in the bedroom and there are more towels on the shelf in the loo.

KELLI Thank you.

GORDON Yes, thank you. I'm sure we'll be fine.

TOMAS Just remember, if ye need anything we're just up in the main hoose.

GORDON We'll be all right. You go and enjoy the weather report.

TOMAS *(As he opens the door, the bagpipes outside become louder.)* Aye, lad, I intend to. *(quietly to GORDON)* You should see the size of her…

KELLI He's still practising.

TOMAS *(nervous)* What's that, lassie?

KELLI The piper, he's still practising.

TOMAS Aye, aye, he is.

GORDON But it's almost midnight. When does he stop?

TOMAS I wouldnae imagine he'd go much longer. He tends to stop around midnight.

GORDON I sure hope so. It sounds like someone wringing out a cat.

TOMAS Wringing out a cat? Are ye sure ye're a true Scot, lad?

GORDON Sorry.

TOMAS A true Scot is proud when he hears the pipes. He feels the fire in his belly grow. He stands a little taller, holds his head high and is willin to face anyone who dares dishonour his land and the pipes.

GORDON Hey, hey, hey! I said I was sorry. I'm just tired, that's all.

TOMAS *(slapping GORDON on the shoulder)* 'Tis all right, lad, I understand. Consider that lesson number one on how to be a Highlander. Ye get your rest and I'll come see ye the morn'. The good Lord took six days to create the world and I suspect I'll need double that to make a Highlander out a ye!

KELLI Could we talk to this MacGregor boy tomorrow and see if he could cut his practising a little shorter?

TOMAS *(thinking quickly)* I dinna think ye want to be doing that.

KELLI Why not?

TOMAS The MacGregors are a wee bit… well… let's just say, it's best we leave well enough alone. Good night now.

KELLI Good night and thanks again.

GORDON Yes, thanks for everything.

TOMAS Dennae mention it. Get some rest, Hamish.

TOMAS exits.

KELLI *(giggling)* Hamish, it sounds so cute.

GORDON *(pouring himself a glass of Scotch)* Yeah, cute like a moose in heat.

KELLI No, really, I like it. Why don't you use it?

GORDON Well, for starters, I'd have to change all my business cards. Besides, how many corporate lawyers do you know called Hamish?

KELLI *(hugging him)* You could be the first. You already said you were going to be the best. If you're the best, you can call yourself whatever you want.

GORDON In that case, when I'm the best, I'll call myself rich!

KELLI Rich Grant?

GORDON *(following her to the couch)* Okay then, how about Moneybags Grant or Wealthy Grant, or even Extremely Wealthy Grant. Oh, I like the sound of that one. Hey, maybe High on the Hog Grant…

KELLI quickly turns and kisses him passionately and they fall back onto the couch.

GORDON Talking about money makes you horny, too, huh?

KELLI No, it just seems to be the only way to get you to stop talking about work lately.

GORDON I just want to do well, for our sake. So we can have the finer things in life.

KELLI When are you going to learn that there are more important things in life than "the finer things"?

GORDON When someone shows me what could possibly be more important than living the high life.

KELLI I know of one thing that's more important than money.

GORDON Nothing is more important than money.

KELLI Family.

GORDON Family?

KELLI Yes, family.

GORDON Kel, you are my family. Until you, I had none.

KELLI You had your uncle and aunt.

GORDON It's not the same.

KELLI Sure it is, family is what you make it.

GORDON And I made you my family. Therefore, that makes you the most important thing. So what do you say we go into that bedroom there and I show you just how important you are.

KELLI You're changing the subject.

GORDON *(moving in for a kiss)* I know. It's amazing how a high-priced lawyer can steer a conversation.

KELLI You're not high-priced yet.

GORDON *(while nibbling her neck)* But someday I will be. Consider this practise. Now are you going to go quietly or am I going to have to start talking about work again?

KELLI *(teasing)* Well, I don't know… Hamish…

During this, GORDON is tickling KELLI and playfully chasing her into the bedroom. She can kiss him between each reference.

GORDON All right then, you asked for it. Legal contracts!

KELLI Hamish!

GORDON Power lunches!

KELLI Hamish!

GORDON Board meetings!

KELLI Hamish!

GORDON Corner offices!

KELLI Hamish!

GORDON Water coolers!

KELLI Hamish!

GORDON *(spoken with KELLI's next line)* Clients! Desks! Paycheques!

KELLI Hamish! Hamish! Hamish!

She exits into the bedroom.

He delivers his final blow as only her arm is seen coming out of the doorway, pulling him in. He flicks the light switch when he goes.

GORDON PAPER CLIPS!

The stage is now empty. During the last banter, the bagpipes should slowly fade out so it's only now the audience realizes they are gone. After a moment, HAMISH, *a large Scotsman, enters from the front door. He pauses, then snaps his fingers to turn the lights back on. He is dressed in old traditional Scottish garb complete with a great kilt. He appears to be in his fifties. He has the air about him that in his younger years he was a giant among men, a fierce and weathered warrior. He's carrying a set of bagpipes. He notices the Scotch on the table and slowly waves his arm, causing the bedroom door to open. He looks in, waves his arm back, causing the door to close. He looks tired as he sets his bagpipes down on the table and picks up the bottle of Scotch.*

HAMISH Humph. *(examining the bottle)*

He drinks from the bottle and spits it out.

He silently walks the room, examining what's changed since the guests have arrived. He pauses at the portrait over the fireplace. He examines the portrait for a moment then imitates the pose. He pauses, looks at his belly then back to the portrait. He sucks in his belly.

Aye.

He makes his way to the pantry door and exits, presumably to visit the washroom. As he goes, he sings.

Noo the simmer's in prime…

The stage is empty for a moment.

KELLI *enters from the bedroom and quickly crosses to the bathroom with her hand over her mouth.*

KELLI I'm sorry, maybe it's the plane ride or something I ate.

GORDON *appears in the doorway with nothing but a blanket wrapped around him.*

GORDON Hey, I know I've gained a bit of weight, but don't you think you're overreacting?

KELLI I'm sorry! I can't help it! *(She's gone out to the bathroom.)*

GORDON Well, that's killed the mood! *(looking at his crotch)* Sorry, Mr. Wiggles, back to sleep. *(He exits to the bedroom.)*

HAMISH *(entering quickly from the bathroom)* Christ, lass, the least ye could do is knock! What makes ye think I want to look at that! Ken the hell's the world coming to?

He crosses to the fireplace with the bottle. GORDON *enters from the bedroom. He is now dressed in pyjama pants and a T-shirt. He does not see* HAMISH.

GORDON *(yelling out to the pantry)* Hon, you okay? Hon? *(crosses to the pantry door)* Look, I'm sorry. Is there anything I can do? *(He exits through the pantry.)*

HAMISH *(sitting)* Dinnae go there, lad. If there's one thing I've learned over the years it's dinnae be bothering a lass when she's going aboot what she's going aboot.

GORDON *(entering backwards from the pantry)* I'm sorry, honey, I was just trying to help.

HAMISH Ah, the younger generation, they never mind.

GORDON *(startled, hearing the stranger's voice)* What?!

HAMISH *(calmly)* Hello.

GORDON *screams, the man jumps from the sofa.*

(looking around) What is it, lad?

GORDON Who the hell are you?

HAMISH *(looking around)* Who?

GORDON You!

HAMISH *(still looking)* Who you?

GORDON You who?

HAMISH Where's who?

GORDON You who, that's who?

HAMISH Fit who, lad?

GORDON *(grabbing a butter knife from the drawer)* Enough of the Dr. Seuss. Tell me who you are!

HAMISH Doctor who?

GORDON Don't start again.

HAMISH Start fit?

GORDON Look, what do you want?

HAMISH For the love of God, lad, who are ya blethering at?

GORDON You, the one holding my bottle of Scotch.

HAMISH *(realizing he's still holding the Scotch)* Ah shite!

He quickly puts the bottle behind his back and begins whistling, trying to be nonchalant.

GORDON What's going on here?

HAMISH Bollocks! *(talking to the picture over the fireplace)* Fit's done is done, I mecht as well ha' some fun wit' it, noo. *(to GORDON as he advances towards him)* So, ye see the bottle, do ye? A bitty eerie, isn't it?

GORDON *(retreating from the advance)* What?

HAMISH 'Tis eerie the way it just floats there, isn't it?

GORDON Stay back!

HAMISH 'Tis a bottle of whisky whooshing through the air. Look oot, it's going to get ye.

He makes roaring airplane sounds as if the bottle's attacking GORDON.

GORDON *(after much high-pitched screaming)* Listen, mister, I don't know who you are and what your story is with the Scotch but I've just about had enough. So why don't you set the bottle down and get the hell out!

HAMISH I'm nae goin' anywhere. 'Tis my hoose. Look oot for the magic flying bottle! Boogie, boogie, boo!

GORDON *(screams)* Oh, I see. You've been at the pub tonight, haven't ya?

HAMISH Fit?

GORDON It's okay. Hey, I like to let loose every now and then, too. The important thing is, we get you home. Let's go up and see Tomas. He'll know who you belong to.

HAMISH *(looking around confused)* Who the hell are ye speaking to?

GORDON Oh, no ya don't. We're not playing that game again.

HAMISH *(realizing, he sets the bottle of Scotch on the table)* By heavens! Ye can hear me! Can ye see me?

GORDON Well, duh!

HAMISH Prove it.

GORDON Why?

HAMISH Because if ye dinnae I'll be showing ye ma dirk, and it's a hell of a lot bigger then your fierce buttering variety there.

GORDON *(setting the knife down)* All right, all right, there's no need for violence. What would you like me to do?

HAMISH Tell me fit I look like.

GORDON If I do, will you let me take you home?

HAMISH I told ye, I am ta hame.

GORDON Listen, sir, we've rented this cottage for two weeks. This isn't your…

HAMISH *(anger building)* Fit do I look like?

GORDON *(retreating)* Okay, okay. You look like a mature man. You are wearing a kilt. A bit of a haircut, shave, and a shower probably wouldn't hurt. You look… ah… ah… kind of mean… ah… maybe a little drunk.

HAMISH Good God, man, I barely touched your whisky.

GORDON What am I suppose to think? You come in here claiming it's your house. Then you chase me around with a bottle and now it comes as a complete surprise that I can see you! I don't know how things work on this side of the Atlantic, but where I come from those clues all point to one of two things. Either you're all wailed up or somewhere out there is an entire village looking for their idiot! Now, if you're not drunk, as you claim, there is only one other choice.

HAMISH Nae, there's more.

GORDON What?

HAMISH *(to himself)* 'Tis amazin. It's ne'er happened afore. He can see me. He can really see me. After all this time and finally someone can see me. The question is why? Why can I be seen the noo? Fit's so special?

GORDON *(opening the front door for* HAMISH*)* Pardon me for interrupting but your village awaits.

HAMISH *(realizing)* Ach aye! That's it! That's why ye can see me, because ye're like me.

GORDON Like you? I don't think so! We're nothing alike. I don't have a village.

HAMISH No, I mean oor situation. 'Tis fantastic! I'll finally have someone to speak wit, other than Tomas's dog of course.

GORDON Of course.

HAMISH 'Tis grand, how long have ye been here?

GORDON How long?

HAMISH Aye, since you made the trip over.

GORDON We arrived this afternoon. Now please, your village needs you.

HAMISH So ye're new.

GORDON Yeah, we're fresh off the plane. I think I hear the villagers calling.

HAMISH We? Ye wifey came with ye?

GORDON Of course. Now, before they light the torches and gather the pitchforks.

HAMISH 'Tis a shame, ye both so young. Ye dinnae have any bairns, did ye?

GORDON No, no kids.

HAMISH Well, thank heavens for that.

GORDON Excuse me, what…

HAMISH *(going to GORDON with his hand extended)* I'm sorry, I havenae introduced masell. Hamish, Hamish Grant.

GORDON Yes, but please, I prefer Gordon.

HAMISH Huh?

GORDON I go by Gordon.

HAMISH *(building anger)* Gordon? You're a Gordon?

GORDON Perhaps not…

HAMISH *(turning menacing)* Gordon, eh? Ye're a wee bitty far from home, aren't ye?

GORDON *(confused)* Yeah, well, you know…

HAMISH What brings ye to the Grant's?

GORDON My wife made me come.

HAMISH Ye wife? Ye Gordons always did ride on your wifey's pinny strings.

GORDON Now just a minute.

HAMISH I ken the real reason why ye're here.

GORDON You do?

HAMISH Aye, and I donae believe it.

GORDON I don't think I do either.

HAMISH *(producing a sword)* So you want ma land, do ye? Ye clan ne'r gives up. Over two hundred and fifty years since I last fought ye off and still ye're trying to get ye filthy hands on it. Nae this time, Gordon. Nae as long as I'm here. Nae body will take this land. It's Grant land!

GORDON Grant land?

By now, HAMISH has GORDON pinned to the kitchen counter or wall or perhaps on a chair, with his sword at GORDON's navel.

HAMISH That's right. I built this hoose and lived in it e're since.

GORDON You built this?

HAMISH That's right, awbody kens it.

GORDON But, it's over two hundred years old.

HAMISH Two hundred and sixty three to be exact.

KELLI enters from the bathroom. She looks exhausted and sick. She immediately crosses as if going to the bedroom.

GORDON Kelli!

KELLI What?

She looks at him. He has arms out as if to show his predicament, but she does not see HAMISH.

Oh, come on, honey, I've just let go of my lunch in there. How can you possibly still be thinking about sex?

GORDON *(pointing at the tip of the sword, which is right at his navel)* Do you think you could help me here?

KELLI *(misunderstanding his gesture)* You're pathetic, Gordon. Take the matter into your own hands if you must. *(She begins to exit.)*

GORDON Do you suppose you could call someone for me then?

KELLI *(as she's exiting)* Not if you want to stay married!

GORDON What the hell's with her?

HAMISH She could nae see me. *(thinking)* Odd.

GORDON Listen. Can't we just talk about it, man to man?

HAMISH I would if there was another man here, but Hamish Grant dinnae speak to the likes of ye.

GORDON What?

HAMISH Ye heard me.

GORDON No, what did you say your name was?

HAMISH I told ye, I'm Hamish Grant.

GORDON You're Hamish Grant?

HAMISH Aye, 'tis ma hoose and ma land.

GORDON How can that be? I'm Hamish Grant.

HAMISH *(pulling the sword back slightly)* Fit do ye mean?

GORDON That's my name: Hamish Gordon Grant.

HAMISH Lad, noo ye're the one nae making sense. Ye said ye were a Gordon.

GORDON I'm not "a" Gordon. I am Gordon. It's my middle name. I'm the last living Hamish Grant.

HAMISH Living!

GORDON Huh?

HAMISH You're alive?

GORDON *(looking at the sword)* Currently.

HAMISH *(thinking)* Quick, fit was your father called?

GORDON Hamish.

HAMISH And his father?

GORDON Hamish. We're all Hamish for as far back as anyone can remember. Some self-absorbed ancestor started the stupid idea of naming the first son Hamish.

HAMISH Mind your tongue.

GORDON Pardon.

HAMISH Mind your manners, boy. It wasnae stupid and I'm nae self-absorbed.

GORDON All right, that's enough. It's time for you to go. *(He picks up a fireplace poker.)* I've had enough of this nonsense.

HAMISH puts the sword away and opens his arms as if expecting a hug.

HAMISH Now, son, is that anywa' to speak to ye grandda?

GORDON Listen, mister, I don't know who you are, or what the hell you're talking about. But my grandfather is dead along with the rest of my family. So I'd be very much obliged if you could find your way to the door.

HAMISH I'm sorry about oor family, Hamish, but I'm nae leaving. I built this hoose and until the man upstairs opens the gates for me, I'm nae leaving.

GORDON The guy who built it is long dead.

HAMISH Aye, the auld gears in that melon of yours are startin' to turn for ye, noo?!

GORDON So, you're telling me that you're over two hundred years old.

HAMISH Actually we dinnae count when we're dead.

GORDON What?

HAMISH Think about it. Really, fit would the point be?

GORDON You're telling me you're a ghost?

HAMISH *(laughing)* Finally! That took ye a while. I see the clan hasnae gotten any brighter over the years.

GORDON A ghost? I don't believe it.

HAMISH 'Tis really nae the issue, Hamish.

GORDON It's not?

HAMISH No, the real question is why nae one could e're see me and then ye waltz in here and bang I'm clear as a bell to ye.

GORDON Only me?

HAMISH Aye, only ye. Your wee wifey didnae see me when she came from the loo and she didnae see me when she went in.

GORDON How do you know?

HAMISH *(raising his voice)* Because I was on the seat when she went to use it. I'll tell ye, transparency has its downsides.

GORDON And no one else has ever seen you?

HAMISH Nay, nary a soul.

GORDON Not even Tomas?

HAMISH *(laughing)* Old Tomas! Nae chance. Of a night I sit on his sofa and watch the weather girl with him. She's got a great set of…

GORDON That's terrible.

HAMISH Ach, just because I'm dead dinnae mean I can nae look.

GORDON I need a drink.

HAMISH *(picks up the bottle)* Grand idea, I'll have one, too.

GORDON You can drink?

HAMISH Sure, I've been drinkin Tomas's for years. His wifey sees the empty bottle in the mornin and tears a strip off him. But the best part, I'm dead. No hangover!

GORDON It sounds kind of cruel.

HAMISH Cruel? I'll tell ye fits cruel. The man up there leavin me down here. Noo, that's cruel! Me wifey and bairns are all up there and I'm stuck here guarding this hoose.

GORDON Guarding it from who?

HAMISH I dinnae ken! The Gordons I suppose. He ne'er really told me.

GORDON You've spoken to the Almighty?

HAMISH Aye. He said I still had important work to do here.

GORDON Guarding the house is important work?

HAMISH He never said fit the work was. The Gordons have been trying to get this land for centuries, I assume that's the important work.

GORDON How long do you have to stay here?

HAMISH Ye guess is as good as mine, laddie. He said that when the time came, I'd ken. Then, when I had completed ma task, I could join ma family.

GORDON You haven't seen them in all that time?

HAMISH No.

GORDON *(noticing the bagpipes on table)* Are those yours?

HAMISH *(His mind is elsewhere.)* Aye.

GORDON *(after a moment)* It was you, wasn't it?

HAMISH Fit?

GORDON Playing earlier.

HAMISH Aye.

GORDON I knew it.

Pause.

HAMISH I play them for Annis.

GORDON Who?

HAMISH Ma wife, Annis. Every night, I stand on the hillock out there, look to the heavens, and play her favourite songs.

GORDON She can hear them? I mean up there.

HAMISH I dinnae ken. *(pause)* I hope so. *(long pause)* Someday I'll get there. *(convincing himself)* It'll happen. *(wiping away tears)* Ach, but fit the hell are we doing here? I have nae spoken to anyone for over two centuries and here we are blubbering like a bunch of lassies at a wedding. Tell me about ye, lad. Fit's the family done since it went to the New World?

GORDON I don't really know.

HAMISH Fit the hell do ye mean ye dinna ken? How could you nae ken?

GORDON What's with this place? Why do I need to keep explaining my life? I was an orphan.

HAMISH So?

GORDON So? My mother's uncle and aunt raised me. There's no one left on my father's side.

HAMISH Isn't that ma luck! Over a hundred years of not seein ma family and when I finally meet one, he's as daft as I am!

GORDON Hey, it's not my fault!

HAMISH Now your starting to sound like your great-great-great-grandda. It was ne'er his fault either. It wasnae his fault about the kuh incident, the Nessie story, or aboot MacGregor's lassie. Hell, it wasnae even his fault he abandoned the family land and headed to the New World.

GORDON No, it's not like that, I mean…

HAMISH I ken fit ye mean. Ye young people today are ne'er willin to stand behind ye actions. In ma day we said fit we meant and stood behind it until the end, right or wrong.

GORDON *(clapping sarcastically)* Your little spook story was well done, mister, but it's time for you to go back to your village or wherever it is you came from. I'm dead tired.

HAMISH I told ye, I'm nae gain'.

GORDON Oh, yes, you are.

GORDON tries to grab HAMISH by the arm but can't as he's a ghost. GORDON realizes his first attempt failed and tries again, only to be face to face with HAMISH. Realizing the truth, he backs away.

What the hell!

Stumbling away from HAMISH.

Shit! You are a… a… a ghost! Shit!

HAMISH I thought we covered aw this?

GORDON Shit!

HAMISH *(moves towards GORDON)* Now, son!

GORDON Stay back! Stay away!

HAMISH I'm nae goin to hurt ye. I'm your grandda.

GORDON No you're not! No way! You're just my imagination. You're just a dream! Hell, I'm probably asleep right now on that sofa. You're nothing but a bad dream. Damn jet lag! How did Scrooge put it? "You're just something I ate, maybe a piece of beef." Well, old boy, I do my best dreaming in bed, so if you don't mind, good night, meathead! *(He starts to exit.)*

HAMISH Whisht, Hamish! We need to speak.

GORDON Sorry, jerky boy!

HAMISH *(raising voice)* Hamish! Wait!

At this point GORDON is about to pass through the doorway to the bedroom when HAMISH raises his arm and the door suddenly slams shut, as if moved by a supernatural force. It hits GORDON squarely in the face, knocking him out cold. He falls to the floor.

Fit is it with ma offspring? They ne'r mind.

He picks up the bottle of Scotch, drinks it all, sets it back on the table, picks up his pipes, and exits out the pantry door. He snaps his fingers as he leaves and the interior lights go out.

SCENE TWO

It is early morning. All is the same as it was before. GORDON is still lying on the floor where he fell. The stage is quiet. It should remain that way during a slow light change that would signify the sunrise and a passage of time. Finally, after a long, quiet moment…

TOMAS *(pounding loudly on the door)* Hamish! Hamish! Hamish, ye awake yet? Hamish!

GORDON stirs and slowly rises. He finds his feet, looks around, and turns on the interior lights. Feeling the bump on his head, he stumbles into the bedroom to check on KELLI. He re-enters the room, scanning to see if HAMISH is still there.

Come on, Hamish. The Gathering will be starting soon. Hamish! Ye want to meet your family, don't ye! Come on, Hamish! Rise and shine! We dinnae want to miss the heavy events! Come on, ma laddie! Let's awa! Hamish!? Hamish? Come on, lad, 'tis a wee bitty chilly out here!

GORDON opens the door, and TOMAS enters. He is dressed in true Highland fashion. He carries a bundle of clothing under his arm.

Christ, lad, I damn near froze the wee one off out there.

GORDON That'd serve ye right for going around without any pants on.

TOMAS 'Tis a kilt, lad.

GORDON *(inspecting the cottage for any sign of the ghost)* What's the occasion?

TOMAS What's the occasion? 'Tis the Gathering today!

GORDON The gathering of what?

TOMAS Ye clan. I told ye last night, were ye nae listening?

GORDON Oh yeah, I'm sorry. I've got a lot on my mind right now.

TOMAS 'Tis all right, just forget aboot your troubles and put this on. *(He tosses a kilt at GORDON.)*

GORDON What's this?

TOMAS Ye kilt. Put it on.

GORDON No really, Tomas, I don't think…

TOMAS Hie on, lad, we'll be late, put it on.

GORDON But I really don't have the legs to pull something like this off.

TOMAS Christ, lad, ye're wed. You don't have to be looking good anymore, the hunt's over.

GORDON But…

TOMAS No "buts." Get in there, get dressed, and wake that lass of yours up, too. She'll be wanting to meet the family I suppose.

GORDON But I really need to ask you…

TOMAS Speak later, dress now. *(hurries him into the bedroom)*

GORDON *(re-entering)* Tomas, I don't know how to put it on.

TOMAS *(pushing him out)* Ye're a Grant! You'll figure it out. Awa wi ye!

GORDON Well, could ya find me some Aspirin, I've got a splitting headache.

GORDON exits.

TOMAS *(picking up the empty Scotch bottle, to himself)* I'm not surprised.

He crosses to the kitchen, sets the bottle on the table, and begins to search for Aspirin. He yells to the bedroom.

Hurry up, lad! A Scotsman doesnae let a hangover slow him down. *(to himself)* If we did, the country would grind to a halt. *(continues searching)*

HAMISH enters through the front door.

HAMISH *(He's in good spirits.)* Mornin, Tomas, ye old bullocks, fit's the weather for today? The dog tells me she was wearing a low-cut green number last night. Sorry I missed it. *(Pause. TOMAS doesn't respond.)* Ach, the silent treatment again? What a shocker. *(as he exits through the pantry)* By the by, the dog left ye a prizzie in the garden.

TOMAS *(finding Aspirin)* Damn, it's getting chilly in here!

GORDON enters wearing the kilt incorrectly with loud boxer shorts underneath. He is holding the kilt up with both hands.

GORDON How's this look?

TOMAS tosses the bottle of Aspirin at him. GORDON lets go of the kilt to catch the bottle and the kilt falls to the floor.

TOMAS *(pause)* Fright, boy! Ye cannae even dress yourself. When ye get a hangover ye really go all out, donae ye?

GORDON Huh?

TOMAS Come, I'll show ye.

During the next bit of dialogue, TOMAS *gets to his knees and helps* GORDON *with the kilt.*

Ye've got to start it this way.

GORDON *(as he stands and* TOMAS *wraps him)* Tomas, something strange happened here last night.

TOMAS *(only half listening)* Aye.

GORDON It was kind of creepy.

TOMAS Could you raise your arm? *(*GORDON *does.)* Ta.

GORDON Yeah, it was kind of, I don't know. *(pause)* Has anything ever happened here before?

TOMAS There, ye're done. Noo ye can lose the shorts.

GORDON I beg your pardon?

TOMAS Drop your drawers.

GORDON I don't think…

TOMAS 'Tis the Highland way. If folk see ye wearing them under ye kilt ye'll be the laughingstock of the Gathering. Now drop them.

GORDON What do ya mean, see them? Who the hell would look? This thing's so high-cut I could traumatize a toddler.

TOMAS Now don't be shy, 'tis the Highland way. Look.

TOMAS *raises his kilt to show* GORDON *just as* KELLI *enters from the bedroom. She is met with a full view of* TOMAS. *She crosses to the pantry quickly, holding her mouth as if to be sick.*

KELLI I'll never eat prunes again. *(She's gone.)*

TOMAS Ach, damnation! *(yelling after her)* Sorry about that. *(to* GORDON*)* I am sorry.

GORDON Don't worry about it, I got the same reaction when I showed her mine.

TOMAS Huh?

GORDON Never mind. I want to know about last night. Has anything strange ever happened here before?

TOMAS *(guarded)* Like what?

GORDON I don't know, like something paranormal.

TOMAS What have ye heard?

GORDON Nothing, it's just…

HAMISH *(entering quickly)* Ach, that's twice the lassie's done that, damn it! *(seeing GORDON)* Mornin, son, sleep well I trust?

TOMAS It's just what? Was that MacGregor boy over here fillin your head wit a bunch of old ghostie tales?

GORDON *(eyes locked on HAMISH)* Huh?

TOMAS Well, donae ye be listening to him. It's just some old wive's tale they tell around here to scare the wee ones.

GORDON It is?

TOMAS Aye, just a bunch of rubbish.

HAMISH Ask him about the bagpipes.

GORDON Ask him yourself.

TOMAS What's that?

HAMISH He cannae hear me!

TOMAS Ask what?

GORDON *(after a look to HAMISH)* What about the bagpipes?

TOMAS What about them?

HAMISH Who was playing them?

GORDON Who was playing them?

TOMAS Why? What do you know?

GORDON *(to HAMISH)* What do I know?

TOMAS Aye, what do you know?

GORDON I don't know, wait a second.

HAMISH Ask again.

GORDON Who was playing them?

TOMAS Why are ye asking such questions? Why can't ye just relax and enjoy your vacation?

GORDON I wish I could, really, but I need to know.

TOMAS No, you don't.

GORDON Yes, I do! You're the one that said I needed to learn about my family. I need to know!

TOMAS 'Tis just an old legend.

GORDON Then spin me a yarn, Tomas.

HAMISH Guid lad.

GORDON You stay out of it!

TOMAS 'Tis nonsense.

GORDON Tell me!

KELLI appears in the pantry doorway unnoticed.

TOMAS 'Tis just an old story about ye grandfather, the first Hamish.

GORDON Go on.

TOMAS Weil, legend says that of a night old Hamish's ghostie stands out on the hillock over there and plays the pipes for his wifey. The story says that he mourns since her death and he plays them for her.

KELLI That's beautiful.

TOMAS 'Tis just the wind blowing through the glen, one of those natural things. It's been happening as long as anyone can remember. The whistling wind just sounds like the pipes.

GORDON Kel, quick, tell me who you see?

KELLI What?

GORDON How many people do you see?

KELLI What are you talking about? Is the plaid effecting your brain?

TOMAS Never mind him, darlin. I've some clothes for ye to try on, too. Come wit me. *(He begins to exit to the bedroom.)*

KELLI *(noticing the empty bottle on the table)* You drank all that last night?

GORDON What?

TOMAS Pay him no mind, lass. It happens round here quite a bit.

KELLI I am not going in there unless you promise to keep that kilt down, Tomas.

TOMAS Come on, come on, I'm sorry about that. We dinna have much time. *(They both exit.)*

GORDON *(going to the bottle)* So you drank the rest of my bottle.

HAMISH Aye.

GORDON Thanks a lot.

HAMISH I had to.

GORDON Oh, you had to, did ya?

HAMISH Aye, if I hadnae I would have been stuck drinking it the night. Now ye've to get a new bottle. Preferably something a little finer.

GORDON A little finer?

HAMISH I dinnae mean to judge your taste, lad, but there's better whiskey.

GORDON *(building anger)* Oh, well, maybe you could make out a list of your preferences and I can show it to the shopkeeper. Oh wait, that wouldn't work, they wouldn't be able to see it because I imagine your ink's invisible, too!

HAMISH Now son, dinnae fash yersel.

GORDON Look at my situation here! My wife drags me to the middle of nowhere, I've spent six hours on a plane and still have no idea what time it is, and I have no way of communicating with the outside world! Now I'm wearing a dress and I'm talking to some kind of hallucination.

HAMISH 'Tis a kilt.

GORDON What?

HAMISH Ye called it a dress. 'Tis a kilt.

GORDON I don't care what you call it. That's not the point.

HAMISH 'Tis precisely the point. The kilt is a proud symbol of ye heritage, son, and ye cannae be bothered to show it respect. This dress, as ye call it, is worn only by a Grant. It shows aw ye meet ye are a Grant and proud of it.

GORDON Proud of it! How can I be proud of being a Grant, I don't know what the hell it means to "be a Grant."

HAMISH And whose fault is that?

GORDON Hardly mine. I told ya, I was orphaned.

HAMISH Fer Christ's sakes, laddie, would ye stop using that excuse! Me fether and mither were kilt when I was a bairn, but I still learned. All ye had to do was read. There'd be photos, letters, books, something would have told ye!

GORDON But what would be the point, it's in the past. It has no relevance in today's society where I come from, whether or not you killed a dozen Englishman or invented golf.

HAMISH More like two dozen.

GORDON Two dozen?

HAMISH Aye, I do nae mean to boast, mind.

GORDON See, that's what I'm saying, it doesn't mean anything to me.

HAMISH It does nae mean anything to you?

GORDON No! Why should it?

HAMISH Because if I hadnae ye probably wouldn't be alive, or if ye were ye'd be sippin tea by the Thames calling yourself a "jolly good chap."

GORDON Well, that sounds better than where I am now, freezing my ass off in some draughty old cottage in these godforsaken Highlands!

HAMISH *(softly)* Son, how can ye ken where to go in life if you dinnae ken where it 'tis ye come from?

GORDON That's crap!

HAMISH Crap?

GORDON Yes, crap! Everything about this place is crap! Even you. You're just paranormal crap!

HAMISH *(starting to draw his sword)* If ye weren't my son, laddie.

GORDON I'm NOT!

This freezes HAMISH with shock.

KELLI *(entering dressed in traditional Scottish garb)* Gordon, who are you yelling at?

A pause as GORDON looks at KELLI and then slowly back to HAMISH.

GORDON *(looking directly into HAMISH's eyes)* No one!

Long pause.

HAMISH *(putting the sword back)* If that's the way of it, then I'll stay oot o' ye way. *(goes to the door and turns, pause)* I'll also consider the family line finished and the clan dead. *(exits out the main door)*

TOMAS enters behind KELLI.

GORDON *(running to the door)* Hamish, wait! I didn't mean that, it's just…

KELLI Gordon, are you all right? Who are you talking to?

GORDON Never mind.

KELLI Why are you so upset?

GORDON I'm NOT.

KELLI Yes, you are. What's wrong?

TOMAS *(suspicious)* Who were you speaking with, lad?

GORDON I told ya, no one.

Pause as TOMAS eyes GORDON.

What?!

TOMAS I 'spect ye'll tell me when ye're ready.

KELLI Gordon, what's going on?

GORDON I told ya nothing's going on. I was just talking to myself, letting off some steam. Can't we just forget it? Don't we have someplace to go? What about the Round Up or whatever the hell it is.

KELLI You mean the Gathering there, Tex.

TOMAS Aye, we should be goin but first I've to go to the MacGregor's to chat wi me son. Get the latest news and bookings.

GORDON Do you want us to come?

TOMAS No, ye two stay here. I'll nae be a minute. The MacGregor's dinna really care much for outlanders. *(He exits out the main door.)*

KELLI Don't you find it odd the way Tomas tries to keep us from the MacGregors, like he's hiding something from us?

GORDON Tomas's behaviour is the least we have to worry about around here.

KELLI I beg your pardon?

GORDON Nothing, Kel. You wouldn't understand.

KELLI Oh really! Come to think of it, you've been acting strange ever since we arrived. What's going on, Gordon?

GORDON Nothing.

KELLI *(falling backwards onto the sofa)* Ahh!

GORDON What are you doing?

KELLI Falling off the turnip truck. *(GORDON walks away.)* Come on, honey, we've been married half a decade. Don't you think by now I'd know when something's bothering you? Cough it up.

GORDON This is a little different.

KELLI Try me.

GORDON It's rather complex.

KELLI *(mock shock)* Oh my God! You're gay!

GORDON What?!

KELLI *(softly going to GORDON)* Relax, Gordon. I'm your wife, your life partner, your soulmate. Remember that day a few years back when you wore your tux to church? I was the one in the white dress! I should hope you could tell me anything. Talk to me.

GORDON *(pause as he thinks how to approach it)* Last night we, I, had a visitor.

KELLI Last night? Someone was here after I went to bed?

GORDON Well, sort of.

KELLI Sort of? Was someone here or not?

GORDON Yes and no.

KELLI Well, that clears it up!

GORDON I told you, it's complicated. He was here but not here.

KELLI All right, Gordon, if you don't want to tell me just say so. Don't play games.

GORDON I am telling you. He was here.

KELLI Who?

GORDON My great-grandfather.

Pause.

KELLI Your great-grandfather?

GORDON Yes.

KELLI Oh, is that all! With all the Scotch you drank, I wouldn't be surprised if the queen herself dropped by for a visit, too.

GORDON Forget it!

KELLI Come on, Gord, you drank the whole damn thing. I mean I don't care if that's what you want to do on your holidays, go for it. Live it up.

GORDON Would you forget about the Scotch? I didn't drink it.

KELLI Oh, really?

GORDON No, he did.

KELLI Who?

GORDON My great-grandfather, or should I say my great-great whatever grandfather.

KELLI Your great-grandfather?

GORDON Yes, the first Hamish!

KELLI Gordon, don't play me for a fool.

GORDON I'm serious, Kel, the first Hamish Grant, the guy who built this house, was here last night.

KELLI The guy who built this house has long been dead.

GORDON Precisely!

KELLI So, what are you saying, that your great whatever grandfather rose from the dead so he could come here and drink all your Scotch?

GORDON Well…

KELLI Besides the obvious flaws in your little tale, there is one glaring problem.

GORDON What's that?

KELLI Your Scotch sucks! A wino drunk on Baby Duck wouldn't cross the street to take a sip of that crap let alone a Scottish Highlander rising from his grave.

GORDON He didn't rise from his grave. He's a, a ghost.

KELLI A ghost.

GORDON Yes, a ghost, a spirit, an apparition! I know it sounds completely crazy but you have to believe me. It's the truth. He was here last night! He was sitting in that chair. He must have drank my Scotch after I passed out on the floor.

KELLI You passed out on the floor?

GORDON Kelli, I'm telling you I wasn't drunk. He was here, he was still here this morning.

KELLI Then where is he? Show him to me. I want to see this Casper in a kilt.

GORDON He left.

KELLI He left?

GORDON Yes, that's who I was yelling at. He left right after.

KELLI If he's your long-lost ancestor, why on earth were you yelling at him?

GORDON It's complicated.

KELLI Oh, well then, forget it. We wouldn't want to complicate a story about a heavy-drinking spook that stalks the Highlands by night looking for cheap Scotch and by day stands around getting bellowed at. Come to think of it, go find him. I could let off some steam right about now.

GORDON Forget it. If you're not going to take me seriously, why'd you bother to ask?

KELLI I'm sorry, Gord, but it's a little out there. When a husband lies to his wife about his drinking, he traditionally tries to make it a little more believable.

GORDON Exactly!

KELLI Well, what did he say? What did he want, other than your Scotch?

GORDON I don't know, really. He was as surprised as I was. He said I was the only person ever to see him.

KELLI The only person?

GORDON Strange, huh?

KELLI Not really. If anyone were to see him, it would make sense it was you.

GORDON Why me?

KELLI Because you are his flesh and blood.

GORDON Lucky me.

KELLI Did you tell Tomas about it?

GORDON No, and I don't plan on it.

KELLI But he might know something about it.

GORDON I'm not telling him. He'll think I'm crazy. That's all we need for the next few weeks. Everyone pointing at us saying, "There go the Crazy Canucks."

HAMISH enters from the main door and immediately starts walking to the pantry. GORDON and he make eye contact. HAMISH stops.

HAMISH I forgot ma pipes.

HAMISH exits through the pantry.

GORDON *(staring off at the pantry door)* Kelli, he's back.

KELLI He is? Where?

GORDON He just went into the pantry.

She begins to exit to the pantry.

KELLI Cool!

GORDON Where are you going?

KELLI To meet him.

GORDON Kelli, no! Don't go in there.

KELLI *(She stops.)* Why not?

HAMISH enters with his pipes and walks past KELLI.

GORDON Well, ah…

KELLI Not good enough. *(She turns and enters the pantry, shouting.)* How do you do, sir. Can I call you Grandpa?

HAMISH Ye've tellt her?

GORDON Yeah.

KELLI *(off, still shouting)* I'm your grandson's wife, Kelli. I've heard so much about you.

HAMISH Tell her I'm dead, na dief. *(begins to exit out the main door)*

GORDON Hamish, wait. I…

HAMISH Ye've said enough already, lad. *(He exits.)*

GORDON But… Shit!

KELLI *(re-entering, still shouting)* I'm sorry about my husband's Scotch. He insists on buying the cheapest stuff. What can I say, he's Scottish. We'll get you some better stuff today. Hey, Gord, I think he likes me.

GORDON He's gone.

KELLI I beg your pardon?

GORDON He left.

KELLI Without even a goodbye? Now I know where you get your manners. What did he say?

GORDON Not much.

KELLI What happened? Did I say something wrong? I was just trying to be hospitable.

GORDON You didn't say anything. It was me.

KELLI What did you do?

GORDON I told him that he was paranormal crap.

KELLI You told your dead grandfather he was crap.

GORDON No, paranormal crap.

KELLI Wow! You don't waste any time getting the dysfunctional aspects of your family working, do ya?

GORDON Not funny, Kel.

KELLI Sorry, I'm just trying to understand. For the first time ever you found a family member and you immediately tell him off. It doesn't make any sense.

GORDON It makes perfect sense. I've told you a hundred times. I don't have any family. I spent my entire life having no one, just me against the world. Every step I've made, I've made alone. Do you have any idea how isolating that is? When I was a kid playing in the park, I'd see other kids playing with their dads, squealing and jumping on them. Their dads carrying them on their shoulders and pushing them on the swings. I had no one. No one I could yell "Higher, Dad, higher!" to. Just once I wanted a shoulder I could ride on. But the worst, the absolute worst was when it was time to go home for the night. All the families would gather up their coolers and blankets and head off to their cars, laughing, running, skipping, whatever, and I knew that they'd probably be singing songs in the car all the way home. Then when they got there, Mom would give them a bath, and Dad would tuck them in and read them a story. I never got any of that. My uncle and aunt did the best they could but they were getting up there. I mean it was a banner day if my uncle stayed awake until my bedtime.

Every night I would lie in bed and imagine what my parents were like; dreaming that it was all a big mistake, they hadn't died and maybe they were looking for me but didn't know where to find me. I'd pray the doorbell would ring and there would be my mother and father standing there, waiting to take me home. Every time that damn doorbell rang, I ran like hell to answer it, ready to jump into my father's arms. *(pause)* But it was never them.

Pause.

KELLI Gord, I'm so sorry.

GORDON Yeah, not half as sorry as the UPS man was.

KELLI But here's a chance, as odd as it seems, to connect with your family, to learn something about yourself.

GORDON I know all I need to know about me!

KELLI But Gordon, this is special, this is rare, this is… completely insane, but it is a chance of a lifetime!

GORDON Whose lifetime? His? His ended a century ago! I'm talking to air here! He's dead, gone, doing the old natural-turf catnap. Hell, I wouldn't be surprised if he came back and broke into a song-and-dance number with bloody Elvis Presley. At least then there would be some entertainment value!

KELLI I've prayed every night that you would develop an interest in your family. That's why I booked this trip. But never did I expect… *(looking to the heavens)* That's good.

GORDON Well, I'm sorry to disappoint you, Kel *(looking up)*, and anyone else involved, but school's dismissed. I'm not interested. I'm skipping class. I don't need some old fossil telling me about me. I know everything I need to know. I don't need someone going and changing things. I know exactly who I am. I'm Gordon Grant, your husband. I live in Canada, where men wear pants for crying out loud! I'm a corporate lawyer and a damn fine one. I don't need him or anyone else telling me different. I like who I am and the way things are and I don't need anyone changing anything. *(starts to exit)*

KELLI Where are you going?

GORDON For a walk, I need some air.

KELLI But Gordon, wait, there is something you should know.

GORDON Stop! I know everything I need to know. No news is good news!

GORDON exits.

KELLI gathers her thoughts and sits at the table. TOMAS enters unseen.

KELLI *(to herself)* "No news is good news." Then I guess it's not a good time to tell you I'm pregnant.

TOMAS 'Tis nae a bad time, lass, just not necessary.

KELLI *(startled)* What!

TOMAS A man would have to be blind as a tree stump not to know that this fine lass is with child.

KELLI You… you know?

TOMAS Aye, I may be auld, but I can still see the shine of a beautiful mither-to-be's face.

KELLI Oh, Tomas, thank you. *(HAMISH enters.)* I was just prattling on to myself there, sorry.

TOMAS He doesnae know yet, does he?

HAMISH Ken fit? Enough to come oot 'a the cold? Nae, the dumb-ass is standing by the moor gettin aw the northerly up his kilt.

KELLI No, he doesn't.

HAMISH Much more 'a the breeze swirlin round his parts and there'll be nae hope of passin the family name on.

TOMAS Well, the younger men dinnae catch on as quickly as us older ones. Gie him time.

HAMISH Aye. He'll mind aw right in aboot fifteen minutes when the wee feller freezes up and falls off.

KELLI I was hoping to tell him while we're here. I wanted him to get a sense of family.

HAMISH Nae hope, lass.

KELLI I mean that's why I booked this trip in the first place.

HAMISH Ach, so 'tis your fault.

TOMAS Dinnae worry, quinie. Ye'll find the right time.

KELLI Please don't say anything to him. I really think it should come from me.

TOMAS Of course, ma lady.

KELLI Oh, but what are we talking about this for? We should get going to the Gathering.

TOMAS Well, aboot that, I dinnae think I can go.

KELLI What?

TOMAS Ye two go on wit' out me.

KELLI But Tomas, we need you there. We won't have a clue what to do without you.

HAMISH He's liable to get a caber upside the heid. Whist, I said that like 'twas a bad thin'.

TOMAS It's pretty straightforward. Ye'll be fine.

HAMISH I'll go wit' ye! *(to self)* This could be more entertainin than the Nessie trick. "The day the cabers fought back." They'll be crack aboot it for years.

KELLI Is something wrong?

TOMAS No, no, everythin's fine.

KELLI Well, you old boys may be able to tell when a girl's pregnant, but us girls know when something's bothering an old man. Speak up.

TOMAS I dinnae want to spoil your holiday, lass.

KELLI Trust me, it's not you that's spoiling it.

HAMISH Spoil awa', me auld laddie.

TOMAS Well, I guess ye've a right to know, being a Grant an' aw. *(pause)* We've lost the hoose.

HAMISH / KELLI What!

TOMAS This hoose. This home. It's being taken over. The Grants no longer have rights to it.

HAMISH Bollocks!

KELLI What do you mean?

TOMAS Well, apparently the trust fund set up many years back to pay the taxes has run dry. We've been in default for some time noo.

HAMISH 'Tis ma hoose, damn it!

KELLI How did it happen? Who does the finances?

TOMAS I do.

HAMISH *(drawing the sword)* Start speakin quickly.

TOMAS I've ne'er had to deal with property taxes because the fund took care of them. The bank set it up years ago.

KELLI But didn't they notify you that it was empty?

TOMAS They've been trying for quite some time but they havenae been able to reach me.

KELLI Why not?

TOMAS My telephone does nae work.

HAMISH Does naebody speak face to face anymore?

KELLI They must have mailed you something.

TOMAS Aye, I'm sure they did.

KELLI Why didn't you deal with it?

TOMAS 'Cause I did nae look at it. I just filed it.

KELLI You didn't look at it?

TOMAS There was nae point. *(pause)* I can nae read! I just filed it like I did everythin else the bank sends. The trust fund was supposed to take care of everythin.

HAMISH I'd file your heid the noo if I could!

TOMAS They have sold the property?

KELLI How, wouldn't they have to advertise it somehow? Wouldn't you have seen?

TOMAS 'Twas sold the moment it became available.

HAMISH / KELLI To who?

TOMAS To ah…

HAMISH *(building anger)* Dinnae say the name, Tomas, dinnae say it.

TOMAS Gordon Family Industries.

HAMISH *(angry)* 'Tis the name.

TOMAS They're going to tear it down and put up some kind of distillery.

HAMISH strikes the sword down on the table, resulting in a thunderous noise and causing everything on it to rattle and fall over.

HAMISH O'er ma dead body!

Pause.

KELLI *(staring at the table)* I think someone's ticked.

TOMAS That's what I 'feert.

Blackout.

End of Act One.

ACT TWO

SCENE ONE

It is several moments later. GORDON *enters through the main door followed by* KELLI. *He is still in his kilt and has gathered it up for warmth around his privates.*

GORDON NO! For the last time NO!

KELLI *(pleading)* But he just went to the house to get the paperwork. The Gordon rep and the banker are coming. Couldn't you at least look at it?

GORDON Couldn't he have told me how quickly things freeze out there!

KELLI He's going to lose all this!

GORDON Me too!

KELLI It's your history.

GORDON Not if I act quickly!

KELLI Gordon! I'm serious!

GORDON So am I! *(exits through the pantry, off)* Look, Kel, I'm sorry he's losing all this. I really am. But what am I suppose to do? This is Scotland. I know nothing about the laws here. *(Enters through the doorway carrying a hair dryer. After a moment he aims it under his kilt.)* I'm from Canada! Hell, if he wants to build an ice rink out back I can do that. God knows it's cold enough, but what do I know about the way things are done here? *(exits back into pantry to return the hair dryer)* Besides, the bank will have a team of lawyers. I'm just one man on vacation.

KELLI Yes, but isn't that one man called "Money Bags Grant"?

GORDON *(re-entering without the hair dryer)* Not now. More like first name: Frozen. Why the hell do they wear these things when it's this cold? I mean Winky could be rendered useless after that kind of exposure! *(lifts his kilt and places the front on the stove)*

KELLI That's fine. Unless you help Tomas, you won't need it anyway!

GORDON Oh, come on, Kel! Don't play that card. You know as well as I do, it's a crock.

KELLI Oh yeah? Try me.

GORDON What, right now?

KELLI Sure. If you think you're man enough.

GORDON But it's daylight out.

KELLI Prude.

GORDON I've just been outside in a skirt for the last hour and don't feel that manly. Besides, Junior's turtled up so far I think he's effecting my breathing.

KELLI He won't warm up there, nestled to that cold heart.

GORDON Wait one second, Kel! One minute you're telling me to relax and enjoy the vacation and the next you want me to work. What gives?

KELLI The man is in trouble. He needs your help!

GORDON My help?!

KELLI Yes! Him and your family!

GORDON begins to exit to the bedroom.

Where are you going?

GORDON To dress like a civilized man. If I act quickly I may be able to save the wee fella. *(He exits.)*

HAMISH enters through the main door, unseen by both.

KELLI Sure. Leave in the middle of a fight.

GORDON *(off)* I'm not fighting! There's nothing to fight about!

KELLI *(to herself)* I thought you Scots were supposed to be fearless fighters. Ugh!

HAMISH is startled by her yell. Then he begins making tea. Throughout the process KELLI notices the spoon moving.

HAMISH Nae when it came to our wives, lass. We ken when to pick our battles. Sure an' the English with their endless stream of armies seemed unbeatable but there was aw a chance, a hope. But with the wifeys… nae chance and nae hope. Why the hell do ye think we spent so much damn time herding the livestock? Think aboot it. The bloody kuhs are on the side of a mountain fer Christ's sakes. Where are they goin to go? Up? Aw that goes up, as they say, must come doon some time. Doon? Well, that just means they're closer ta hame. Nae, lass, the real reason we were awa' the herdin was to avoid the hurtin we'd get the hame. A good Scot knows when to pick his battles and the're never ta hame.

KELLI *(seeing the spoon move but not seeing HAMISH)* Oh my God! Hamish, is that you?

HAMISH Damnation. O'er two centuries and I still forget. Nae wonder I dinnae mind aw the herding when I was alive. I've the memory of an ox.

KELLI *(not hearing him)* It's you, isn't it?

HAMISH relents and holds the spoon in front of her face then moves it up and down, causing her to nod as she follows it.

Oh God! Oh God! This is so cool! Hamish? Grandpa? Can I call you Grandpa?

HAMISH uses the spoon again.

Cool! This is so cool! There is so much I want to ask you. This is totally amazing. I don't know where to begin. Ah, Grandpa, what are you doing? Are you making tea?

HAMISH We finally bridge the paranormal generation gap and the best ye can come up wit' is "Are ye makin' tea"? *(uses the spoon to signal yes)*

KELLI Oh my God! Gordon was right! It's true! You're here. I don't know what to ask. *(pause)* Are you a friendly ghost?

HAMISH Well, ma mither aw said I dinnae play well with others but I reckon I'm friendlier noo. *(uses the spoon)*

KELLI Do you mean us any harm?

HAMISH Ye no. That husband, the ungrateful seed, ach, wiel, let's just say 'tis undecided.

He uses the spoon to signal then moves around the room with KELLI in close pursuit of the spoon. It has become a fun game.

KELLI *(sitting back at the table)* This is so overwhelming.

HAMISH sets tea and spoon on the table in front of KELLI then moves off.

(looking at the tea) Two sugars and no cream. How did you know?

HAMISH Boogie, boogie!

KELLI This is too much! I, I don't know what to say! I never expected anything like this. I was just hoping for… I don't know. It's that damn job. Work has become his whole life. It's all he seems to think about now. He's lucky if he gets home in time for supper and then, after he eats, he's on the damn computer all night. It's like all he's interested in now is work. I know, I shouldn't complain. He's doing it for us. So we can have a decent life, but what kind of life is it when you never see him. It's like we said "I do" and then we never do.

HAMISH *(repeatedly bangs on whatever is available)* Hey! *(moves away)*

KELLI *(She goes to wherever the sound was made.)* Oh sorry. I guess you don't want to hear that being his grandfather. It's just that I wish he'd take an interest in other things. That's why I booked this trip. I hoped he'd find something of interest here. Maybe make a connection with his roots.

HAMISH He connected aw richt. If I wasnae dead I'd connect right back. *(He bangs again.)*

KELLI *(She moves to the new sound.)* Don't get me wrong. I know he loves me and he means well. It's just, I don't know. I mean, we're hardly ever intimate anymore. I even have the dates written down.

HAMISH *(bangs repeatedly)* Aw richt! That's it! Ye're blethering aboot sex again.

KELLI *(goes to the sound)* I'm sorry, I didn't mean to bring it up again…

HAMISH No, no, I reckon 'tis best we stop the noo!

GORDON enters, he does not see HAMISH.

GORDON That's better. Now I feel normal, or at least Canadian. Is that tea I smell? Hon, did you make tea?

KELLI No.

GORDON Then what's this?

KELLI Tea.

GORDON Kel, don't be juvenile.

KELLI I'm not. I didn't make it.

GORDON Oh really, then who did? Hamish?

HAMISH Boo.

GORDON Do you have to go around scaring the hell out of everybody? Is it a job requirement?

HAMISH Nae, just a wee perk.

GORDON Is there enough left for me to have a cup?

KELLI Depends.

GORDON On what?

KELLI If you are going to help Tomas and your grandfather.

GORDON Don't start that again. *(goes to the kitchen and gets a cup)*

KELLI Grandpa, can you talk some sense into him?

GORDON What? You're talking to him now?

HAMISH Nae point, ma dear. If he doesnae care, I cannae make him.

GORDON See, he agrees with me. Now can we drop it?

He pours his tea, sits on the sofa, and flips through a magazine. Long pause as KELLI and HAMISH stare disapprovingly at GORDON.

Your silent treatment isn't going to work. *(long pause)* Stare all you want. *(long pause)* All right! All right! I'll take a look at his damn paperwork, but that's it. I'm supposed to be on vacation, remember.

KELLI *(hugging him)* Thank you, Gordon, that's all we ask.

GORDON Why do you care so much? It has nothing to do with us. What difference does it make if they tear this place down?

KELLI Because it's part of us. It's part of you. It's family, and family's important, don't you think?

GORDON What's with you lately, Kel? That's all you talk about, family this and family that.

TOMAS hurriedly enters through the main door carrying a file box.

TOMAS Aw right, lad! I think I got everything. It won't take a wee minute. I do appreciate this. They'll be here soon. Havin a legal type around here is rather rare.

GORDON Oh Tomas. Look, I ah…

TOMAS *(opening the box)* They're all here, every last one. I kept everythin.

GORDON *(reaching in the box and pulling out a handful of papers and receipts)* Yes, and so beautifully organized.

TOMAS Be prepared. That's what ma mither always said.

GORDON I'm sure she did.

KELLI Gordon.

GORDON *(relenting)* All right, let's take a look. What do you have here?

TOMAS Everythin! I kept everythin! Those bloodsucking bankers. I knew they'd try somethin. They're aways looking for ways to screw ye!

GORDON What's this, a receipt for dog food? Why did you keep this? Are you claiming the dog as a dependant?

TOMAS *(hopeful)* Can I?

GORDON No.

TOMAS Ah. I told ye, I kept everythin. Everythin the bank sent me. Every damn receipt. Everythin. If I were to die the noo, everythin you need to know about me is in that carton. Maybe I cannae read, but at least I'm organized.

GORDON notices a month from a calendar taped on the side of the box. He reads it.

GORDON August.

TOMAS Aye, do ye need the rest of the year, too?

GORDON Not right now. These statements from the bank aren't even opened.

TOMAS What's the point? I cannae read them.

GORDON *(picking out another piece of paper and reading)* What's this, a video-rental receipt, *Weather Girls Gone Crazy.*

TOMAS *(quickly grabbing the receipt and eats it)* We don't need to claim that one.

GORDON No, I don't suppose so.

TOMAS *(embarrassed, looking for an escape, and with his mouth still full)* I think I'll go get the rest of the year. *(He exits.)*

GORDON Good idea.

KELLI What do you think, Gordon?

GORDON It's hopeless. It would take months to figure all this mess out.

HAMISH Ye donae have months, they're on the way the noo.

GORDON I know, I know. That's why it can't be done.

HAMISH Lookie here, laddie, I've been fichtin those Gordons off our land for o'er a century. I'm nae aboot to lose it to them noo. Ye say it's hopeless, well that's fine. In ma day many folk said 'twas hopeless to fight the English but we did and today this land is still in oor name, so dinnae speak to ma about hopeless.

GORDON Then why don't you grab your sword and go save the world and leave me out of it?

HAMISH You're fit's hopeless here! Ye! Ye're the end of our name and if ye're the result of centuries of family evolution, then I'm aw glad ye're the last! I'm glad it's ending! Ye sit roon here pissin and moanin aboot how ye were orphaned and the world's agin ye. Well, I think 'tis ye and that damn chip on that shoulder of yourn that have somethin agin the world.

GORDON Would you cut me some slack! I'm on vacation! Where the hell's the beach? Where are the bellhops and bikinis? Where's my all-inclusive bar?! No, I couldn't ask for something that good! No, what do I get? Some lecturing paranormal piper in the middle of nowhere in a drafty old barn! That's apparently all I get!

HAMISH Noo ye mind me, lad.

KELLI *(crying)* I'm sorry, Gordon, I just thought that if you had a chance to… you might feel differently about…

Knock at the door.

HAMISH 'Tis the Gordon.

KELLI exits to the bedroom weeping.

GORDON *(following, closing the door behind him)* Hon, wait. I didn't mean that, it's just… my blood is boiling.

More knocking.

HAMISH A moment. Someone maun get the door. For the love of God. Hamish! *(pause)* Be damned if I'm goin.

The door opens and slowly and timidly Mr. SHELBY *Sutherland appears. He is a very nervous and meek man. The classic comical pencil-pusher. He is carrying a briefcase.*

SHELBY Hello, Tomas? It's Shelby Sutherland. I'm with the bank. I'm here with Mrs. Gordon from Gordon Industries. We spoke to you earlier. Anyone home? Mrs. Gordon is in the car. She's on the phone. Hello, anyone? Tomas? We have the paperwork we discussed. Hello?

HAMISH *(at the bedroom door)* Hamish, get oot here. The Grim Reaper's here and ye would nae believe it. Aw the auld photos of a creepy hooded guy with a huge sickle, let's just say they were a wee bit off! Hamish? *(knocking on the door)*

SHELBY *(startled)* Hello? Who's there?

HAMISH Ooh, a nervy one noo, are ye? Weil, mayhap I h've a fichtin chance after aw. Good day, Mr. Reaper, do ye mind if I call ye Grim. Here Grim, let me move that carton for ye. *(picks up a box from the table and begins to carry it around)* Lookie, Grim, isn't it creepy the way it flies through the air? Scary aye, a wee bitty scary. Come on noo, Grim, scream for me, scream like a wee bitty girlie.

GORDON *enters from bedroom. By this time* SHELBY *is cowering on the sofa and* HAMISH *is overtop of him.*

GORDON What the hell! Give me that!

He takes the box from HAMISH.

HAMISH Fit! Nae body was aroon to help him. I was just showin him oor paperwork.

GORDON Not funny.

SHELBY That box… What… What's going on? Who are you?

GORDON I'm sorry, I'm Gordon, Gordon Grant.

SHELBY The box… it moved.

GORDON Sorry about that. *(thinking fast)* I'm an illusionist. I was just practising. I didn't mean to startle you like that. I'm terribly sorry. Just practising my magic, you know, abracadabra and all that.

HAMISH Illusionist? 'Tis the best ye could come up wit'?

GORDON *(under his breath)* Shut up! I had to think of something.

SHELBY *(visibly shaken)* Magic, yes, well I can't say I've ever been one for magic. Just a bunch of silliness, really.

HAMISH quickly begins to exit to the bathroom.

GORDON Oh yes, just silliness. *(seeing HAMISH)* What are you doing?

HAMISH Are ye oot of ye're mind!? 'Tis a joy! I'm going ta do more "abracadabras"!

HAMISH exits through the pantry.

SHELBY What am I doing?

GORDON Beg your pardon?

SHELBY You just asked me what I was doing.

GORDON What are you doing? Ah, what are you doing… ah, what are you doing… here! Yes, what are you doing here?

SHELBY I have some business to conduct with Tomas. Is he around?

GORDON No!

SHELBY Oh. Now did you say your name was Grant?

GORDON Yes, Gordon Grant. Kind of ironic, don't you think?

SHELBY *(uninterested)* Yes, I suppose so. Do I take it to mean that you stay here?

GORDON Oh no, no. We're from Canada. We're just renting it for a couple of weeks.

SHELBY We?

GORDON My wife is in the bedroom lying down.

SHELBY Would you excuse me for a moment? Your magic kind of, well, I feel a need to splash some water on my face. Would you mind if I used your restroom?

GORDON I would prefer you didn't.

SHELBY I beg your pardon? Why on earth not?

GORDON *(thinking quickly but coming up with nothing)* I don't know, really. What the hell, it's out that way.

SHELBY Thank you. *(exits)*

HAMISH *(offstage laughing)* Me too!

GORDON Oh God.

TOMAS enters hurriedly. He's precariously balancing more file boxes.

TOMAS Hamish! Hamish! They're here! Someone's gettin oot of a car there! They're here!

GORDON I know, the banker's in the bathroom!

TOMAS Ma God, we're infested! What are we goin to do? They're aw here! We're nae ready! Ye've nae had a chance to look at aw this stuff!

GORDON We need to stall them, I need time. Is that the rest of last year in the boxes?

TOMAS No, just the spring.

GORDON I need the rest ASAP!

They start to exit out the main door but…

ANNETTE *(offstage)* Okay, fine… I'll ring you back as soon as we're done here. Yes, five o'clock would be fine. All right, great. Bye.

TOMAS They're here!

GORDON Quick, the boxes, hide them!

TOMAS Where?

GORDON The bedroom! Then get the rest! *(They both exit.)*

ANNETTE enters. She is a very attractive woman in her forties, sharply dressed in business apparel. She has the air of being all business. She is carrying a cellphone.

ANNETTE Hello, anyone here? Shelby? Hello.

TOMAS quickly enters. He freezes when he sees ANNETTE.

Hello.

TOMAS Hello. *(runs out the front door)*

Short pause as ANNETTE absorbs what just occurred.

KELLI *(offstage)* Why do I have to go?

GORDON *(offstage)* Because I have to look through all this stuff.

KELLI *(offstage)* Let me at least clean myself up.

GORDON *(Offstage as KELLI comes through the doorway being pushed by GORDON against her will. The door should slam shut behind her.)* No time!

ANNETTE *(pause)* Hello there.

KELLI looks as if she's been crying and in fact still is. She hides her face in a tissue, facing against the bedroom door. She doesn't turn around but acknowledges her with a small wave.

Excuse me, is something wrong?

Still facing the door, KELLI *shakes her head.*

I'm Annette Gordon. We spoke to someone earlier. I'm with Gordon Industries. We've recently purchased this property.

KELLI Ah-huh.

ANNETTE Would you know where Mr. Sutherland went to?

KELLI *shakes her head.*

Oh.

There is a sudden loud screech of a bagpipe coming from the bathroom followed by a scream. SHELBY *Sutherland races out of the bathroom. The front of his shirt and pants are covered with water.*

SHELBY What was that?

ANNETTE Shelby!

SHELBY Annette!

GORDON *(entering, crashing into* KELLI *in the doorway)* Kelli!

KELLI *exits.*

SHELBY Mr. Grant!

GORDON Mr. Sutherland!

ANNETTE Mr. Grant?

GORDON Ms. Gordon?

ANNETTE Mrs.

GORDON Gordon.

ANNETTE Yes.

GORDON Gordon Grant.

ANNETTE Gordon Grant?

GORDON Yes.

ANNETTE Shelby?

SHELBY Annette?

ANNETTE *(referring to* GORDON*)* Who is this?

SHELBY *(referring to the noise)* What was that?

TOMAS *runs in with several more boxes and immediately exits to the bedroom.*

SHELBY / ANNETTE
Who's he?

GORDON Tomas.

ANNETTE Tomas?

SHELBY *(calling after him)* Tomas!

GORDON Whoa! Stop it! I'm getting a headache.

SHELBY Mr. Grant, what on earth was that noise?

GORDON *(trying to cover)* What noise?

SHELBY That noise that came from the bathroom. I nearly soiled myself.

They all look at the front of him.

(wiping himself off with a handkerchief) It's water. What was that explosion?

GORDON Explosion?

SHELBY Yes, explosion. A huge noise and water flying everywhere.

GORDON It must have been the pipes. They're old and tend to make weird sounds.

SHELBY Pipes?

GORDON Yeah, pipes.

SHELBY I think you need a plumber.

GORDON *(to himself)* Or an exorcist.

SHELBY I beg your pardon?

GORDON Nothing. I'm sorry about that. Let me get you a towel.

ANNETTE Am I to understand that you are a Grant?

GORDON *(getting a towel from the bathroom)* Yes, Gordon Grant.

ANNETTE *(shaking hands)* Annette Gordon. Pleasure to meet you. Do you have some connection to this old place?

GORDON Not really, we're from Canada. Apparently an ancestor of mine built it. We're just renting it for a couple of weeks, a vacation of sorts.

ANNETTE It is a quaint wee place, I suppose. I prefer to vacation in Spain myself.

GORDON Me too.

ANNETTE It does have its charms. Too bad we'll be tearing it down.

GORDON Tearing it down?

ANNETTE Yes. We'll be erecting a distillery. Our business is growing and we are just bursting at the seams in our current location. The natural spring outside makes it a perfect location. But don't worry, nothing will be done immediately, so I'm sure you'll be able to finish out your stay.

TOMAS enters during the next line and immediately starts to the front door.

GORDON But this place has so much history, it would be a shame to just tear it down.

Hearing this, TOMAS stops, turns, and gives them a defiant grunt. He then exits.

SHELBY *(following)* Tomas, wait. We have some documents to go over here.

ANNETTE That Tomas sure is a busy fellow. What is he doing? He knew we were coming.

GORDON He's just preparing.

ANNETTE Aye, well I wish he would sit still soon, I need to get back to my office this afternoon. I have a great deal of work to get done before construction starts.

GORDON Speaking of work, would you excuse me, I have some work to do in the bedroom.

ANNETTE I guess you do.

GORDON Excuse me.

ANNETTE Well, she seemed quite upset.

GORDON Oh that, well yeah, she's the emotional type, you know.

ANNETTE I noticed.

GORDON Yeah, well. *(starts to exit)*

ANNETTE *(noticing the picture of HAMISH)* It's not a bad thing.

GORDON Pardon?

ANNETTE Being emotional. It shows passion. It's good to be passionate about things, don't you think?

GORDON I suppose so.

ANNETTE I remember a time when I was passionate about things, but that was a long time ago.

GORDON What were you passionate about?

ANNETTE Oh, nothing. Forget it.

GORDON starts to exit.

It's silly really.

GORDON What?

ANNETTE Dancing, Highland dancing. I wanted to be the best in the country, even the world.

GORDON Highland dancing, eh?

ANNETTE Aye, ever since I was a wee girl I loved the sound of the pipes. I mean really loved it. I know every Scot is supposed to love the pipes but it was more than that. It was strange. I would hear them in my sleep. It was always the same song over and over and it made ma dance, like I had no control over it, like that, you know. I could nae help masel', even when I was awake. The sound of the pipes just made me dance. Me mither enrolled me in classes and I took to it like a fish to water. The instructors always told me parents that I really didn't need much coaching, that I was a natural. Strange, isn't it?

GORDON So, what happened?

ANNETTE Ah, you know, you grow up, meet a boy, fall in love, get married, and then, well, I went to work with his company and that takes up most of my time. I haven't heard the pipes in my dreams for years noo.

A pause. She looks behind herself, as if she heard something.

Ah, but listen to me prattling on.

GORDON It's okay.

ANNETTE It's strange, I don't even know you, I've never seen you before, but somehow I feel I've met you before.

GORDON Oh?

ANNETTE Have you been to Scotland before?

GORDON No, it's our first time.

ANNETTE Maybe it's some kind of kindred spirit.

GORDON How so?

ANNETTE My maiden name was Grant.

GORDON Maybe we're related.

ANNETTE I dinnae think so. It would be like thirty times removed if we were.

GORDON How can you be so sure?

ANNETTE Because aw round here know that Hamish Grant built this place. He was legend, a huge hero many years ago. My grandfather used to tell my sisters and I all the stories. It's amazin everythin that he did. He would have told us if we were related. It would have been a huge honour to be descendants of the grand Hamish Grant.

GORDON Really?

ANNETTE Why am I telling ye? Ye are a descendant.

GORDON Yeah, I guess so.

ANNETTE Now, you go and cheer that wee lass up.

GORDON *(lost in his thoughts)* Huh?

ANNETTE The weepy one.

GORDON Oh yeah.

ANNETTE I'm just going to go and walk the property and take a look around till Tomas and Shelby can sit down for a wee time.

GORDON Thanks.

ANNETTE For fit?

GORDON The passion. *(exits to the bedroom)*

ANNETTE Nay bother. *(exits out the front door)*

The stage is bare for a moment until HAMISH *enters from the pantry.*

HAMISH Where the hell is awbody? Hamish, where are ye? *(goes to the bedroom door)* Hamish, ye in there? Fit's goin on? Did I scare the jackass awa?

GORDON *(entering)* Quiet. Kelli's fallen asleep.

HAMISH Hamish, I'm dead. *(shouting)* She cannae hear me.

GORDON Oh yeah.

HAMISH Where is everyone? Fit's goin on? Did they awa?

GORDON No, Mrs. Gordon is snooping around and your little playmate is chasing Tomas.

HAMISH And fit are you doin?

GORDON Going through this mountain of papers.

HAMISH Find anythin?

GORDON Nothing yet, I don't think there's much hope.

HAMISH Dinnae start that again.

GORDON Hey, I didn't say I was giving up, I just don't see anything.

HAMISH Well, get back in there and keep looking, I'll brew us a cuppa.

GORDON I'm on it. *(turns to exit, stops and turns around again)* By the way… thanks… Grandpa. *(He exits.)*

HAMISH looks confused about the last statement, shrugs it off, and begins to make tea. SHELBY enters exhausted through the main door.

HAMISH Ach weil, if 'tisnae me wee frien. Dried off yet?

SHELBY *(out of breath)* Hello, Annette? Mr. Grant? Where are you? Tomas ran away. I chased him but I ran into some woman who wouldn't stop talking. She talked and talked. Then I ran away, but she chased me. She was quick, she didn't break a sweat, and she just kept talking the whole way. This is the most bizarre place I've ever been. *(after a moment, to himself)* Well, I'll be ready the next time he runs through.

SHELBY goes to the table, opens his briefcase, and begins pulling out files.

HAMISH 'Tis "play time"!

HAMISH watches SHELBY for a few moments.

Fit ye got here, lad?

He pulls the paperwork away from underneath SHELBY and sets it down on the table in front of him and begins to read it. Noticing, SHELBY scans the room for someone, grabs the paperwork and pulls it back.

Whisht, I was readin that.

SHELBY begins to write on the paper.

Gie it back, I wasnae finished.

SHELBY *(raising a finger to feel for a breeze)* Where in the dickens is that breeze coming from?

HAMISH The afterlife. *(blowing on finger)* Now whisht and let me read.

SHELBY *(takes the paper back)* Gee whiz.

HAMISH Noo that's just plain rude.

He stands and moves to read over SHELBY's shoulder, reading as SHELBY writes.

By the stars, it's an eviction notice! Ye're evicting Grants from oor own land! O'er me dead body! *(pause)* 'Tis just an expression.

He takes the pen from SHELBY's hand and throws it across the room.

SHELBY What in the world…?

HAMISH Nae, the afterworld.

SHELBY *(yelling)* These magic tricks, Mr. Grant, are wearing thin.

He bends down to pick up the pen.

HAMISH Fore!

He mimes swinging a golf club at SHELBY's behind. SHELBY falls.

SHELBY That is just about enough!

GORDON *(entering)* What's going on out here?

SHELBY As if you didn't know. I've never been treated with such disrespect in my life. This magic of yours is truly appalling.

GORDON Disrespect? *(to HAMISH)* What's going on?

HAMISH Just doin ma duty.

SHELBY "What's going on"? These pranks of yours are not going to change my resolve. I appreciate the fact that you may not like what I'm doing here but, none the less, I have a job to do so I would appreciate if you would stay out of my way and let me do it. Besides, it is none of your business. This is between the Gordons and the Grants. You and your opinions are irrelevant. Therefore, I would suggest that you stay out of my way and let me conduct my business. When I'm through, you may take your leave and return to the pathetic, wild wasteland you call a home.

GORDON Irrelevant? Pathetic? Wow! *(to HAMISH)* Go to town. Just try not to break anything. *(exits)*

HAMISH rubs his hands with glee.

SHELBY "Go to town"? What is that suppose to mean?

HAMISH stalks SHELBY like a cat as SHELBY returns to the table and resumes work. HAMISH is about to pour a pitcher of water over his head when TOMAS enters with two more boxes through the main door and immediately exits to the bedroom.

Tomas, where've ye been? I need you to sign these papers. *(following to the bedroom door)* You can't just ignore the situation. Gordon Industries will be taking control of this property regardless.

ANNETTE *(entering the main door)* Shelby, there you are. Are you done yet? Can we be on our way?

SHELBY I haven't been able to pin Tomas down, but he's in the bedroom now and he's not getting out of this cottage until he signs the papers.

HAMISH *(stalking both from behind)* Ah, the Gordon. I get two fer one.

ANNETTE While we wait, can we review the plans? I have a few questions.

SHELBY Sure, they're in me briefcase.

HAMISH *(as ANNETTE and SHELBY both turn to face HAMISH)* Ah ha!

HAMISH stops and drops the water pitcher. His gaze is frozen on ANNETTE. Both ANNETTE and SHELBY stop and look at the dropped pitcher.

SHELBY Where did that come from?

ANNETTE I havenae a clue.

SHELBY walks by. ANNETTE picks up the pitcher and feels something, maybe a cold breeze. She freezes.

SHELBY It's probably that Mr. Grant.

HAMISH *(eye to eye with ANNETTE)* Annis… 'tis you. Annis, can ye hear me? Annis, say somethin. Can ye see me?

SHELBY *(producing plans from his briefcase)* Other than some minor adjustments I think everything should go as planned. *(noticing ANNETTE hasn't moved)* Annette, are you all right?

ANNETTE I don't know. Shelby, do you feel anything?

SHELBY Other than the slight headache Mr. Grant has caused me? No.

HAMISH Annis, 'tis me, Hamish… Annis.

SHELBY Annette?

HAMISH Annis?

ANNETTE *(pause)* Shelby. I think we need to go. Noo.

SHELBY What's the matter?

ANNETTE I can't explain it.

SHELBY Could you try, I mean we drove thirty minutes to get here and we've accomplished nothing.

ANNETTE I think I have. Please, we need to leave. We'll come back next week. There's something I need to do. *(She feels the air around her.)* I'll be in the car.

She exits out main door. HAMISH remains frozen. SHELBY begins packing up his briefcase. TOMAS enters from the bedroom.

TOMAS All right, Mr. Sutherland, what did you have to show me?

SHELBY I'm sorry, Tomas, but it will have to wait. Something has come up.

TOMAS You want to wait?

SHELBY Yes.

TOMAS Well 'tis fine with me. Take aw the time ye need. I'm in nae hurry.

SHELBY No, I don't imagine you are. We'll be returning next week and I expect that you will be able to sit down like a proper adult and conduct business in a mature way.

SHELBY exits through the main door.

TOMAS *(mocking)* "In a mature way," I highly doubt it. Arsehole! *(knocking on the bedroom door)* They're gone!

GORDON *(entering)* Gone?

TOMAS Aye, but they'll be back.

GORDON What happened?

TOMAS I reckon ma stalling tactics worked. I tell ye, when he followed me oot I didnae think I'd ever lose him, but I did.

GORDON Yeah?

TOMAS Aye, I introduced him to the missus and she started the yapping. I wandered awa' when his eyes started to glaze over.

HAMISH It was her, Hamish.

GORDON Who?

TOMAS *(sitting proudly on the sofa and putting his feet on the coffee table)* The wife, the old clattering teeth herself. Handy to have around every now and then, I tell ye.

HAMISH Annis.

GORDON Annis?

TOMAS What's that?

HAMISH Aye, ma wife… your grandmither.

GORDON Annette?

TOMAS Oh, her, I dinnae know. When I came out here she was already gone.

HAMISH The woman that was here, she was ma wife.

TOMAS Weil, I'm going into town to get some whiskey. I feel a need to celebrate.

HAMISH breaks from his freeze but is still quite puzzled.

GORDON Good idea, Tomas. Would you mind getting me one as well? Here's some money.

GORDON gives him several bills. HAMISH looks at him disapprovingly. Pause. Gives him several more but HAMISH still gives him a look.

(gives him all the money) Tell you what, buy me two of the best they got. Something tells me we'll need them. Pick up some food for everyone also.

SALES DRAFT - FACTURE

4514 0936 0325 5098

DO NOT WRITE ABOVE THIS LINE - NE RIEN ÉCRIRE AU-DESSUS DE CETTE LIGNE

05/13

DAVID HOLTON

EXPIRY DATE CHECKED ✓ DATE D'EXPIRATION VERIFIÉE

CLERK-COMMIS

DEPT.-RAYON

AUTHORIZATION NUMBER / NO D'AUTORISATION

M	D-J	Y-A
05	31	11

PLEASE RETAIN THIS COPY AS RECORD OF YOUR TRANSACTION
CONSERVEZ CETTE COPIE COMME PREUVE DE VOTRE TRANSACTION

CUSTOMER COPY
COPIE DU CLIENT

31304516 613-421-6121
PLAYWRIGHTS CANADA PRESS
TORONTO ON

2088121

DESCRIPTION	AMOUNT-MONTANT
books	44 06

X
CARDHOLDER'S SIGNATURE - SIGNATURE DU TITULAIRE

CARDHOLDER WILL PAY TOTAL AMOUNT SHOWN TO CARD ISSUER ACCORDING TO CARDHOLDER AGREEMENT WITH CARD ISSUER.

LE TITULAIRE S'ENGAGE A REMBOURSER L'ÉMETTEUR DE LA CARTE DU MONTANT TOTAL FIGURANT SUR CETTE FACTURE, CONFORMÉMENT À LA CONVENTION REGISSANT L'UTILISATION DE LA CARTE.

VISA MasterCard

TOTAL $ CDN CAN ▶ 44.06

recycled recyclé

370134

DATE 31/05/11
TAX REG. NO.

FOB | VIA

		PRICE	UNIT	AMOUNT
				18 00
				10 00
	Grassroots			16 00
			GST	
			PST	
			TOTAL	44 00

STAPLES 51E

INVOICE

Playwrights Canada Press
215 Spadina Avenue
Suite 230
Toronto, Ontario
M5T 2C7
FX (416) 408-3402

SOLD TO	SHIP TO
ADDRESS	ADDRESS

CUSTOMER'S ORDER	SOLD BY	TERMS

QUANTITY	DESCRIPTION

TOMAS Ye bet. *(exits)*

GORDON What are you saying, that Annette looks like your wife?

HAMISH She dinnae look like her. She is her. She's Annis.

GORDON I hate to bring it up but you're dead! Mrs. Gordon's still playing on my side, Team Alive!

HAMISH The woman that was standing right here is ma wife and she kent it, or kent somethin anywa'. I could see it in her eyes. She sensed I was here.

GORDON Could she see you?

HAMISH No, I don't reckon so, at least nae in the proper sense, but she kent somethin. *(moves to the fireplace)* That's why she left. I think it scared her.

GORDON That's your job. Do you need a manual on how to be a ghost? Where are you going?

HAMISH Nowhere. I need to play the pipes. *(starts to exit)*

GORDON Hey, wait. After you're done there, do you think you and I could, you know, talk?

HAMISH *(pause)* Fit aboot?

GORDON Oh, stuff. I just got some questions.

HAMISH I'd enjoy that, son.

GORDON Me too.

HAMISH exits. GORDON goes to investigate the fireplace. After a moment we hear bagpipes in the distance. KELLI enters.

KELLI Where did everybody go?

GORDON Oh, how are you doing?

KELLI shrugs.

They all left. We managed to stall them. I'm sorry I said… I know you went to a lot of effort to make this trip happen and that you did it for me and…

KELLI It's okay.

GORDON Can I get you anything?

KELLI Yes, out of this puddle. What's with the water?

GORDON I beg your pardon?

KELLI There's water all over the floor.

GORDON It's like having a kid around here. I'll get a towel.

KELLI I'll get it. Speaking of the kid, is that him playing the pipes?

GORDON Yeah.

KELLI cleans up the water while GORDON is touching the walls and stones around the fireplace, searching for something.

KELLI What are you doing?

GORDON I don't know. He was over here looking for something.

GORDON feels around the mantle until he accidentally dislodges it, revealing a hidden compartment.

Damn, I broke it.

KELLI *(looking in the hole)* What this? *(She produces a pile of old papers.)*

GORDON What is it?

KELLI *(sitting on the sofa)* Some old letters.

GORDON *(joining her on the sofa)* Let's see.

KELLI Do you think we should?

GORDON Hell, yeah! *(He unties them.)*

KELLI What do they say?

GORDON I can't make it out.

KELLI *(holding one up to the light)* It looks like a letter. Oh my, look here at the bottom, it's signed "Hamish." Your grandfather wrote these. It's a poem. A poem to a lady named Ann… Annie… Angie…?

GORDON Annis, it was his wife.

KELLI *(reading)* "As the day's last light falls behind the hill,
The wind gusts up and I feel a chill,
It comes from…"

HAMISH enters and immediately begins reciting the poem along with KELLI.

HAMISH	It comes from deep within my heart,	**GORDON**	*(taking the poem)* Kelli?
	It comes from being pulled apart,	**KELLI**	Yeah?
	But as sure as the mist on the hills above,	**GORDON**	He's here.
	In the morn my heart will send it's love,	**KELLI**	He is? What's he doing?
	And although I'll awake far, far away,	**GORDON**	Reciting the poem.
	I'll be carrying yer	**KELLI**	Really?

love throughout the day,
Just as the moon that
travels the night,
I too shall travel till I
see the light,
The light that guides me
on our journey far,
The light in yer eyes
My shining star.

GORDON *(softly)* Shh.

Pause.

GORDON That was beautiful.

KELLI But I didn't get to hear it.

GORDON Trust me, Kel.

HAMISH I wrote it for Annis.

GORDON We know.

KELLI What's he saying?

GORDON Shh.

KELLI But I didn't get to hear the poem.

HAMISH Ye found 'em.

GORDON Oh, yeah, yeah we did.

HAMISH Nae one e'er has afore.

GORDON Oh, you know, dumb luck.

HAMISH Ye were snoopin?

GORDON Well, actually… Yes, yes… Kelli was.

KELLI What, what about me?

GORDON Kelli, quiet, can't you see I'm talking here?

HAMISH It doesnae matter. I havenae opened it in probably one hundred and twenty years mesel.

GORDON You haven't?

HAMISH No.

GORDON How could you possibly remember it after so long?

HAMISH Son, when ye write somethin like that, ye dinnae write it with this. *(indicates his head)* You write it with this. *(indicates his heart)* And when ye write from there, truly from there, it ne'er leaves ye. Ye remember it, aways. It becomes a part of ye.

A pause as GORDON *absorbs this.*

KELLI Could you write down what he's saying? I'll get a pen and some paper.

GORDON I'll tell you what. You go meet Tomas when he gets back and tell him we've decided to dine alone here tonight. Tell him we're doing the romance thing. Tell him it's our anniversary, whatever, just get him to go home for the night. Then, when you get back I'll tell you everything, okay?

KELLI Promise?

GORDON Scout's honour.

KELLI You were never a scout.

GORDON Honey, I promise.

KELLI *(kissing him on the cheek)* I guess it's the best I can hope for.

KELLI *exits through the main door.*

GORDON *(returning to the sofa)* Well...

HAMISH Well.

Long awkward pause.

GORDON Scotch should be here soon.

HAMISH Guid.

GORDON Yeah.

HAMISH Aye. *(pause)* Should one of us be writin this doon?

GORDON No, no. It's fine.

HAMISH Oh guid.

GORDON Yeah.

HAMISH *(long awkward pause)* So lad...

GORDON Yeah?

HAMISH Ye said ye had some questions. Fit do ye want to ken?

GORDON *(pause, collecting thoughts)* Everything.

Blackout.

SCENE TWO

The next week. The cottage is in a state of cleanliness except for a half-empty Scotch bottle and two empty glasses sitting by the sink. There is a stack of hardcover legal books on the table. Mid-morning light streams in the windows. HAMISH *enters from the pantry carrying a vase of white heather. He is singing "The Braes O' Balquhidder." He places the vase on the mantle and exits back out the pantry.*

HAMISH Let us go, lassie, go
Tae the braes o' Balquhidder
Whar the blaeberries grow
'Mang the bonnie Hiela'd heather
Whar the deer and the rae
Lichtly bounding tegither
Sport the lang simmer day
On the braes o' Balquhidder.

He's gone.

TOMAS *(from offstage)* Hello, are ye not up yet? For the love of God buy an alarm clock, Hamish! Hamish? Kelli? Hello? Anyone? *(in the window)* Oh, for crying oot loud, cock-a-doodle-doo!

GORDON *enters from the bedroom. He is fully dressed and carries a couple of bags of luggage.*

GORDON Just a minute.

He sets the bags by the door and then answers it.

G'morning, Tomas.

TOMAS *enters carrying a hardcover book, which he sets on the counter face down.*

TOMAS Well, 'tis aboot time. At least ye're dressed. Are ye aw ready for the meetin?

GORDON Now, Tomas, I don't want you getting your hopes up.

KELLI *(entering from the bedroom)* Good morning, Tomas. Would you like some tea?

TOMAS Oh, no lass. I dinnae want to be a bother.

KELLI It's no trouble, I've just steeped some in the pot.

TOMAS Aye, that would be fine then, ta. Actually, I came over to see how Hamish made out last night.

GORDON Not the best. The books we got at the library weren't much use. They're rather dated.

TOMAS 'Tis too bad. But it was worth the trip to see the old biddy, Mrs. Cottleworth's face when I laid the books in front of her. I mean me, signing these books oot. Hell, I've ne'er been in there afore and she kens it, the damn busybody. I thought the bun on the back of her head was going to explode.

GORDON Actually, the best part was when you looked her in the eye and without even a smirk said, "Oh, just a wee bit of light reading to get me through the weekend." She damn near fainted right there on the spot.

They all laugh.

TOMAS I have ma moments.

KELLI I wish I had been there.

TOMAS Sorry ye missed it, lass. But ye say they werenae any good?

GORDON No, I've been pouring through them for the last four days and haven't come up with much. I'm sorry.

TOMAS Dinnae be. Ye did the best you could and I 'preciate it. I'm the one should be sorry. If it was nae for me, ye wouldnae have had to spend the last week and a half trying to find a way to save the place. I cannae thank ye enough.

HAMISH enters from the bathroom.

HAMISH Morning, son.

GORDON, noticing TOMAS, catches himself before saying anything and acknowledges HAMISH with a nod.

Now I get the silent treatment from ye, too. 'Tis like living in a troupe of mimes.

GORDON waves his head in TOMAS's direction, signifying he doesn't want to speak in front of him. TOMAS sees him.

TOMAS Ye aw right, lad?

GORDON Huh?

TOMAS You're waving your hied around like one a them bobble-head things.

GORDON Oh, that, just stretching, you know.

KELLI *(catching on)* You always want to stretch before going into battle.

TOMAS Battle? Ye're not planning anythin violent, are ye?

KELLI *(She copies what GORDON had been doing.)* No, no, no, it's good for the blood flow.

TOMAS Really?

KELLI Oh yeah, gets the blood flowing to the brain. Helps you think. Try it.

TOMAS does, reluctantly at first but starts to get into it.

HAMISH Ye got yoursel' a guid lassie there.

KELLI That's it, Tomas.

GORDON I know.

HAMISH I'd better be oot a here 'fore I'm the cause of a body's injury. When does the Grim Reaper come?

GORDON *(quietly)* Any time now.

HAMISH I'll keep an eye ta the road. I'm on ma way to the garden to see the dog. He's the most interesting interpretation of how our foreign policy could cause an economic decline within all of western Europe. 'Tis quite a remarkable theory. But what else would ye expect of him. He's a Highland terrier! *(He exits.)*

GORDON does a slashing motion across his neck to KELLI.

KELLI All right, that's it. How do you feel?

TOMAS A wee bit light-headed and woozy.

KELLI That's just a side effect. Trust me, your brain will be working overtime now.

TOMAS Right noo I feel a bitty blottered. Maybe that's why I seem a lot smarter when I'm drinking.

GORDON Now remember, Tomas, when they get here, let me do the talking. Okay?

TOMAS But I just primed ma old noodle up. I'm ready to go.

GORDON Leave it to me.

TOMAS Aw right then. Can I at least gie ye a hand with those bags?

GORDON Sure, that would be great.

TOMAS I'll just put them in the boot. *(stopping at the door)* Ye know, 'tis a pity ye have to leave so soon. All the trouble we've had with this auld place, you never got the chance to do what you set out to do.

KELLI What's that?

TOMAS Well, ye know, learn about your history and such.

GORDON You'd be surprised.

TOMAS exits.

KELLI Was he here?

GORDON Yeah, he's over discussing world politics with the dog now.

KELLI It's unbelievable.

GORDON Apparently, the dog is quite right about his views on politics. Even though they tend to lean heavily to the left.

KELLI Not that.

GORDON I wonder if the dog ever read *Animal Farm*. If Tomas has any pigs in the barn, that dog could stir up a whole heap of trouble. I've never trusted pork products.

KELLI Would you stop it? I'm not talking about livestock, I mean about Hamish, your grandfather.

GORDON What about him?

KELLI How do we explain it to people? When we get back home, I mean.

GORDON We don't.

KELLI No?

GORDON God NO! People will think we're nuts. I've got a career to think about. I don't want to be known as the lawyer that talks to dead people. Who would hire me in a murder trial? I could talk to the victim.

KELLI You're a corporate lawyer.

GORDON Even worse, half the board members look like they're already dead.

TOMAS enters running.

Hey, slow down! Is the missus after ya again?

TOMAS Worse, two cars just pulled up. 'Tis the banker and the lady from Gordon Industries.

KELLI Oh, dear!

GORDON Oh, God!

TOMAS *(fearfully)* Oh, shite!

HAMISH enters through the front door and immediately moves downstage left.

HAMISH *(mimicking a boxing announcer)* It's time for the main event!

TOMAS Hamish, the paperwork?

GORDON It's on the bedside table.

TOMAS I'll get it.

HAMISH *(bouncing like a boxer preparing for a bout)* In this corner, weighing in at a paranormal weight similar to a dust particle, from the far reaches of the Other Side. The Spooky Stinger, the Apparition of Submission, the Heavenly Highlander…

GORDON Would you get serious?

KELLI What?

GORDON He's back.

HAMISH And larger then life in more ways then one! ME!

TOMAS *(carrying papers, which include the letters that were found in the fireplace)* Here ye go, Hamish. Do ye best.

All wait nervously for a knock at the door.

HAMISH *(still bouncing)* And in that corner, weighing in at a whopping ten stone, originating from somewhere under a rock, the Pencil Pushing Little Prick, the Bottom Dwelling Pond Scum *(a knock at the door)*, the Seat Cover Wearing Wiener.

KELLI answers the door and SHELBY enters.

The Grim Reaper!

SHELBY *(timidly)* Good morning.

KELLI Good morning, come right in.

GORDON ushers HAMISH to the corner and sets the papers down.

ANNETTE Good morning.

KELLI Good morning.

GORDON Good morning. Mrs. Gordon, have you meet my wife, Kelli?

ANNETTE No, not from the front.

KELLI Oh yes, that. I'm sorry, it was a bad day for me, jet lag and all.

ANNETTE Aye, of course, I understand.

SHELBY All right, Tomas, I see you're rather stagnant this time so maybe we can get this over with quickly. I do have other appointments today.

HAMISH Fit, are ye meetin wit' the other three horsemen?

GORDON chuckles.

During the following conversation, ANNETTE wanders the room, studying it as if looking for something. HAMISH watches her intently.

SHELBY Pardon me, Mr. Grant, do you find something amusing?

GORDON No, sorry, carry on.

SHELBY I won't have any of your silly pranks today either. So, let's sit down and conduct our business like grown adults.

HAMISH Ye may want to get a telephone book fer his chair.

GORDON chuckles again.

GORDON I'm sorry, really.

SHELBY 'Tis is no time for juvenile behaviour. 'Tis is a grave situation.

HAMISH Hell, I'm dead. Everythin's a grave situation fer me.

GORDON Please, Mr. Sutherland, have a seat. Tomas, please join us.

SHELBY What are you doing, Mr. Grant? 'Tis a matter between Tomas and myself.

GORDON I'm working as Tomas's legal council.

SHELBY You? What gives you the right?

GORDON Well, I practise law back home and I am the direct descendant of the man who built this home.

SHELBY Fine, whatever, but it is pretty simple. Tomas has not paid the taxes on the property fir a substantial stretch of time and has not responded to any of our attempts at communication. Therefore, the government has seized the property, which is well within its legal right. I'm working on their behalf to find a buyer. Actually, in this case, the buyer found me.

GORDON May I see the statements?

SHELBY Certainly.

KELLI, who has been eavesdropping, now sees ANNETTE.

KELLI Mrs. Gordon, may I offer you tea?

ANNETTE That would be lovely, ta, and please, call me Annette.

KELLI Annette, fine, how do you like it?

HAMISH Black.

ANNETTE Black. *(pause, taking in the room)* 'Tis a lovely auld place, dinnae you think?

KELLI *(getting tea)* Oh yes. It's just perfect.

ANNETTE It feels so cosy. It's like an old blanket that you love to wrap around you. It makes ye feel safe, doesn't it?

KELLI It does.

ANNETTE I dinnae ken what it is about this place, 'tis like, ach, I dinnae ken. I cannae explain.

KELLI *(giving her the tea)* I know.

ANNETTE *(noticing flowers on the mantle)* Oh look, white heather! Aren't they beautiful? They're my favourite, always have been, ever since I can remember.

HAMISH Since ye were sixteen and I fetched ye a bouquet. Ye kept a vase full in this very hoose every summer after until… I could nae bare to keep them after.

ANNETTE Where did you get them?

KELLI Well, ah…

TOMAS *(hearing)* They grow wild out back over the cairn. There's a whole hillside of them.

HAMISH I planted them for ye.

ANNETTE I must see it before we go.

> *ANNETTE becomes engrossed with studying the flowers and is in deep thought. HAMISH moves beside her, keeping his eyes fixed on her. She seems to sense his presence.*

GORDON Right then, this all seems to be in order.

SHELBY Of course.

TOMAS *(beaten)* Of course.

GORDON I do have several questions and concerns though.

TOMAS That's ma lad!

GORDON My first concern is that we have a royal document regarding the deed to this land.

SHELBY You do?

TOMAS We do?

GORDON Yes, we found it hidden in the cottage.

SHELBY You did?

TOMAS We did?

GORDON Yes, it states that this land is deeded to the clan Grant and therefore exempt from all taxes and, as far as I can understand from these books, it could possibly be declared a landmark.

SHELBY *(skeptical)* You have a letter from the queen?

TOMAS The queen?

GORDON *(retrieving a document from the paperwork)* No, not exactly.

SHELBY Who then?

TOMAS Aye, who?

GORDON The Scottish king, Robert the Bruce.

SHELBY The Bruce?

TOMAS The Bruce?

GORDON Yes.

SHELBY Really?

TOMAS Really?

GORDON *(to* TOMAS*)* Would you stop that?

SHELBY Nonsense. Let me see that. *(He takes the document.)* I can't make this out. How can ye possible suggest these are from the Bruce?

GORDON Hold it up to the light.

TOMAS *(whispering to* GORDON*)* Where the hell did ye find that?

GORDON It's a long story, I'll explain later.

SHELBY has set the love letters down on a table and holds the letter up to the light.

SHELBY I don't know. 'Tis pretty hard to read.

He moves to a window for better light.

GORDON Look at the bottom. It has his seal clearly marked. I cross-referenced it with some documents at the local library.

SHELBY *(studying)* Yes, I think I see it. But it doesn't matter, the rest of the document is too damaged with age. It's not legible. Years of studying it wouldn't prove a thing. *(moving back to the table)* It may draw a crowd of believers to the museum but it wouldn't stand a chance in court.

During the next exchange ANNETTE picks up the love letters that are in the paperwork and examines them.

GORDON *(defiant)* You may be right. Are you willing to take your chances in court?

SHELBY Most definitely.

GORDON Oh… well then…

GORDON rises and paces the room while ANNETTE is still studying the letters. GORDON pauses and looks at KELLI for a moment, then…

What does Tomas owe you?

SHELBY What?

GORDON What does Tomas owe you, the government or whomever?

SHELBY gives GORDON a statement. After looking at it, he gives TOMAS a shocked look. TOMAS responds with an innocent shrug.

Pause.

I'll pay it.

TOMAS / SHELBY
FIT!

GORDON I'll pay it. I'll cover all that's owing, provided that he keeps the place.

KELLI I love you, Gord.

SHELBY That's a very generous offer but...

ANNETTE Where did ye get these?

TOMAS I'm sorry?

ANNETTE Where did ye get these letters?

GORDON We found them here, in the cottage. I think an old ancestor of mine wrote them.

ANNETTE Impossible.

GORDON Why?

ANNETTE *(pause)* Because I wrote them.

KELLI What?

ANNETTE These poems, I wrote them, to my husband before we were wed.

KELLI You did?

ANNETTE These are all poems I wrote to him. How did ye get them?

GORDON We found them here in the cottage.

TOMAS Where?

GORDON Right over here.

GORDON takes ANNETTE to the mantle.

SHELBY I think we're getting off topic here. 'Tis very generous that you have offered to pay the debt, Mr. Grant, but the fact remains that Tomas does not have the financial ability to sustain the place and continue to pay the taxes, not to mention that the Gordons have a proper and legal offer to buy the land. It's all but theirs now. You're too late.

TOMAS How do you ken I dinnae ha'e the money?

SHELBY Because I'm your banker, too.

TOMAS Damn. *(to himself)* Arsehole.

ANNETTE This place does nae belong to us.

SHELBY Na, not yet, but I've drawn up the papers and as soon as we all sign, it will.

ANNETTE The offer is off the table.

TOMAS 'Tis?

ANNETTE Aye. I will also be setting up a trust fund to sustain this place just the way it is, in the Grant name.

SHELBY But why?

ANNETTE I can nae explain it.

SHELBY Would ye try? Your husband will be quite upset. Think this through!

ANNETTE I dinnae care! I'm a Grant by birth. He kens that. Lord kens it would nae be the first time he's came against the Grant resolve.

SHELBY He'll kill us both! This was the opportunity your company has been waiting for and now you're going to throw it away on some foolish girlie whim just because ye found some stupid, sappy love letters? Leave it to a woman!

ANNETTE gives SHELBY a sharp look, the rest freeze waiting for the attack. TOMAS dives behind the sofa for safety.

ANNETTE *(sternly)* Nae! 'Tis no girlie whim. I would nae expect ye to understand. 'Tis about family; about human emotions and human decency. Values that I suspect would be lost on a simple buttock-kissing bean counter like you.

HAMISH That's ma lassie.

TOMAS *(as he raises his head above the back of the sofa)* I really like her.

GORDON Me too.

SHELBY Well, I never.

ANNETTE Maybe ye should. It might help ye relax.

SHELBY I'm not going to stand here and take this. I'm leaving. *(begins to collect his paperwork)*

TOMAS That was kind of what we were hopin for.

SHELBY Mr. Gordon will be hearing about this.

ANNETTE Guid, saves me telling him.

SHELBY exits, HAMISH begins to follow.

GORDON *(whispering)* Where you going?

HAMISH I'm the only one who dinnae get a shottie at him. 'Tis the grand finale. *(turns to leave, then)* Aye, and Hamish, that quinne is definitely your grandmither. Trust me. *(He's gone.)*

KELLI *(noticing)* What's going on?

GORDON The grand finale.

TOMAS Mrs. Gordon, I'm deeply moved and thankful that ye would do such a thing.

KELLI Yes, it was very kind.

GORDON Yes, thank you.

ANNETTE 'Tis no need to thank me, this place needs to be here. It's a monument to our past. It's our history. It seems the landscape's getting more and more crowded wit' factories and offices and such. We need to preserve more places like this, untouched in our Highlands. Besides, I cannae explain it but I feel a connection here. The whole place is familiar, and the flowers and the poems.

TOMAS Aye, 'twas kind of eerie.

ANNETTE No, 'tis nae eerie, 'tis… strangely enough… comforting.

SHELBY screams, we hear a dog and perhaps a car horn or such from outside.

TOMAS *(looking out the window)* Fit's he doin? Ma God, the dog!

He exits, KELLI looks out the window.

KELLI Oh my goodness! *(She exits.)*

GORDON It's a wonderful thing you did.

ANNETTE Just seemed right.

GORDON Will your husband be as angry as Mr. Sutherland says?

ANNETTE Dougie, heavens nae. Shelby talks like he's an ogre. Truth is he made me the controller for the division. He trusts me. The only one who's angry is Shelby. He has a hard time doing business with women. He's of the "old school." *(pause)* Anyway, I think I've taken up enough of your time. I should go.

GORDON But you wanted to see the flowers.

ANNETTE Aye.

GORDON They're just out back. Come, I'll show you.

ANNETTE If ye dinnae mind, I'd kind of like to see them masel'.

GORDON Yes, yes of course. I understand.

ANNETTE I'm nae sure I do. *(She starts to exit then stops.)* You know, Mr. Grant…

GORDON Call me Gordon.

ANNETTE Gordon, right. I just…

GORDON No, better yet, call me Hamish.

ANNETTE Hamish?

GORDON It's my first name. I've always gone by Gordon but I'm thinking I'll start to use Hamish.

ANNETTE Hamish, 'tis a beautiful name. I've always adored it.

GORDON What can I say, some of us are slower off the mark than others.

ANNETTE I was going to tell you that since our last visit, I've signed on for dance classes.

GORDON Really?

ANNETTE Aye, I'm taking an adult class three times a week and I've ne'er been happier.

GORDON That's terrific.

ANNETTE Of course, I'm pretty rusty but I think I've still got it. At least I've got the sore muscles so I figure it's a start. It never hurt like this when I was younger. Gettin old stinks sometimes.

GORDON Yeah, but we're also getting wiser so it's an even trade.

ANNETTE I wonder. Thanks for everything. *(She exits.)*

GORDON No, thank you *(after looking at a picture)*, Grandma?

GORDON gathers up paperwork and tea cups and sets them on the table and counter. HAMISH enters laughing.

HAMISH That was priceless! That, ma laddie, made wanderin the afterlife for a hundred and fifty years all worthwhile. Ah, ye shoulda seen it. *(noticing ANNETTE is gone)* Where'd she go?

GORDON She's out back, looking at the flowers.

HAMISH Ah, fine, I think I'll join her. *(rising)*

GORDON She wanted to be alone.

HAMISH And so she will. *(exits)*

TOMAS *(entering with KELLI)* I would nae ha'e believed it if I hadnae see it with ma own two eyes. Fit the hell was the dog doin?

KELLI You got me, but I never knew a dog had that much strength.

GORDON Hey, you two.

KELLI Hi, hon.

TOMAS Here's the man a the hour, or should I say the year. 'Twas incredible. I don't know exactly what happened, it was all so fast but, my, my!

I cannae thank ye enough for puttin up the dosh. I'll pay you back every pence.

GORDON No need, it's my family's croft after all.

TOMAS Aye, but 'twas me arse ye pulled out of the fire.

GORDON It's okay.

TOMAS I mean, ma family made a commitment o'er a hundred years back to care for the place. 'Twas the least we could do but I dropped the ball. I feel horrible.

GORDON Don't. If you want to make it up to me, just book us here every year.

KELLI Really?

GORDON You bet.

TOMAS Book it?! I'll gi'e ye the royal red-carpet treatment every time. Whisky on the house, guaranteed!

GORDON You're on.

KELLI *(hugging him)* Gord, you're wonderful! Oh dear, what time does our plane leave?

GORDON *(looking at his watch)* We're going to have to get going soon.

TOMAS I do 'preciate ye two taking the later flight to help me oot. I could nae have dealt with that weasel by masel'.

KELLI You would have done fine.

GORDON What do you say to one last sip before we go, to celebrate our victory?

TOMAS Sorry, I'd best nae be doin that. I need ma wits about me today. You see, since watching ye these past few weeks I've learned that I need to have better control of the situation here, so to rectify the problem I signed on for night classes. I start the night, right after I drop you at the airport.

KELLI Night school?

TOMAS Aye, I'm goin ta learn ta read!

KELLI *(giving him a hug and a kiss on the cheek)* That's wonderful!

GORDON Way to go, Tomas!

TOMAS Here now, fit do ye ken, 'tis true. College boys do get aw the lassies!

KELLI Oh, quit it.

TOMAS Listen, ye two get yoursel's ready to go, I've to get the dog back on its leash and make sure the old yapper is set for the day, aw right?

GORDON That would be fine, thanks.

TOMAS All right then. *(He exits.)*

KELLI Thanks for everything, college boy.

GORDON Well.

KELLI Yeah, well.

GORDON That was one hell of a vacation.

KELLI I'm sorry it wasn't what you wanted.

GORDON Maybe not, but it's what I needed. Thanks.

KELLI *(getting her bag from the bedroom)* There's just the small bag in the bathroom?

GORDON Yes.

KELLI Where'd Grandpa go?

GORDON He's out in the wildflowers with Grandma.

KELLI What?

GORDON I'll tell you later. Do you want me to put that in the car?

KELLI *(She picks up the bag by the door.)* I can do it. You gather up those books so we can drop them off at the library. I'm going to miss this place, and Tomas, not to mention Hamish and his poem. I have still never heard it and you promised me.

GORDON I'm sorry. I…

KELLI Relax, Gordon, it's okay. I'm just teasing. This was really a trip of a lifetime and that's more than I hoped for.

She exits through the main door. Gathering up the books, GORDON *pauses and looks around.* HAMISH *enters and stays in the doorway, unseen by* GORDON.

GORDON Well, old place. You and your spook and Kelli are all I got for family. You've all taught me that. You also taught me just how important it is. Hopefully everything will be all right now with the taxes and stuff. You'll all be safe, and hey, I'll be back, every year from now on. You can count on it. Maybe Tomas would let us retire here. What do ya think of that?

HAMISH I would enjoy that.

GORDON *(surprised)* Huh?!

HAMISH So would the local shoppy fit sells the whiskey.

GORDON Sorry, I didn't realize you were there, I was just talking to myself.

HAMISH Ah, ye dinnae have to explain to me about talking to yersel'.

GORDON No, I guess not. I thought you were out back with Grandma.

HAMISH I was. Turns oot she'll be back. She's decided to visit the meadow regularly.

GORDON She told you.

HAMISH She dinnae ha'e to.

A car horn honks.

GORDON I've got to go.

HAMISH I ken.

GORDON Look, Hamish… Grandpa, I don't know what to say, I…

HAMISH I ken.

GORDON What you've done for me, what you've shown me…

HAMISH I ken. Ye've done the same fer me.

Car horn.

GORDON I wish I could, I don't know, shake your hand or give you a hug or something.

HAMISH Aye, so do I.

GORDON I mean, you're the closest thing to a family. Well, I guess you are. You're the… you're like… like, my grandpa.

HAMISH I am your grandda.

GORDON Yeah. Yeah, you are. Look, I've got to go, but we'll be back next year, I promise.

HAMISH That would be grand.

GORDON *(picking up the books)* Yeah. Yeah, it will be. *(pause)* Bye. *(starts to exit)*

HAMISH *(when GORDON reaches the door)* Call him Hamish.

GORDON I beg your pardon?

HAMISH Yer son, call him Hamish.

GORDON I don't have a son.

HAMISH gives a sly shrug.

(suspiciously) What are you saying?

HAMISH Let's just say, I can see things.

GORDON You mean Kelli's…!

HAMISH Boogie, boogie!

GORDON Of course, that's why we're here! That's why she booked this trip. All her talk about family… I was so stupid!

HAMISH *(laughing)* Aye.

GORDON I'm going to be a dad! Me, a dad! Can you believe it?! Me!

HAMISH *(handing him the poem)* Read it to her often.

GORDON *(pause as he takes the poem)* Aye, Grandda, I will. Kelli! Kelli! Kelli! *(He exits.)*

HAMISH goes to the door and watches him leave. After a moment he turns back in and begins to sing. He crosses to the picture of St. Andrew and retrieves the flask from behind it. He drinks and goes to the white heather, touching it delicately as he sings.

HAMISH
Noo the summers in prime
Wi' the flooers richly bloomin
Wi' the wild mountain thyme
A' the moorlan's perfumin
Tae oor dear native scenes
Let us journey tegither
Whar glad innocence reigns
'Mang the braes o' Balquhidder.

Lights slowly change during the song so we now see a bright light coming from the main entrance. During the next line, HAMISH is joined in song. He stops singing and turns when he hears it. ANNIS enters singing. She is dressed in the same era of dress as HAMISH. It is his wife, ANNIS, played by the same actress as ANNETTE. While she sings, she raises her hand to HAMISH, beckoning him to come. He does, he rejoins her singing and after a moment they both exit out the main entrance.

Let us go, lassie, go…

ANNIS
…Let us go, lassie, go
Tae the braes o' Balquhidder
Whar the blaeberries grow
'Mang the bonnie Hielan' heather.

HAMISH / ANNIS
Whar the deer and the rae
Lichtly bounding tegither
Sport the lang simmer day
On the braes o' Balquhidder.

They exit.

Fade to black.

The end.

NEVER SUCH INNOCENCE AGAIN

BY J. MICHAEL FAY

NOTES

J. Michael Fay left the United States in 1970, leaving behind a nation torn between patriotism and opposition to the Vietnam War. Thirty years later, he started writing *Never Such Innocence Again*, shortly after the "coalition of the willing" invaded Iraq in a war that promised to end terrorism. He finished the play at about the same time the American president declared "Mission Accomplished."

Fay sets the scene in the Haliburton Highlands where he now lives, examining ordinary people in 1914 as they watch the emergence of yet another war—the Great War, the war to end all wars. His characters are echoes of historical residents of the Highlands area, including Sir Sam Hughes, Canada's minister of militia during World War I, whose nephew was killed in France during the war and whose niece was a suffragist and leading peace advocate. The title *Never Such Innocence Again* is the ironic last line of Philip Larkin's poem about World War I—"MCMXIV."

This play was produced by Highlands Little Theatre in 2005. After being adjudicated by Ron Cameron-Lewis in the Eastern Ontario Drama League Festival, the play gained new life. Cameron-Lewis was hired to continue dramaturgical work, and a second version of the script (also available from the author) was performed as a staged reading by the Sheridan/UTM drama program in 2006.

J. Michael Fay has spent his life as a community organizer, writer, and student of creative writing. He lives in Minden, Ontario, and is a member of the Conjurors, a co-operative community theatre.

For Fay, as always.

Never Such Innocence Again was first produced by Highlands Little Theatre in Haliburton, Ontario, in March 2005, with the following cast and crew:

Tom Ross	Benton Brown
Lila Ross	Cathy Cox
Robert Ross	Mark Johnston
Ada Ross	Chris Archer
Nan Payne	Maureen Johnson
Vera Payne	Kathryn Boyd
Johnny Payne	Michael Johnson
Mr. Willoughby	Tim Nicholson

Director: Caryl Miller
Stage Manager/Props: Heather Smith
Set Design: Doug Brohm
Set Construction: Tim Nicholson
Lighting: Curtis Eastmuir, Craig Saunders
Sound/Special Effects: Ray Miller
Costume Design: Caryl Miller
Seamstress: Karlene Cooney
Wardrobe Mistress: Debra Dart
Drill Instructor: M.W.O. Mike Flowers
Poster Design: Brian Atyeo

CHARACTERS

In order of appearance:

TOM Ross, youngest son of the highlands resort manager
LILA Ross, daughter of the manager
ROBERT Ross, oldest son of the manager
ADA Ross, the manager of the resort
NAN Payne, a guest, the mother of Vera and John and sister-in-law of the minister of war
VERA Payne, a guest, the niece of the minister
JOHNNY Payne, a guest, the nephew of the minister
Mr. WILLOUGHBY, a new arrival, a business associate of the minister

SETTING

The action takes place at a lodge overlooking a lake in the Haliburton Highlands, late in the afternoon of August 1, 1914. Although the playwright has attempted to maintain historical accuracy, the characters and events in the play are strictly fictitious.

ACT ONE

SCENE ONE

The sounds of a lake; a loon call. Spotlight up downstage left.

TOM sits on the ground with his legs crossed and a rifle cradled in his lap. He reaches for the cloth in his back pocket, raises the rifle, and begins to shine the barrel, then the stock. He lifts the rifle to his shoulder and looks down the barrel at several spots in the audience, pretending to fire. He seems very pleased with the rifle and with himself. He stands and begins to handle the rifle like a soldier, in a boyish way: lifting it to his shoulder, holding it across his chest, clicking the butt on the ground. He seems satisfied with his work, bends over, picks up an empty canvas bag, and exits stage left.

Spotlight down. Lake sounds continue for a few beats, then a gunshot.

Lights up centre stage.

A table is being set on the summer porch of the lodge. The table sits at an angle downstage right, with the head facing the audience. There is a side table for serving, situated upstage right, and a Muskoka chair and stool on level ground downstage right. LILA is moving water glasses from the side table to the place settings at the dinner table. She is young and sprightly, wearing a bright long dress and moving with light gaiety. She looks away from the dinner table to a framed photograph she is carrying in her hand, curling a strand of her hair on her finger. ROBERT enters from the lodge upstage right. He wears workmen's clothes and cap, but is neat and clean-cut, an unlikely workman. He has a telescope slung over his shoulder.

ROBERT I caught you, Li.

LILA You caught me what?

ROBERT I know who that is.

LILA sets the photograph down and joins her brother. She takes him by the hand, leads him to the chair, and sits him down. She stands over him and places her hand on her hip, ready to admonish him.

LILA And I caught you.

ROBERT Caught me what?

LILA Staring.

ROBERT lifts the telescope, as if to look at the sky.

ROBERT At the stars?

LILA No, dear Robby, the stars were in your eyes. And they brighten every time Vera Payne comes into the room.

ROBERT The same way yours brighten when her brother—he of the famous photograph—strikes a crochet ball on the lawn.

LILA *(sighing dreamily)* Oh my, it's true. It must be the way the lazy sun has been sitting in the bright blue sky these past few days. It must be the long starry nights. August has been just perfect for all the songs Mother bought for our new Victrola. Why, it's a time—

ROBERT *(interrupting)* To fall in love?

LILA Oh, Robbie, don't we wish?

ROBERT For you, perhaps. *(standing, holding the telescope in his hand like a protective wand)* For me, that's a different matter.

LILA Why? We're young and it's never been this lovely in the highlands. It's a perfect time for—

ROBERT *(interrupting again)* Working on the railway.

LILA circles him, takes his free hand, and holds it tenderly.

LILA But you've bankers' holiday free, Robbie. It's your time away from the men of the rails.

ROBERT It may be a free weekend for me, Li, because I'm young. But the men have families to feed and things to worry over. Why, I bet they're in camp right now, worrying over what's going to happen in London after the holiday weekend—

LILA *(interrupting now)* Let's not talk about those nasty rumours of war. *(She slips away, gay again, and waves her hand over the table.)* We have John and Vera and Nan for the dinner. Mother is cooking yummy things in the kitchen. We have a guest coming on the train. We have the night before us. We have the moon and the stars. And we have the music.

ROBERT Yes, we have the music.

ADA enters upstage right from the lodge and stops to inspect the table. She is an attractive woman with a strong sense of her maturing femininity. She wears a fine dress with an apron over it.

ADA Where are the wine glasses?

LILA I'm chilling them with the wine, Mother. I'll get them when we're ready.

ADA Everything must be just so for dinner.

LILA Everything will.

ADA Where's your brother?

LILA Tom went up in the woods with his friends. He had his gun, so there may be rabbit for your stew.

ROBERT Why the fuss, Mother?

ADA We have a guest coming on the train. He's an associate of the minister. And. And I have business with him tonight.

ROBERT Business?

ADA *(flustered)* It's not… not for us to discuss… yet.

LILA Is the minister coming as well?

ADA No. He's detained in Ottawa.

LILA Do you know why?

ADA I can only guess.

ROBERT And the guessing is about the war?

LILA Please, Robbie. Let's not talk about this stupid war tonight.

ADA *(smoothing down her apron and scanning the table again)* Robert, will you take the carriage down to Rail's End to pick up the guest?

ROBERT Certainly, Mother. His name?

ADA Willoughby. Mr. Willoughby.

ROBERT hurries off into the lodge.

I'll ask Vera to help you with the table, dear.

LILA I can manage, Mother.

ADA She needs to make herself useful, that girl. She spends far too much time in the window seat with those labour periodicals.

LILA As you wish.

ADA surveys the table, adjusts a place setting, then exits into the lodge.

LILA begins to dance from the side table to the dinner table, bringing the rest of the water glasses and a stack of plates. She stops at the side table and picks up the framed photograph again and studies it carefully, joyfully. VERA enters from the lodge and considers LILA. She folds her arms across the bodice of her dress and watches. She is pretty, but dressed severely in a long black skirt and plain white blouse. She has wire-rim glasses on a chain around her neck. LILA notices her, then sets the photograph down.

Oh, Vera, Johnny looks so handsome in his uniform.

VERA He looks just as handsome without the uniform.

LILA But—

VERA *(interrupting)* But nothing, Lila. I don't like that uniform.

LILA How can you say that?

VERA The uniform means he's preparing for war. A war that should be stopped before it begins.

LILA Oh, that silly war again. All I know is that he's the most handsome man who comes here. And the uniform… it just does something.

VERA It beats the drums of war.

LILA You argue just like your uncle.

VERA The famous minister of war.

LILA and VERA begin to roll and slip napkins into napkin rings, then place them on the table at an easy, relaxed pace.

LILA Robbie's just left for Rail's End.

VERA He's not going back to work, is he?

LILA No, silly. He's with us for the whole weekend. He's off to meet our guest at the train. *(beat)* Robbie and I were just having a chat.

VERA You were?

LILA About love.

VERA drops the napkin on the floor behind the table. She bends to pick it up.

VERA Love? What *about* love?

LILA We were talking about songs and the stars in the bright clear sky.

VERA Oh, yes. The stars. Robbie's become quite an expert with that telescope of his.

LILA The stars we talked about were in his eyes.

VERA His eyes?

VERA hurries to the side table, fusses over the tablecloth, and pours herself a glass of water. LILA, enjoying the teasing banter, approaches in a confidential, sisterly way.

LILA It's you, my dear Vera. Robbie's eyes light at the mere sight of you. He watches the way you walk, the way you slip into the window seat with your magazines, the way you perch those pretty glasses on your nose.

VERA I rather doubt it, Li. He's such a serious young man.

LILA Oh, there's part of him that's serious, yes. But there's another part—

VERA *(interrupting)* That's not serious?

LILA You've guessed it. A side that likes to watch a pretty girl like you.

VERA slips the glasses on her nose.

Does that help you see what I'm saying?

VERA You're such a tease, little Lila.

LILA I may be a tease but I'm not so little anymore.

VERA That's true. None of us are so little anymore.

ADA *(calling, offstage)* Lila dear, I need you to help me with this fish.

LILA gives VERA a squeeze on her arm. She turns to go.

JOHNNY enters downstage left from the grounds, wearing cricketing pants and sweater, with a croquet mallet over his shoulder. LILA stops in her tracks.

JOHNNY There you are. *(pausing at the sight of LILA, then looking at VERA)* Sister.

LILA rushes off in a wave of flustered energy.

VERA You've worked your magic on her.

JOHNNY Oh, V.

VERA Well, you have.

JOHNNY She's a child.

VERA A very beautiful child.

JOHNNY Oh, V. Stop it. Let's just enjoy the lake.

JOHNNY takes VERA by the hand and turns her towards the lake.

What a magnificent day!

JOHNNY points to the lake.

I love the lake in the light at dusk, with the hills stretching to the sky like a wondrous dream. And there's the island, round and green, rising from the lake like life itself.

VERA Ada told me a tale about the island today.

JOHNNY Tell me, V.

VERA Her father told her that Indians brushed against each other in this very spot.

JOHNNY Brushed?

VERA They fought, Johnny. They fought over the hunting in the hills and the fishing in the lakes and rivers.

JOHNNY raises the mallet, aims it like a gun towards the island, and mimics a shot. He drops the mallet to his side.

JOHNNY They weren't so different from us, after all.

VERA Oh, yes, they were. The elders made them stop the fighting for a while. They went to the island and shared a feast of fish and talked and smoked their pipes and talked some more.

JOHNNY And what came of all this talk and smoke and fish?

VERA They settled their differences. And they didn't carry on with that awful, bloody war.

JOHNNY *(pulling away)* There you go, V. You never stop. You know how I feel about serving the king. And you know the value of honour.

VERA The men on the island had to leave honour behind, in order to talk. And the talking led to a way without war.

JOHNNY Please, V. Just leave it.

LILA enters from the lodge, composes herself, and stops midway between JOHNNY and VERA, obviously pleased about something.

LILA Your mother wishes you to dress for dinner.

JOHNNY Dress?

LILA She wishes you to wear your uniform.

JOHNNY slips the mallet to his shoulder, holding it like a rifle.

VERA *(exasperated)* Oh, heavens.

JOHNNY *(suddenly more formal)* I'll dress right now.

JOHNNY marches away and, as he nears the door, NAN enters from the lodge. She is dressed formally for dinner, with a shawl draped over her shoulders, her hair in a tight bun. Although dressed somewhat severely, she is attractive and carries herself with that awareness. JOHNNY stops when he sees her.

I'm going to my room to dress for dinner.

NAN You're a dear, Johnny.

JOHNNY exits into the lodge. NAN looks at the table and fusses over one of the table settings. LILA slips beside VERA. NAN looks up and notices them.

You've heard?

VERA There's news from Ottawa?

NAN No, dear, a… a guest will be joining us for dinner.

VERA That news we've heard.

NAN He's a… friend of your uncle.

VERA Robbie's gone to Rail's End to fetch him.

NAN Yes, young Robbie.

VERA He's not so young anymore.

NAN *(looking carefully at her daughter)* I guess you're right about that. Ada tells me he's thinking of entering the clergy.

VERA Is he, Lila?

LILA It's news to me. But, with Robbie, anything's possible. I would rather doubt it.

VERA *(turning to NAN)* Mother, must Johnny wear his uniform at dinner?

NAN We have a guest. It shows respect.

VERA How can you encourage him so? I thought you were for peace.

NAN I am.

VERA Then how can you prepare your only son for war?

NAN, looking confused, walks away from her daughter, then stops. VERA has followed her.

NAN He's my son and I want for him what he wants for himself.

VERA Even if it's war?

NAN Even…

VERA And what of me, Mother?

NAN Of you?

VERA I'm your daughter. Do you want what I want?

NAN Of course, I do.

VERA I want peace.

NAN Vera, must you be so exasperating? Can't you simply enjoy this fine summer evening with us, with our guest?

VERA Oh, how I wish I could.

LILA The evening will be exciting, won't it, Vera?

VERA looks at LILA abstractly, as if she didn't hear.

VERA Exciting?

LILA A guest. The table. The wine. The thought of it all makes me want to sing. Surely, it's a time for singing.

VERA I wish it were, Li. I really do

NAN *(turning to* LILA*)* Would you see if your mother needs help?

LILA Yes, ma'am.

VERA I'll go, too. We can see to the wine and the glasses.

NAN Ada will appreciate that.

LILA and VERA hurry into the lodge. NAN turns to the table and, like ADA, begins to fuss over the place settings. ADA comes out of the lodge and joins NAN.

Do the children know that the lodge has been lost?

ADA I didn't have the heart to tell them.

They drift towards the chair downstage right. NAN sits and begins to rock. ADA remains by her side.

NAN What will you do with this Mr. Willoughby?

ADA I'll hear him out about his plans, now that he owns the place. I'll try to see if I fit into those plans. And I hope there's still room for Tommy and Lila to help with the managing.

NAN It's such a job, running the lodge. He needs you and he'll want the children to help. And surely he'll pay them, as we've always paid them.

ADA You were such dears to us. For all those years, I almost felt that we somehow owned this place together.

NAN We trusted you. We got to know you so well. We got to know the children… I'll never be able to understand how my John allowed his brother to take this place from us.

ADA Brothers will do such things.

NAN Allowing the minister to have the deed to our precious lodge to cover a debt! And then for him to lose the place to Willoughby to cover another debt! I'm sure the stress of that had a part to play in John's death.

ADA It came so suddenly, the heart attack. Such a blow to you.

NAN And to the children. Vera reacted with a cold fury, a fury she seems to transfer to this war.

ADA And Johnny?

NAN The opposite. But then, they've always been opposites. He seems to need to be up and doing—marching with the militia, shining his boots and belt, endlessly oiling his rifle.

ADA I'm glad you could visit and get away for a while, from wills and lawyers and all of that.

NAN I was only too happy to come. We have time with our children and, together, we can face this man.

ADA Mr. Willoughby must be a clever man.

NAN Let's hope he's fair, as well as clever.

ADA Hope is all we have left as women.

NAN A pity, but true.

ADA Goodness, I hear them now.

NAN rises. She takes ADA's hand and begins to move towards the table. ROBERT and WILLOUGHBY enter from the lodge. WILLOUGHBY wears a dark suit and fills the stage with his presence. He carries a cane and walks gingerly ahead of the younger man. ADA steps towards him, extending her hand.

Welcome, sir. I'm Ada Ross, manager of the resort.

WILLOUGHBY Yes, and I'm Willoughby. The minister's mentioned your management.

ADA *(shaking his hand)* May I introduce my good friend, the minister's sister-in-law, Nan Payne.

WILLOUGHBY *(taking her hand)* Yes. It's an honour to meet you.

ADA May I offer you a whiskey?

WILLOUGHBY Indeed. The dust on the train dried my throat. *(rapping the cane on the stage)* And the cramped seat sharpened the misery of my gout. Whiskey, indeed. For the throat, for the pain.

ADA Robbie, would you see to the gentleman's whiskey.

ROBERT exits into the lodge, leaving the new guest with the two women. WILLOUGHBY considers the women as the young man leaves, looking them over with a connoisseur's eye. The women are keenly aware of his careful study.

WILLOUGHBY The boy tells me he's working on the railway?

ADA He's repairing rail beds and at night helping teach the men to read and write.

WILLOUGHBY Where are they?

ADA Just below Rail's End in that horrid swamp. It's awful, back-breaking work for the men.

WILLOUGHBY That swamp was a terrible drain on capital. I spent far too many hours with investors in London trying to explain that miserable swamp.

NAN Imagine those poor men trying to lay steel across it.

WILLOUGHBY I daresay they are richer for the pay packets from the investors in London.

ADA And I suspect that their wives don't appreciate the paltry size of those pay packets.

WILLOUGHBY My, my. Ladies in the country have such sharp wit.

ADA We widows learn to live by our wits, sir.

WILLOUGHBY Pity that. *(looking at them carefully)* With so much else you have to offer.

NAN What we have, sir, is no longer on offer.

WILLOUGHBY Pity that, too. *(clearing his throat)* Now, enough of this banter. We've business to attend to, Mrs. Ross.

ADA Business can await dinner, can it not?

WILLOUGHBY Marvellous idea, that.

ROBERT swings back and offers a whiskey to WILLOUGHBY. He takes a careful sip, then empties the glass.

ADA The whiskey suits you?

WILLOUGHBY Fine whiskey it is.

ADA Robert, please refill his glass.

ROBERT takes the glass from WILLOUGHBY and exits into the lodge again.

WILLOUGHBY That's kind of you, my dear.

ADA *(coyly)* We try to be kind as we can at the lodge.

WILLOUGHBY It looks like one only gets the best at… my lodge. The train has sharpened my appetite. *(tapping his cane on the stage)* And this standing makes me yearn for my place at the table.

JOHNNY enters from the lodge and approaches them. He is more stiffly formal in his brown woollen uniform, brown boots, and leather belt.

NAN *(moving closer to WILLOUGHBY)* My son, sir. Johnny Payne.

WILLOUGHBY A young man ready to serve, I see.

JOHNNY Indeed, sir.

WILLOUGHBY The king will need young men of your cut.

ROBERT enters from the lodge with a second whiskey for WILLOUGHBY. He also has whiskies on the small tray for himself and for JOHNNY. He offers one to JOHNNY and takes one for himself.

(raising his glass) To His Majesty!

JOHNNY *(joining the toast)* His Majesty!

ROBERT empties his glass without honouring the toast.

LILA and VERA enter with the chilled wine glasses and a bottle of white wine. They set them down on the side table and join the others.

NAN Sir, my daughter, Vera.

WILLOUGHBY takes her hand, looks at her, and kisses her hand.

WILLOUGHBY A pleasure, young lady.

ADA And sir, *my* daughter, Lila Ross.

WILLOUGHBY repeats the hand kissing.

WILLOUGHBY Such lovely young things. Such lovely company all round.

JOHNNY *(gesturing towards the table)* Let's sit for this feast of fish.

VERA And hope for talk of peace?

JOHNNY *(sharply)* Talk, certainly. There will always be good talk at my table.

LILA Oh, yes there will.

They begin to arrange themselves at the table. ADA shows WILLOUGHBY to his place at the head of the table, facing the audience, then exits. VERA and ROBERT sit to his right, NAN and JOHNNY to his left. ADA enters, holding a large platter that she sets on the side table. LILA begins to set the wine glasses at the place settings. ADA takes the bottle of wine to the head of the table and pours a bit into WILLOUGHBY's glass. He lifts the glass, rolls the wine, sips, and nods appreciatively. ADA fills his glass and begins to fill the others. LILA takes her place at the table next to JOHNNY, managing to brush against him, drawing his immediate attention. They settle in at the table, for a moment. ADA continues to fill the glasses.

TOM suddenly hurries up the stairs from the grounds downstage left to the porch, wearing coveralls, cradling a rifle in his left arm and, with his right hand, holding a small burlap bag.

ADA Tommy!

TOM I bagged a beauty, Mother. We'll have stew for a week for sure.

ADA Tom, we have a guest. Can't you see we're sitting for dinner?

TOM *(noticing the dinner table for the first time)* Oh, my. I do apologize, Mother. I meant no offence.

WILLOUGHBY *(rising)* Don't scold the boy. Come show me, son.

TOM So I will, sir.

TOM moves quickly to WILLOUGHBY. JOHNNY rises and joins them. They frame TOM, who proudly opens the bag for the men to see.

JOHNNY Fine one, Tommy. Where did you nail him?

TOM I went up the ridge with my mates. We only had my rifle, so it was me that done the nailin'.

WILLOUGHBY How many shots, son?

TOM One shot, sir. That's all I ever need.

WILLOUGHBY You must take lessons from the minister.

TOM I do, sir. He takes me out with the targets every time he stops at the lodge.

WILLOUGHBY raises his cane like a rifle and "shoots" across the table.

WILLOUGHBY And soon he'll have all the boys in the Dominion target-shooting the Hun.

JOHNNY Well put, sir.

VERA squirms at this.

ADA Enough of this, you men. My trout is chilling in the air. Take that… whatever it is, to the kitchen for cleaning.

TOM It's a hare, Mother.

VERA *(to no one in particular)* There you have it: first, the hare… then the Hun.

ADA On with you, Tom, or you'll be doing the cleaning.

TOM It's women's work, Mother.

WILLOUGHBY And shooting is men's.

ADA Enough of this jabbering. I'll not serve cold trout at my table. I have a reputation to maintain.

TOM exits hurriedly into the lodge. WILLOUGHBY sits down and JOHNNY returns to his seat. As ADA tops up WILLOUGHBY's wine glass, he looks up at her with interest. LILA rises, goes to the side table, and picks up the platter with the fish and trimmings and begins serving the guests. As she serves JOHNNY, she manages to touch his hand.

WILLOUGHBY That boy of yours will make a fine soldier.

VERA *(snapping around)* Please, sir, not that.

WILLOUGHBY I beg your pardon?

VERA The boy is only fifteen.

WILLOUGHBY A strapping, strong fifteen, I might say. And a fine shot. His Majesty will need boys like him from across the Dominion.

VERA *(interrupting)* I won't have it.

NAN Vera! Your manners, please.

VERA The gentleman is singing the siren song of war. It's no time for manners. Soon Johnny will be singing that song.

JOHNNY Vera! I can… sing for myself. I fancied joining up as soon as I heard the call might come.

NAN Joining up?

JOHNNY I meant to tell you after dinner, Mother. But Vera…

LILA finishes serving entrees and listens closely to JOHNNY.

NAN What is it, son?

JOHNNY The minister needs a contingent to fight the Hun, Mother. My friends are joining up after holiday Monday. And I hope that Mr. Willoughby, acting as Father would if he were still alive, may just write a reference to the major.

WILLOUGHBY I'd be honoured, young man. The major is a man I know well.

VERA *(rising, with a growing anger)* Father, rest his soul, would write no such reference, Johnny. He believed in peace, not war.

NAN Vera, please sit down. I won't have this kind of argument at the table.

VERA sits promptly.

ROBERT *(quickly interrupting)* Mother, it's time for your trout. May I offer the blessing?

ADA Why, yes… yes, indeed.

The table stills. ROBERT rises and the guests bow their heads; ADA and LILA stand still, bowing their heads, too. The storm at the table is averted.

ROBERT Lord, we're gathered in the highlands, blessed with the bounty of your waters and fields. We seek a blessing tonight for the men who risk life and limb to bring your gifts to their own tables, and soon may be asked to risk even more. And we ask for your help in finding a way to keep those men safe from the storms of war.

ALL *(except Mr. WILLOUGHBY)* Amen.

ROBERT, pleased with himself, sits down. After LILA finishes serving, she sits next to JOHNNY, paying special attention to him and his needs. WILLOUGHBY makes a display of shaking open his white napkin and tucking it under his chin. He lifts his knife and fork in front of him, framing his speech with silverware.

WILLOUGHBY While I appreciate the fine sentiment of your blessing, young man, I must quarrel with the logic. These times require clarity in logic. If you allow me, I'll share that with you.

JOHNNY It may help to keep it simple, sir, as well as clear; so my dear mother can follow.

VERA Your "dear mother" doesn't need to be patronized, Johnny.

ROBERT *(quickly, to deflect the tension)* Please, sir… continue.

LILA Yes, sir, please continue.

WILLOUGHBY Very well, then, let me begin this way.

ADA *(by his side again)* Sir, before you begin, may I determine interest in dessert?

WILLOUGHBY *(looks up at her, with a sudden interest in his eyes)* What do you have in mind?

ADA Berries from the bush, with rich cream.

WILLOUGHBY There's no doubt, my dear. Dessert, it is.

JOHNNY And now, sir, may we hear from you. You've spoken to Uncle recently?

WILLOUGHBY I saw the minister in the city just a week ago… about a matter relating to this… property. And, after that, we went over events in the world. He's studied world events ever since his years in South Africa with those bloody Boers.

ADA Sir!

WILLOUGHBY Beg pardon. I've never been able to separate that miserable noun from that truly useful adjective. But I wish no offence.

ADA Thank you, sir.

WILLOUGHBY The minister sees this war as the challenge of our time. On one side is the way of the West. *Our* way. On the other side, the way of the East. *Their* way.

VERA Your obliqueness is charming, sir. But what do East and West have to do with the assassination in Sarajevo?

WILLOUGHBY Ah, the young lady reads more than the droppings of the *Daily Star*.

VERA I read labour journals, sir.

WILLOUGHBY I should have guessed by the bias in your question.

ROBERT Bias?

WILLOUGHBY Indeed. The biased rhetoric of Labourites never considers that the East is the seat of fanatics and assassins and anarchists. Franz Joseph was struck down by just such a fanatic assassin and the war the minister saw brewing long before will come within days.

JOHNNY Sir, now I find myself confused. I thought we were going in to fight the Hun. And the Hun is neither West nor East. Why, the Hun is right in the middle of Europe.

LILA Yes. The middle… of Europe.

WILLOUGHBY Technically correct. The Hun sits in the centre. He looks like us and acts like us, but, rest assured, his deep-seated values spring from the East, where the cost of a man's life is never measured, always expendable.

VERA This is astonishing. First, there's mumbo-jumbo about East and West. And now you say that our side values life, and the other side doesn't value life at all. Is that correct?

WILLOUGHBY You seem to be listening now. We must declare war against the Hun precisely because he has no respect for human life.

VERA Let me try this "logic" myself. Johnny, are you listening?

LILA Of course he's listening. We're all listening.

VERA Allow me, then. *(beat)* We must go to war and kill the Hun because the Hun has no respect for human life. Is that correct, sir?

WILLOUGHBY I could not state the argument any better.

VERA I rest my case. *That* is the total insanity of war. We kill them, because they'll kill us, because they have no respect for human life. And what, may I ask, does that say about us?

NAN Vera, you must stop this. I feel a migraine coming.

ROBERT *(interrupting again)* She's saying nothing more than the scriptures.

LILA Robbie, it's not time for preaching. It's time for listening.

JOHNNY Indeed. It's time to listen to the wisdom of an older man.

VERA Wait, Johnny. Can't you see? The older generation will always find a way for the younger to go to war. *We* must put a stop to that. We're a new generation with new ideas. This is our world.

WILLOUGHBY You live in *my* world now, young lady; circled by the cables of communication, bound by the steel of the rails, served by ships on the seven seas. We'll stand together to defend our beliefs against the Hun and the hordes of the East. If we don't stand firm now we'll be overrun and live our lives in subjugation.

NAN *(suddenly standing)* I'm sorry. My head is hammering with pain. Please excuse me.

NAN rushes from the table, exits into the lodge, leaving the others in stunned silence.

LILA Oh, dear.

JOHNNY Look what you've done, V. Go to her. We can't have Mother suffer another of her attacks.

VERA There'll be more of them, if you have your way about this war.

JOHNNY As you wish, then. I'll see to Mother.

JOHNNY rises, bows, hurries around the table, and exits into the lodge. LILA follows him.

ADA My fine meal has turned to shambles.

WILLOUGHBY *(lifting his fork and knife)* Not for me, my dear, not for me.

He begins to eat again. TOM enters and approaches his mother.

TOM Nan's crying and Johnny and Lila are having no luck with her.

ADA Come with me, Vera. Please.

ADA exits into the lodge. VERA rises and follows her.

After a moment JOHNNY enters and makes his way back to his seat. TOM sits absently in VERA's seat at the table. He begins to pick at the plates on the table like the hungry adolescent he is.

TOM What happened?

WILLOUGHBY Think nothing of it, son. The women have retreated to the kitchen. We'll just carry on.

ROBERT Carry on?

WILLOUGHBY Men will be men and women, women. Isn't that said somewhere in that Bible of yours?

JOHNNY Perhaps Robbie spends too much time with the New Testament and not enough with the Old.

ROBERT Beg pardon?

JOHNNY I'll explain. The Old Testament is filled with the battles of ancient times, with the victors and the vanquished, and the harsh justice of the one true God. The New…

ROBERT *(interrupting)* Vera *is* right. From you, sir, we get the East and West; and from you, Johnny, the Victors and Vanquished. This is what I say. Christ preached peace for three long years, from the shores of Galilee to the heights of the holy Mount.

After eating through this exchange, WILLOUGHBY *sets down his knife and fork.*

WILLOUGHBY Gibberish. We only need to know one thing, young man. The king will call upon men to take up service in the battles to come. Real men will take up that service willingly. Like John, here. And, I suspect, like young Tom.

TOM Gladly, I'll go. And it won't be soon enough for me. Eh, Johnny?

JOHNNY This is not for the table, Tommy.

ROBERT Was Vera right?

JOHNNY About what?

ROBERT About Tommy?

WILLOUGHBY Sir, you may feel protected by that Bible of yours from the need to defend your country, but there are many of us who don't see it that way. And young Tom here may just be one of them.

TOM Well said, sir. I just may be. Eh, Johnny?

ADA *enters, comes back to the table, and stands next to* WILLOUGHBY. TOM *jumps up quickly, slips away, and exits into the lodge.*

ADA We've calmed her down enough to return to the table, gentlemen. But there'll be no more words of the sort that drove her away. This is my table still and I will have none of it.

WILLOUGHBY There'll be no more trouble at your table, my dear. Why, we've got berries and cream to come!

ADA Just what I would expect from a gentleman.

WILLOUGHBY A gentleman who needs to have a chat with you after those berries and cream.

ADA Yes, indeed.

NAN *enters, followed by* VERA *and* LILA. *They resume their seats and, for a moment, eat in silence.*

(taking control, changing the tone at the table) I was hoping we might hear Johnny strum on his guitar after dinner.

JOHNNY Hmm. I think of it as plucking, but strumming has a nice ring to it.

NAN Oh, will you, Johnny? We need light music on an evening such as this.

JOHNNY To soothe you, Mother, I'd do anything.

VERA *(interrupting)* Anything?

JOHNNY V! We've had enough! I'll get my guitar and "strum" while Ada gets dessert.

NAN Will you play something special?

JOHNNY Just for you, Mother.

JOHNNY hurries away and exits into the lodge. Once again there is silent eating, with tension still hanging over the table. NAN is particularly tense, eating in a mechanical, jerky way.

TOM enters from the lodge, bursting back onto the porch.

TOM May I, Mother?

WILLOUGHBY Let the boy join us, my dear. He's bagged his game and should be able to join us in song.

TOM sits at the table.

JOHNNY enters and goes around to his chair and pulls it back from the table. He lifts his leg onto the chair and strums the guitar, beginning to tune it.

LILA *(clapping her hands in joy)* Sing, Johnny!

NAN Give us "In the Good Old Summertime."

LILA Oh, glory be! I couldn't be happier.

JOHNNY begins to pick out the basic chords, and, as he starts to sing, is joined by the others. He plays "In the Good Old Summertime" by George Evans with lyrics by Ren Shields and wanders around the table like a minstrel, intent on charming the women.

JOHNNY *(singing)* "In the good old summertime…"

ALL *(except VERA, who continues to look glum)* "In the good old summertime."

JOHNNY "Strolling through the shady lanes
With your baby mine,
You hold her hand and she holds yours,
And that's a very good sign,
That she's your tootsie wootsie…"

ALL "In the good old summertime."

JOHNNY *(starting over)* "In the good old summertime…"

ALL "In the good old summertime."

JOHNNY "Strolling through the shady lanes
With your baby mine,

You hold her hand and she holds yours,
And that's a very good sign,
That she's your tootsie wootsie…"

ALL "In the good old summertime."

Guitar music plays during the following dance.

WILLOUGHBY rises, sets his cane aside, circles the table, and holds out his hand to NAN. Although surprised, she nods in question. He nods in answer and then leads her away from the table. They begin to dance.

JOHNNY, as if taking the cue from the older man, sets down his guitar, takes LILA by the hand, and begins to dance as well.

ADA goes to TOM, bows, and takes him to dance.

ROBERT and VERA look at each other and continue singing for a moment instead of joining the others. However, they too get up and begin to dance. The scene is joyous, light, and free.

ADA drops TOM's hand, finds WILLOUGHBY and NAN, and taps NAN on the shoulder. ADA takes up dancing with WILLOUGHBY, while NAN finds TOM and takes up with him.

LILA breaks away and, after picking up his guitar, JOHNNY follows her upstage right. The dancing continues as the lights fade to black.

SCENE TWO

Spotlight up downstage left.

JOHNNY and LILA reach the dock bench downstage left and sit. JOHNNY slips his guitar behind the bench and puts his arm around her shoulder. They look at the water flickering in the moonlight, mimicked by the warm yellow of the torch.

LILA I'm so happy you followed me down here. I was beginning to think that you didn't notice me.

JOHNNY I've been noticing you for years. How could a man not notice what a sweet thing you've become? I couldn't wait to get away from the table and come down to the water with you. And I'm happy you didn't run away.

LILA Run? How could you think that? I wanted you to follow me down here, away from Mother, away from the rest of them. Where we could be alone.

JOHNNY Well, you've got me here now.

LILA The talk at the table was so upsetting tonight. All this wretched talk of war.

JOHNNY The war won't take long, Li. I'm sure of that.

LILA But I get so confused about the way Vera speaks about it.

JOHNNY Don't worry yourself. This war won't take long. I'll be home by Christmas. We'll get the Hun running and he won't stop until he's back where he belongs in Berlin. V doesn't know a thing about war.

LILA leans into him and sets her head into the tuck of his neck.

LILA John? When it's… when it's over, will you come back here?

JOHNNY It would be one of the very first things I'd do.

LILA Would you… would you be coming to see me?

JOHNNY Of course, I'd be coming to see you. And Tommy and your mum and Robbie… and the boys in the village.

LILA Could we sit out here by the lake at night? Just you and me?

JOHNNY I could think of nothing I'd rather do more.

LILA I'm so happy to hear that. I worry about this war, though. I worry it will take you a long way from here. And I worry that you'll forget about…

JOHNNY *(overlapping)* You? There's no chance of that.

LILA Even if this war takes a long time?

JOHNNY I told you, Li, we'll be home by Christmas. That's what all the lads are saying. That's what the men at the lodge are saying. That's what Uncle is saying. I couldn't be surer of anything. And then I'll be back and we'll be together again.

LILA I just know you're telling me the truth. I just know.

JOHNNY That's one thing you can count on from me. The truth.

LILA There's another thing.

JOHNNY What's that?

LILA I know this may sound funny and all, but when I was in the village this morning, I saw the cutest young baby boy, the son of one of my classmates at school.

JOHNNY Yes?

LILA She was always the prettiest and the smartest and managed to find the most handsome man in the county… I mean of those men who live here all the year round… I mean that don't come to the resorts like you.

JOHNNY They sound like a handsome couple indeed.

LILA Oh, that they are. But I was wondering. Do you ever think about children?

JOHNNY *(standing)* Indeed, I do. I know that Mother longs for a grandchild. And, Lord knows, Vera isn't about to provide one soon.

LILA How can you say that?

JOHNNY I mean nothing nasty or mean-spirited. I love my V. But, being a man who knows what's in the minds and in the hearts of other men, it leads me to think that she's taken her education too far. She's become a type who can look to being a spinster. Not the marrying type at all.

LILA I don't know. She has a strong will, certainly, and talks in a way that's hard to understand, but there is still a softness sometimes.

JOHNNY *(interrupting)* One could certainly hope for that.

LILA But you, do you think of children?

JOHNNY I do, I do. But, with my age, with the war, with so many things unsettled, it's hard to say.

LILA But you think that maybe sometime, when the time is right.

JOHNNY *(interrupting)* That's the way to put it. Sometime, when the time is right, Mother will get her grandchild after all.

LILA I knew you were the type of man who would love children.

JOHNNY That's me to a tee, the type of man who loves children.

LILA What will you do when you return?

JOHNNY Do?

LILA What work will you take up?

JOHNNY Oh, Li, there's more studying to do. I'm reading economics at the university now, and there'll be more reading when I return.

LILA And then? After the reading?

JOHNNY *(becoming stuffy, patronizing)* Even more reading. Likely the law at Osgoode.

LILA Would you be a lawyer then?

JOHNNY I wouldn't think so.

LILA Then what? I don't understand.

JOHNNY *(sitting down, taking her hand)* Don't trouble yourself with all of this. You'll bring on a migraine like Mother.

LILA *(getting exasperated)* But, with wanting children and all, and getting married and all, how will you bring food to the table?

JOHNNY There's little to worry in that regard, Li. There'll be opportunities for a man of my cut.

LILA Cut?

JOHNNY For a man who's read economics and the law, there'll be railways to build and factories to put up and capital to raise in the markets. Opportunities will abound.

LILA I see. I mean, I think I see.

JOHNNY The real choice will be when to follow Uncle.

LILA Follow?

JOHNNY Into the House, into Cabinet.

LILA House? What house?

JOHNNY I'd like to enter politics after the war and get myself elected to parliament and become a minister of the Crown. I want to build Canada into a great country, Li. I want to see us with the best railroads, factories, and industry. I want to see us open the west and the north. Why, I believe Canada is the country of the twentieth century. And I hope to be one of the leaders of that country. But first I have to defend it. For us, for the king, for the future.

LILA *(beginning to beam)* Oh my, what a future! *(clapping her hands together in joy)* I love my mother, I do, but she has so little and there are so many things I want, so many places I want to see, such a grand life I've dreamed of. This would be a life like *your* mother's, *your* father's.

JOHNNY stands quickly, walks away, becoming pensive, sad.

What is it?

JOHNNY Nothing, nothing at all.

LILA What is it, John? You can confide in me.

JOHNNY It's nothing. I… I sometimes forget about father's… death. It was so sudden. He was so young. There was so much to decide. I… I relied on him like a boat at sea relies on the beam of a lighthouse.

LILA I'm sorry, John.

JOHNNY It's not for you to be sorry. It's just that I haven't been able to talk to Mother about this. I haven't been able to talk to Vera. I've tried to keep busy, to stay… strong. I've tried to be like him.

LILA *(interrupting)* I'm sorry for bringing up your… father, John.

JOHNNY I'm happy you call me John. Mother called father John. I feel stronger and braver and truer just hearing that name in the air.

LILA It will be John always.

JOHNNY For that, my dear, I'll grant you a wish.

LILA Any wish?

JOHNNY I swear by the light of the moon.

LILA Will you sing for me?

JOHNNY Sing?

LILA You sang for the others and now I wish a song just for me.

JOHNNY And what song would you wish?

LILA "By the Light of the Silvery Moon."

JOHNNY *(reaches for his guitar)* I'll strum, but you've got to sing.

LILA Oh, but I can't carry a tune.

JOHNNY Anyone with a voice as sweet as chocolate candy can certainly sing a simple song.

JOHNNY begins to strum out the chords.

LILA "By the light of the silvery moon…
I want to spoon.
To my honey I'll croon love's tune.
Honey moon, keep a shinin' in June.
Your silv'ry beams will bring love dreams.
We'll be cuddling soon, by the silvery moon."

JOHNNY sets down his guitar and takes her hand, lifting her from the bench. They stand face to face for a moment and then JOHNNY dares a kiss. She pulls back, startled. She looks up to the moon, smiles, and then quickly kisses him. He leans towards her again and they kiss lightly, gently. She becomes flustered with her boldness, hurries away, and exits stage right.

JOHNNY picks up the guitar and strums the chords of "By the Light of the Silvery Moon" again, and then picks up the tune, playing like a balladeer, happy and carefree, in love with the music, with the night, with LILA. He begins to serenade the audience with the song, like he had serenaded the table, picking out people in the audience for special smiles.

JOHNNY "By the light of the silvery moon…
I want to spoon.
To my honey I'll croon love's tune.
Honey moon, keep a shinin' in June.
Your silvery beams will bring love dreams.
We'll be cuddling soon, by the silvery moon.

By the light of the silvery moon…
I want to spoon.
To my honey I'll croon love's tune.
Honey moon, keep a shinin' in June.
Your silvery beams will bring love dreams.
We'll be cuddling soon, by the silvery moon."

Lights fade to black.

JOHNNY exits stage right.

SCENE THREE

Spotlight up downstage right.

LILA wears a nurse's dress, with a stiff white cap and white apron. She is carrying a small tray of medicine bottles.

LILA My God, there are so many of them with the flu on the ward, and so few of us in service.

They keep coming on wagons, and in carriages, and even on the rattling old Queen car. They come with their pale yellowing children clutching their hands. They come with their frail mothers and fathers. They come with their loved ones. They come alone.

The *Daily Star* says that the flu is taking more Canadians than the war. It's not hard to believe that. The war took the men, the young men, but the flu knows no difference between men and women, young and old. We see them all here at St. Michael's.

They come through the door, past the statue with the great white wings and fierce silver sword, and, most of the time, they leave through the back door, on the bed of one of the wagons that takes them up to the cemetery on Mount Pleasant or out to the potter's field north of the city.

My, my, it's sad.

I remember the horror the night I saw my own mother on the ward. She had come down to the city to do business about the resort, but was so upset by what that man Willoughby had done that she suddenly felt dizzy, and she got scared and she had to get to the hospital right away. We were able to send her back home after a short while, it was just a minor upset; but, oh dear, it was frightening to see her among all the strange faces on the ward.

But even that was nothing compared to the day Vera came to see me in the highlands, before I came to the city, before I took up my work here as an aide in the hospital.

She was wearing black that day. I knew the worst as soon as she stepped off the carriage from Rail's End.

John had become such a fine officer, such a wonderful leader of men, but there weren't many who came back after that horrible time at Ypres.

Missing. The word was so much harder to take than *dead.*

My John, my beloved John, was *missing.*

Vera was cool and reasonable, and I, of course, broke down and wept and wept and wept, and went to the bench by the lake and wept some more. After a while, she came down to me and said I should come to live with them in the city and she would help me find something to do to keep my mind from him.

She was helpful. She was kind. She was brave, too.

Nan was broken by the news from Ypres and never recovered. She could not live with that word—*missing*—for all those months.

Yes, she woke in the morning and ate at the table and mentioned the weather, but she never stepped outside again and she kept the house dark, day and night, until… until Vera had to take her away to the institution down on the Lakeshore, where she sat under a tree and stared at the flat, grey lake day after day.

Vera helped me find my way to St. Mike's, and with my skills, and with all these hundreds of people on the ward, they found me work as an aide. I dispense these pills, but I don't know if they do anything at all for these men and women, with their flat, sad faces.

I don't mind the smells anymore. I don't mind the yellowing of their eyes. I don't mind the sight of bone through pale skin. But there is something that I do mind. *(beginning to rock her body)* And there's no thanking God or any living soul. What I do mind is the thought of maybe never seeing my sweet John again, never hearing his beautiful voice, never hearing the strumming of his guitar. *(crying now)* I do mind that, I do; and I will mind that for a long, long time.

Blackout.

SCENE FOUR

Spotlight up downstage left.

ROBERT and VERA are on the dock. He holds the spyglass, surveying the sky. VERA is by his side, hands on her hips. As he scans the sky with the glass, she moves with him.

ROBERT The heavens are a wonder tonight. Ah, there's Jupiter, as big and bold as can be.

VERA I wish you'd let me have a turn with the glass.

ROBERT Certainly. I'm sorry.

ROBERT drops the glass to his side, then hands it to her and positions himself behind her, guiding the glass through her. There is a moment of intimate closeness, with VERA dropping her eye from the glass, noticing his hand on her elbow.

There. Right there. He should be in the centre of the glass now.

VERA He?

ROBERT Jupiter.

VERA Jupiter is a "he"?

ROBERT Why, yes, Vera. And Venus is a "she." While Mars is another "he."

VERA Boys and girls in the sky?

ROBERT I never thought of it that way. I just picked it up from the books left behind at the lodge.

VERA And I bet those books said that boy stars did one thing and girl stars did another.

ROBERT Likely, yes.

VERA *(dropping the glass to her side, but staying in his grasp)* Well, this girl is an exception to all of those rules.

ROBERT I suspected that.

VERA And this girl is beginning to wonder why a boy like you would hide away in a divinity school.

ROBERT Hide away?

VERA Yes, away. At least, away from the wiles of women.

ROBERT I never much thought about that, to tell you the truth. I was too busy thinking about other things.

VERA Well, I'd watch out, if I were you.

ROBERT Watch out?

VERA For the wiles of a woman.

ROBERT *(realizing that he's holding her, drops her elbows)* And what are those wiles?

VERA Have you seen the way Lila looks at Johnny, with her eyes slightly down?

ROBERT Yes.

VERA Wiles.

ROBERT No.

VERA *Yes.* Have you see the way she managed to slightly touch his hand when she served his food?

ROBERT Yes.

VERA Wiles again.

ROBERT It can't be.

VERA *It can be.* And have you seen the way she curls her hair around her ear while she's listening?

ROBERT Why, yes I have; especially when your brother is talking.

VERA Wiles. All of them, wiles of a woman.

ROBERT Perhaps I should pay more attention to these so-called wiles.

VERA There's no "perhaps" about it. *(beat)* I've got my own particular set, too.

ROBERT No.

VERA That's what your sister tells me.

ROBERT It would be hard to believe that, from a sort such as you.

VERA A sort such as me uses words for wiles, sir.

LILA holds the glass up again, but this time swings around and begins to search across the lake. She moves for a moment, then stops.

There.

ROBERT What? What is it?

VERA Look.

VERA gives the glass to him, then repositions herself behind him, guiding the glass through him, as he had done with her just before.

ROBERT I see the island, Vera; with the splash of planets and stars on the horizon framing her soft, round shape.

VERA My, my. I've never heard the island described so well. You handle words just like a poet.

ROBERT I'm glad it's dark down here on the deck.

VERA Why?

ROBERT So you can't see the crimson rushing to my cheeks.

VERA *(looking up at his face)* We need no more light than the stars to see *that*, Robert. But I'm wondering what it means.

ROBERT It means I'm embarrassed by the compliment.

VERA It may mean more than that.

ROBERT What are you talking about?

VERA I'm talking about you. I'm talking about me. I wonder if that's the reason for the crimson on your face.

ROBERT *(dropping the glass)* Goodness.

VERA "Goodness." I thought you might say something like that. Do you know how refreshing you are as a manly sort?

ROBERT Manly sort?

VERA Most men are formal and rigid like my brother. They'd rather be marching with other men than spending time with a woman. I honestly was despairing of meeting such a man as you've come to be. Honestly.

ROBERT I simply don't know what to say.

VERA I don't mind that. I don't mind my men being speechless. In fact, I rather like it.

There is momentary silence as ROBERT *raises the glass to the sky again.*

What do you see now?

ROBERT You'll find this amusing.

VERA Amusing?

ROBERT It's time for Venus to rise on the horizon. And, sure enough, she's rising right now, just above the giant white pine on the far side of the lake.

VERA Oh, please, may I see?

ROBERT *drops the glass and gives it to her and, like before, slips behind her to guide her into place. He has his hands on her elbows, and she leans back slightly, brushing against him.*

ROBERT Have you got her? She's brilliant and bursting with brightness, even to the naked eye.

VERA Oh, I see her, I do. She's wonderful. So clear and strong in the sky.

ROBERT *(quickly, in a whisper)* Like you.

VERA What did you say?

ROBERT Nothing. I said nothing.

VERA I thought I heard something. Could it be just the rippling of the water?

ROBERT Yes. It was only the rippling of the water.

VERA *(moves the glass slightly, brushing into him again)* And what do I see now?

ROBERT I'll need the glass to tell you.

VERA drops the glass to her side now. He takes it and she moves in behind him, holding his elbows, gently pressing into his back.

VERA There. Do you see it? It's red and angry, following behind the lovely Venus.

ROBERT I can't see it. *(adjusting)* Oh, yes, there, *(focusing)* there it is, *(offering the glass)* the red planet. Mars looks especially angry tonight.

VERA I wonder if they can see that angry planet across the ocean: the British and French *(pointing left)*, the Germans *(pointing right)*. I wonder.

ROBERT They can, if only at a different angle. Mars is in Scorpio just now.

VERA What does that mean, Mars in Scorpio?

ROBERT lowers the glass. VERA holds her hands on his elbows for a moment then drops them to her side. He moves slightly left and stops near the lantern. She follows him.

ROBERT The man who's showing me how to teach the navvies to read and write told me about it this summer. He found out in a letter from his cousin up in Algonquin. He said that she knows the meaning of the stars. She learned it from her father's people. It's one of the family secrets.

VERA Secrets?

ROBERT Her father was very dark, and very handsome. Her mother was fair and fell in love with him and ran away with him to the Ottawa Valley.

VERA That happens all the time. That's not much of a secret.

ROBERT The secret is coming. Her father was not just handsome and dark, he was Metis. The townspeople cut her mother off when they found out. She sunk into a deep depression and finally killed herself. That's the secret. And then, his cousin went to live with her father's people and learned about the stars from them.

VERA Oh my.

ROBERT How did we get to this? Where did this start?

VERA With that red, angry planet in the sky.

ROBERT Mars in Scorpio.

VERA What does it mean?

ROBERT She said it signals cruelty, revenge, and jealousy.

VERA Oh my.

ROBERT I know it seems bizarre and certainly not very logical, but that's what we're feeling right now, isn't it? The men seem blind to thought, to anything but this kind of dark, red rage.

VERA They do seem blind.

ROBERT They say that a man must go or else face the harsh righteousness of the night.

VERA Oh, please don't talk like that. I just know this war can be stopped. No one really wants it. The banks don't want it, the industrialists don't want it, the politicians don't want it.

ROBERT Yet, we're flying towards it like Icarus towards the sun.

VERA What will you do?

ROBERT Me?

VERA Will you join a regiment?

ROBERT Certainly not.

VERA What then?

ROBERT Can you keep a secret?

VERA Of course I can.

ROBERT My friend's cousin has a cabin way up in the woods. He wants me to come with them to the cabin and stay there. When the time comes, we'd go into the logging camps where his father once worked. We'd organize the men. Try to stop the war that way. This seemed like madness to me at first, but now it seems to make the finest sense. The struggle for peace and the struggle for justice may just come together in those logging camps.

VERA Will you go?

ROBERT I believe I will. The men may be eager for war now. But, at some point, they may simply stop wishing to go.

VERA I believe this war will be a war stopped by labour, too. They can see the truth through the propaganda.

ROBERT And the truth just glares at you.

VERA *(finishing his sentence)* Like those stars.

ROBERT Yes, like those stars.

There is silence for a moment. They are perfectly still, looking closely at each other. They stay close, looking out towards the water.

VERA Oh, how I wish for peace.

ROBERT As do I.

VERA With peace there would be time, and, with time, there would be more moments like this, moments to cherish and share.

NAN *(calling out)* Vera, dear! Washing-up time.

VERA quickly kisses ROBERT on the cheek and then hurries up to the lodge, leaving him alone on the dock. He touches his cheek with wonder, then looks up at the sky.

ROBERT I wonder what star brought that on.

He pulls a book from his back pocket and consults it, then moves the telescope across the night sky again.

Mercury? No, not Mercury.

ROBERT consults the book again and shifts direction with the telescope.

Saturn? My, I can even see the rings tonight. But not Saturn either.

ROBERT slips the book into his back pocket again. He turns the telescope to the moon.

And the moon is pocked and freckled and sad. No, not such a sad moon.

ROBERT swings the telescope around.

Yes, that's it. Venus, in all her glory.

ROBERT moves the telescope a bit higher.

I just hope that nasty old Mars gives us time for Venus to work her magic.

ROBERT picks up the lantern and exits left.

Blackout.

SCENE FIVE

Spotlight up down centre.

VERA wears a long coat and hat. She is holding a sign: "KEEP OUT OF WAR." She holds the sign above her head and walks back and forth three times, as in a demonstration. She comes to centre stage and stops, letting the sign rest on her shoulder, much as a soldier would rest his rifle.

VERA We thought we were making a new world in those first few months of 1915, those of us who travelled to Europe to try to stop the war.

The press wrote about us as if we were madwomen, but, believe me, in those early months of the war, the men in unions in England and France, and even in Germany, were anxious to meet with us and listen and try to stop this war.

We even met with politicians.

We explained our hope for peace as one would explain something to a troubled child, and those serious men, with their paunches girdled by their stiff black suits, listened like children, asked the right, smart questions, and wished us well.

VERA steps forward, lifts the sign, and shakes it, as one does in a demonstration, then slings it on her shoulder again.

There was a time when we believed we could stop it all, but that time went away by the spring of '15, sad to say. Then the meetings with the men who could stop the war ground to a halt as hatred grew across the divides.

We packed our trunks and sailed for home. We left the slaughter behind. And it was a slaughter. It took so many millions, lost on the battlefields of Belgium and France, of Russia and Austria. And it wasn't all from rifles and cannons and bombardments.

No, much of it was from stupidity.

The Russians were the worst. The czar sent his men without boots, without proper clothing, without horses, without wagons, without guns, without food.

They sent them into a killing field that stretched for thousands of miles. They believed those men were little better than mules, and now they've paid with their own lives, with a revolution that has swept generations of injustice into the dustbin.

VERA steps to the left, shakes the sign, then slings it over her shoulder.

When we came home, we went to work in the factories to try to keep the women who filled those factories with a naive excitement, safe and sound and healthy.

Oh, yes, we waged a struggle against conscription, against further expansion of the war, against the seeming madness of military decisions, but, to be blunt and honest, no one was listening.

My mother was not alone on that lovely last weekend in August with Johnny. Every single mother of a son in uniform, in the highlands and in the city, in the East and in the West, all of them, taunted those of us who were trying to stop the war.

Those women wore their white ribbons and talked at recruitment rallies and gathered their savings to buy bonds and let their sons and husbands have their war, month after terrible month.

VERA steps to the right, swings the sign around to reveal another slogan: JUSTICE FOR ALL, EVEN THE GERMANS.

And now the heads of state have come to Versailles to make the peace. And the papers report that there will be no peace made in that palace in France. No peace at Versailles. Instead, the victors wish to punish the vanquished.

They long for reparations, which will punish Germany for a generation and, believe me, out of that punishment something nasty will rise.

They say that the real enemy in the world now is revolution, such as the one sparked in Russia. Germany is crawling with revolutionists they say. I say that those men who were at the front, like our men at the front, will come to their homes and find themselves impoverished by their enemy, and, instead of seeing justice, will seek revenge, with ugly militarism again, setting off another soaring flare of violence and, sooner than anyone will be able to believe, we'll find ourselves at war again.

They say I'm a fool for being in the cold with this sign, but this is what the world needs right now, fools like me who yearn for mercy when the crowd cries for retribution. They've burned much out of me, these men of war, but they haven't burned out hope. We women never found our peace, but maybe, just maybe, we'll find justice for our Johnny.

Blackout.

SCENE SIX

Spotlight up stage right. An oil lamp sits on a table.

NAN sits in a rocking chair. TOM sits on a stool at her feet. They're winding a ball of wool through the first part of the scene and then, after they finish, TOM watches her begin to knit.

NAN You're back in school soon?

TOM No, ma'am. I mean, yes, ma'am. I mean, school starts up again in a week.

NAN You're nearly finished with the early grades, aren't you?

TOM I sure am. I'd be going into grade eight this year, with my mates from around the county.

NAN Do you have plans?

TOM Plans?

NAN What do you hope to do with yourself?

TOM I'm not quite sure yet, ma'am. I want some time to think about these things. Some time away, maybe. Yes, that's it. I want some time away.

NAN Where would you go?

TOM Go? Why… why I'd go… I'd go on down to the city.

NAN A good choice. The minister might find something for you to do. He has his fingers in so many pies in the city. I'm sure he could find something for a boy like you.

TOM *(as if appreciating the hidden meaning of this)* I'm sure he will. I'm right sure of that. He'll take care of all us boys, he will.

NAN He has a fond spot in his heart for all the boys in the highlands. When my dear husband was alive, the minister sought his opinion on what to do with the boys. With their education. With their prospects. Yes, he has a fond spot for the boys of the highlands.

TOM And for all the boys across the whole Dominion, ma'am. Why, he's got boys in militias in every tiny town, all the way from sea to sea. We got ours here in the highlands, and there's one down in King, and one even in Chester, and then there's a bigger one down in the city.

NAN My husband used to say that militia training in the summer made men of boys.

TOM That it does, ma'am.

NAN He said that boys learned everything in the militia camps—hygiene, exercise, precision in following instructions, the discipline of marching.

TOM There's loads of marching in the camps, ma'am. Just loads.

NAN I've often thought that marching teaches the same skills as the mastering of a musical instrument.

TOM That could be, ma'am. But we didn't have a lot of musical instruments in the camps. We had guns, though. And good ones. The minister paid special attention to getting the best guns for the boys. They're the best for hitting targets, but they're not as good for game or—

NAN *(interrupting)* My husband never cared much for the guns. Or the shooting.

TOM The boys like the guns and the shooting, ma'am. All my mates like guns. But they can't shoot like me. The minister made sure of that.

NAN Yes, indeed. The minister has always been fond of guns and targets and young boys.

TOM He'll have a whole army of them soon, ma'am.

NAN *(in a correcting tone)* No, Tommy, he won't. Sad to say, summer's almost gone. There'll be no more militia camps till next summer. No more shooting. No more marching.

TOM *(appreciating the irony of what he's about to say)* I don't know. There just may be, ma'am. There just may be marching, and shooting, and hitting the old bull's eye. Johnny thinks so, too.

NAN suddenly stops knitting and rocking.

NAN I beg pardon?

TOM I said that Johnny thinks there'll be marching and shooting. And uniforms. *(suddenly remembering the scene at the table)* What is it you're knitting, ma'am? A sweater?

NAN *(relaxing, beginning to rock again)* No, Tommy. I was asked by my club to begin to knit woollen stockings for the boys.

TOM The boys going over, eh? *(remembering again, quickly recovering)* Isn't it a fine August we've had this year, better than I can ever remember.

NAN *(distracted again, looking out on the lake)* Oh, Tommy. I've seen so many Augusts in my life, and this, the first without my dear husband. And yes, of all of them, this has been the finest and most pleasant. It's the kind of summer a poet would wish to record for posterity.

TOM *(looking out at the lake, too)* I don't know much about poetry, ma'am, but I do know that it's been such a summer for songs. Lila's been buying sheet music with her wages and mother treated us to the Victrola and a set of recordings.

NAN It is lovely to hear music coming from the lodge, filling the air with sweet sounds.

A shot rings out, followed by a second.

NAN is startled.

TOM It's okay, ma'am. A few of the men are on the ridge tonight with their rifles.

NAN It startled me.

TOM They're trying to take deer, ma'am. There are no jobs anymore. Times are tough. The men are out most nights trying to take game. As they say in the village, every little bit helps.

ADA *(offstage, distant)* Nan, dear, we're ready.

NAN sets her knitting in her lap.

NAN *(rising from the chair)* Well, my boy, now I've got to help Lila and Vera in the kitchen, while the men have their cigars.

TOM I'll be with the men tonight. According to Johnny, that is. Will you let Mother know?

NAN That should be a treat for you, Tom. Go along with the men.

TOM I will, ma'am. Oh, yes, I will.

NAN exits into the lodge. TOM picks up the knitting. He sits down in the rocking chair and measures the sock against his own foot and sees that it would fit perfectly. He pulls a corn pipe from his back pocket and a small sack of tobacco from his breast pocket and packs his pipe. He lights it and listens to the music for a moment. He begins to tap his feet. He stands up, sets the pipe in an ashtray on the table, and picks up a broom by the door.

TOM begins play-acting soldier, starting with marching, with the broom stick over his shoulder, then moving to various positions for "shooting"—standing, kneeling, and lying on the ground, working his way back and forth on stage. He aims the broom at the audience and makes the sound of a shot each time. He returns to marching then, picking up the rhythm of the music. As he begins to march, LILA comes to the porch to collect more dishes. She sees him and stops to watch, a smile spreading across her face.

LILA Aren't you the one.

TOM stops playing immediately, obviously embarrassed.

TOM And what's that supposed to mean?

LILA Aren't you a little old for playing toy soldier?

TOM I wasn't playing anything.

LILA *(laughing)* You were.

TOM I wasn't.

LILA You were.

TOM Was not.

LILA Tommy, I saw you with my own eyes. You were playing like the little boys down in the village.

TOM Practising is not playing.

LILA Practising for what?

TOM You'll see, smarty pants. Just you wait.

LILA I wouldn't bet on it, little boy.

TOM Well, I would, old lady.

Two shots ring out.

LILA *(startled)* My God, that scared me!

TOM smiles, raises the broomstick, and aims it at her.

Two more shots ring out.

Blackout.

ACT TWO

SCENE ONE

Lights illuminate centre stage.

ADA enters from the lodge, wiping her hands with a dishtowel, and looks at "her" place at the foot of the table, then at the head of the table. She nods, then moves to the head of the table. NAN enters from the lodge, sees ADA, and takes her place to her right.

ADA How are you? I shouldn't have called you into that hot summer kitchen.

NAN I'm fine now, my headache gone… When the tone of my children's bickering becomes shrill, my head starts to pound. I should be sharper with them.

ADA The bickering is everywhere now. I don't remember this when the men went off to South Africa to fight Willoughby's Boers.

NAN I was busy with two small children then, but there was little mention of that war at all. But now… it's unnerving. Especially with… my John gone.

ADA His passing was such a shock… When I lost my Harry, the children were too young to really know him. But, for you… for your children…

NAN John always knew what to say to them. He didn't mind that Vera worked with those women for peace while Johnny marched the summer away in the militia camp. But now that he's gone, I don't know how to manage their differences. I simply want to love each of them for who they are, not what they believe.

ADA And you do. That's your great strength. Always hold on to that.

NAN I'll try, dear. I'm so thankful for this weekend. Even with all the turmoil of Mr. Willoughby.

ADA I felt fear when I first found out. And a kind of betrayal. The minister is so loved by so many people. How could he do that to his own brother? To his brother's family? And to me?

NAN He's a Janus; one face for the parlour and another for the study. He knew how to tie a string around John's logical self and pull that string until there was nothing but a babble of support for his "elder brother's" plan.

ADA It must have been a terrible blow for you. To find out… after he was gone.

NAN It was. But, like all such blows, one lets time take its healing role.

ADA And experience.

NAN We've had our share of that, haven't we, dear? And now, this Willoughby.

ADA We'll come to a meeting of the minds. I've promised to give him some time tonight. We'll see where that goes. *(looking towards the door)* I hear the girls coming. We'd do well to brighten up.

LILA and VERA enter and join them, sitting on opposite sides of the table.

LILA I'm glad that work's done.

ADA As am I. Many hands make for quick work.

NAN I couldn't have put it better myself.

ADA *(leans back in her chair)* I've always wanted to sit at the head of the table at a dinner such as tonight. But—

NAN *(interrupting)* It's not meant to be.

VERA Why?

NAN Vera, dear, please don't start up again. We heard quite enough around the washing-up basin.

VERA But it's silly, Mother. Ada is the head of her household. Why can't she sit at the head of the table?

NAN Because the head is reserved for a man—

VERA *(interrupting)* And the heart for a woman?

NAN There, Vera, you seem to be getting it now.

VERA The only thing I'm "getting" is exasperated, Mother. I hate the way roles are determined by gender. I'm a suffragist. We're going to change all that.

LILA And wear pants?

VERA Yes, Lila, "and wear pants."

ADA But where does this take us?

VERA Into the modern era. It's 1914, after all. And the future—

ADA *(interrupting)* The future seems to be rushing at us this weekend. And it's not a future that looks friendly for women, or for men.

NAN Here, here! Ada is right. The men will have to defend us from the—

VERA *(interrupting)* Hun?

NAN From the—

VERA *(interrupting)* Go ahead, Mother, say it. The men need to defend us from the Hun. You *did* hear what that man was saying at the dinner table.

NAN I always try to listen when a man of standing speaks. But, with your constant interruptions—

VERA *(interrupting)* And challenges…

NAN *(interrupting)* There you go, Vera. You're doing it again. You're interrupting me, as you interrupted Ada, as you interrupted Mr. Willoughby. Do suffragists have no manners?

VERA Mother, men have been doing it for thousands of years. It's only when a woman dares do it that it somehow becomes wrong.

NAN Vera, I don't know what I'm going to do with you. Your head is filled with icy words and your heart is filled with angry flames. Why can't you be a normal young woman who says normal things in a normal tone of voice? Just why?

VERA Mother, I was never normal. I have Father to thank for that. And this is not a "normal" time. We have to decide what we're going to do about this war. I'm sorry for my urgency, but I'm not sorry for my arguments.

ADA Arguments will divide us, dear.

VERA There comes a time when we need to be divided, I'm afraid.

ADA The good on the one side, the bad on the other?

VERA Please, Mrs. Ross, you know enough not to mock me.

ADA I'm not mocking you, dear. I'm simply trying to understand.

VERA Let me try another way. Willoughby says that we must go to war to "defend our values." Do you honestly believe that Johnny will go to war for that?

NAN Of course he will, Vera.

VERA Johnny will go to war because he feels fine and grand in his uniform. But we know that, under the uniform, he is just a boy.

LILA *(emotionally)* A boy he is not.

VERA Oh, Li, romance is blinding you, but Johnny is not yet a man.

LILA I know otherwise—

ADA *(shooting a quick glance at her daughter, interrupting)* How otherwise?

LILA *(regaining control)* He has plans… to read… to study the law… to build a house.

ADA You've been having a chat?

LILA Yes, Mother. We were down by the water after supper and we were *(sounding like her mother)* "having a chat."

ADA I see. And what else were you "chatting" about?

LILA About the future, about Canada, about railroads and factories, about babies, about—

ADA *(interrupting)* Babies? What about babies?

LILA I told John I saw Clara Connelly in the village with her new baby.

ADA And?

LILA I wondered if John wanted—

ADA *(interrupting again)* What?

LILA Whether he wanted a…

ADA Baby?

LILA Oh, Mother, must you. We were "chatting" and John was explaining about many things, about the war, and all.

VERA What did he say about the war?

LILA He said it wouldn't last long. He said he would… come back and see me… and Mother and the boys in the village.

NAN I just know that Johnny will make a fine officer. I just know it.

VERA Mother, please listen. Johnny will be an officer. And safe because of that. I'm worried about Tommy.

ADA *(snapping to attention)* What about Tommy?

VERA You heard what Willoughby said at the table.

NAN He said many things.

VERA And the most important was that the king would be calling on boys from across the Dominion—

LILA *(startled, interrupting)* I just saw him.

VERA Who?

LILA Tommy. Why, he was playing at soldier out on the porch. Marching up and down with a broom over his shoulder like a rifle.

ADA Tommy is a boy, dear. And boys play.

VERA We're getting to the point now. Tommy *is* a boy and boys should not be left in the clutches of men like Willoughby.

ADA I wouldn't be too harsh about Mr. Willoughby, dear.

VERA You find him agreeable?

NAN Vera, have you lost your mind? Have you no manners at all? No sense of decorum?

VERA I'm only asking. I can see as well as you can see.

NAN Vera!

ADA Leave the girl, Nan. I can answer her question. Yes, I find him agreeable. I find men of his sort who come to this resort most agreeable.

VERA *(laughing)* I'm happy to hear it's not his smile or his intellect or his manners.

ADA *(laughing with her now)* You'll understand some day, my sweet, that there's more to life than a smile, intellect, or manners.

NAN Touché!

VERA Mother!

NAN Well, dear, you may have been asking for that. We have eyes, too.

VERA I fail to see what you're talking about.

NAN We're talking, Vera, about you *(smiling at ADA)* and Robbie. We saw your eyes widen and brighten when he arrived. And my, hasn't he become a handsome man—

VERA *(interrupting)* Talk all you wish, ladies. That doesn't make it anything other than hot air.

ADA My, my. I think we touched a nerve here, Nan. And I wonder if we can find a nerve to touch with my Lila? I heard singing down by the water before washing up. Were you singing to yourself, my dear?

LILA I… I—

ADA *(interrupting)* I also heard someone strumming by the water. Would that be a hidden talent, my dear? Or the work of someone we all know? Well?

LILA I… I…

LILA becomes exasperated and rushes from the table to the building. ADA and NAN begin to laugh, and, with their infectious playfulness rising, VERA joins in.

ADA How I long for a cigar!

NAN What was that, dear?

ADA Oh, nothing. Just the fantasy of an older woman.

Blackout.

SCENE TWO

Lights shine on a dock, downstage left.

ROBERT aims his spyglass low, looking across the lake. TOM is kneeling by his side, watching him. JOHNNY is behind them, holding an unlit cigar. WILLOUGHBY is away from the rest, sitting in a Muskoka chair, the only one smoking a cigar.

TOM What's out there, Rob?

ROBERT It's just the island.

JOHNNY Vera told me a tale about that island today.

ROBERT She did?

JOHNNY She said that Indians held peace talks out there.

TOM Did they, Robbie?

ROBERT That's what Grandfather always said. He heard it from travelling tinkers when he was scratching out the homestead up on the ridge.

JOHNNY It sounds a mite fanciful to me. I suspect they fought on that island, not talked.

ROBERT Grandfather said the island was a sacred place for them. They held their circles out there, too.

TOM Circles?

ROBERT When a member of a band was caught in a crime like stealing, the elders called a circle.

TOM Was it like the court in town?

ROBERT Nothing could be more different. There was no judge in a powdered wig, no lawyers with their briefs and their bafflement, no jury to decide about something they didn't know first-hand.

TOM How did it work, then?

ROBERT They made a circle. The elders, in the east and west, the offender in the south, the victim in the north.

TOM What happened?

ROBERT The elders helped the offender admit to the crime and show a sense of shame and remorse. They helped the victim to agree to a way to restore his dignity and integrity. When they reached that moment, they passed a pipe to seal the agreement, and then everyone in the band saw that the terms were met.

JOHNNY That certainly sounds like a fairy tale.

ROBERT Grandfather wasn't one to tell tales.

WILLOUGHBY Well, they're not like the Indians I know from the men I sent west to find routes for my rails. They said they drank themselves senseless and stole anything for more whiskey. No justice in that circle, my friend.

ROBERT This happened before we took away their land and fenced them in. And, you know what? The circle might be the way to settle the disputes that are leading us to war.

JOHNNY It sounds Marxian to me, Robbie. But now, it's time to find out where you stand on the war.

ROBERT I stand for social justice, against the greed of militarists.

WILLOUGHBY Well, sir, I wonder where you'll stand when the king calls upon us to defend the empire. The call will come when the Hun runs through Belgium and touches the sacred soil of France.

ROBERT *(laughing)* Did I hear the words, "sacred" and "France," in the same sentence? From an Orangeman such as you?

WILLOUGHBY I'm losing patience with your mental gymnastics, sir. I don't think you understand the gravity of the moment and the importance of making the right decision. We'll have no patience with slackers, sir. I assure you of that.

ROBERT Slackers?

JOHNNY I've been up to the Orange Lodge, Robbie. The men told me they won't tolerate slackers. We all have to answer the call, and those who don't will be searched out, found, and treated with the harsh righteousness of the night.

ROBERT I'm beginning to get the whole picture now. We have to blindly follow the king and kill those he says have no respect for human life. If we object, we face the righteousness of the night. And we call this freedom and liberty, honour and justice. Correct?

TOM leaves ROBERT and edges towards WILLOUGHBY.

JOHNNY You're twisting things like my sister, Robert; but let me remind you that there are far more of us than those on your side.

ROBERT Another one of your principles? The strong crush the weak?

WILLOUGHBY Jabber all you wish, sir, for at the end of the day we will prevail. Right, Tommy, my boy?

TOM *(nearing WILLOUGHBY)* I couldn't put it better myself, sir. Prevail. That's the word, sir. Pre- *(pausing for emphasis)* vail!

ROBERT You don't know what you're saying, Tom.

TOM Oh, yes, I do.

ROBERT You're just a boy.

TOM I may have been a boy when you left to work on the rails, but I'm not a boy now.

ROBERT Tommy, stop being so foolish.

JOHNNY Robbie, that's where you're wrong. He's not the fool. You're the one with that cap now.

ROBERT Look, Johnny. We're old enough to decide for ourselves. But Tommy, he's just a boy.

TOM I'm not just a boy, Rob. I looked after Mum. I did the chores. I brought rabbit to her table. And I'm ready.

ROBERT Nonsense. I'll speak to Mother.

TOM It's too late for talking, Rob. Far too late now.

ADA *(offstage)* Tommy!

ROBERT There's Mother now. Go to her.

WILLOUGHBY And make it snappy, son. I've got business with your mother in just a little while.

TOM exits stage right. WILLOUGHBY bends down and douses his cigar in a can of water, sending a hiss into the silence. He takes a silver flask from his coat, draws deeply on it, and then holds it up like a chalice.

A nip for my health. Boys, do you wish to indulge?

JOHNNY takes the offered flask and has a shallow drink, making a face as he does so.

ROBERT I'm curious about what brings you here, sir? Besides your "health," that is. Certainly not my company.

WILLOUGHBY Plans, young man.

ROBERT What sort of plans? Beyond promoting war, that is.

WILLOUGHBY Aren't you a clever one, my boy. I bet you were a smart one in school. I bet you were a devoted one in church. I—

ROBERT *(interrupting)* Bet you have some capitalist scheme up your sleeve.

WILLOUGHBY There are enough "capitalist schemes"—as you so ably put it—to keep me busy in the city.

ROBERT Then what draws you north?

JOHNNY I suspect it's mining or logging.

WILLOUGHBY No, Johnny. I'm not interested in the dwindling resources of these rock-filled hills. I've got something else in mind.

ROBERT And that something has to do with my mother?

WILLOUGHBY Perhaps. But it has more to do with my dreams. You have dreams, don't you, boys? Johnny?

JOHNNY My dreams are of a great country. A country that will one day lead the world. We have the natural riches, a strong people, a vast land. I dream of a great and prosperous future for Canada.

WILLOUGHBY And you, Robert? One can guess.

ROBERT If you guessed a world with justice, a world with fairness, a world that cared for the poor and the sick, a world that took care of workers, you would have guessed my dream.

WILLOUGHBY My, my. A dream worthy of Karl Marx.

ROBERT Or Jesus of Nazareth.

WILLOUGHBY Or Lenin of Zurich. But enough of *your* dreams. This one is mine. I've spent a lot of time in Europe raising capital. A good deal of that time in hunting lodges in the old forests of Austria.

JOHNNY Father was there as a young man. He skied the Alps at Schurns.

WILLOUGHBY I know the place. But the place I had in mind was in the foothills of the Alps. The place became my dream. I dreamed of building a lodge in these highlands where a man could hunt bison and wild boar.

ROBERT This dream should take you back there then. There is no such game in Canada. The bison all but gone. The boar never arrived.

WILLOUGHBY My dreams have my will to make them come true. And where there's a strong will, there's a straight way.

ROBERT Does this way of yours involve an ark, with two bison, two boar, two—

JOHNNY *(interrupting)* It's possible, Robbie. I've read of men who bring such animals to America.

ROBERT This is not America.

WILLOUGHBY Boats dock at Montreal, young man. Why it's but a short trip by boxcar to Rail's End from our docks on the St. Lawrence. I could have animals here in no time.

JOHNNY Such a dream!

ROBERT The capitalist's animal kingdom, shooting boar for sport.

JOHNNY laughs spontaneously. WILLOUGHBY joins in.

WILLOUGHBY I've got one better than that, young man.

ROBERT The bar is high, sir.

WILLOUGHBY How's this, then. The socialist's animal kingdom, shooting workers in war.

ROBERT Clever, sir, but without humour.

WILLOUGHBY Young man, humour always depends on perspective.

ROBERT And sir, justice depends on truth.

Blackout.

SCENE THREE

Lights up centre stage.

WILLOUGHBY sits in ADA's chair at the foot of the table, holding a brandy snifter in his hand. There is a brandy bottle on the table. ADA is standing by his side, interestingly close. WILLOUGHBY drinks steadily through the scene, emptying the snifter and quickly filling it again. The drinking wears on his diction and acts on his libido.

WILLOUGHBY You're an interesting woman, Mrs. Ross.

ADA Is that the brandy talking?

WILLOUGHBY There may be brandy in my glass, but there's no brandy in my words. They come from deep down in this lonely heart of mine.

ADA *(moving away, crossing her arms)* There's no comfort from that wife of yours in Toronto? With her furs and jewels and soft leather shoes?

WILLOUGHBY *(surprised)* You've seen her?

ADA I have. I don't miss a thing on my business trips to the city. I saw her once at the Payne's home, gabbing like a monkey and ordering the help around like a queen. A real crank.

WILLOUGHBY Crank. *(savouring the word like brandy)* The word rings true. I'm pleased that you are no such thing, Mrs. Ross.

ADA In this business, sir, being a crank gets you nowhere. I've learned to please my guests.

WILLOUGHBY It's certainly pleasure you provide. The lovely meal. The wine. The smooth brandy. I can be proud to be the owner of a resort such as this.

ADA *(holding her arms more tightly, backing away)* I must say that we were all shocked to find of your ownership.

WILLOUGHBY Things were not as they appeared.

ADA John Payne was a generous and kind owner. Nan was always so kind and thoughtful. They treated me as family. They were good years for the business, good years for me, good years for my family. Losing my Harry to the hunting accident when my children were so young was a terrible blow. The Payne's made it easier, smoother.

WILLOUGHBY *(sipping brandy eagerly)* I'm glad of that. *(pausing, becoming more businesslike)* I've had to make many financial arrangements to get these railways built and, many times, deeds and notes were the fuel to fire that frantic building.

ADA So we were fuel for that fire?

WILLOUGHBY *(laughing, likely from the brandy)* That country wit again. Yes, you might put it that way. The minister and his brother had the kind of relationship that let the deed pass from hand to hand. And there was the matter of my note, solved by his deed.

ADA Notes and deeds and fuel and fire.

WILLOUGHBY You're a hot sketch, my dear.

ADA A sketch maybe, but certainly not hot. *(smoothing her apron, as if to go)* Now I must—

WILLOUGHBY *(interrupting)* Discus these matters further. We've only just begun.

ADA *(becoming more playful)* So far, sir, we've talked about your heart and your wife, your deeds and your notes, along with my hot… sketch.

WILLOUGHBY You do have a way with words, my dear.

ADA They say I have a way with other things, as well. After a time, that is.

WILLOUGHBY A time? I wonder how much time that would be.

ADA *(still playful, coquettish)* That would be more time, sir, than a night with a snifter of brandy.

WILLOUGHBY Indeed, I may be spending considerable time here. The minister knows the game of war, but not the game of capital. He needed the cash; I took a note on the property. He needed more cash, and, by writing another note on property he no longer actually owned, deceived his poor brother. Need drives it all.

ADA The old devil, need.

WILLOUGHBY I had no choice but to exercise the right of property.

ADA Need does the driving and rights steer the way.

WILLOUGHBY But tonight I begin to see a way to reach a dream with this place. I was telling the boys that I wish to build a hunting lodge some day, a place for a man of the world to hunt big game and breathe sharp autumn air. Of course, this would require considerable development work on my part and take considerable "time."

ADA Ah, but such work would have to wait out this war that is coming.

WILLOUGHBY No, my dear; that's where you're wrong. War presents opportunities. When the men are called to fight in Europe, there'll be fatigued officers who might just fancy a time in the northern woods after the rigors of battle.

ADA It's beginning to sound like you have a new plan for the place.

WILLOUGHBY A plan that will take "time."

ADA *(playful again)* You are a clever one, aren't you?

WILLOUGHBY With all due modesty, that I am.

ADA And "time" *is* starting tonight?

WILLOUGHBY What a lovely way to put it. "Time" is starting tonight.

ADA What's to become of the resort in this new plan of yours?

WILLOUGHBY I thought we might take the place down. My lodge would arise on this very site, between the ridge and the lake, with those islands to amuse the eye. The boys could guide the shooters and anglers, the girl could serve at the table, and you, well, you could run it all. I suspect that it will take a lot of "time" on site to realize my plan, away from my home in the city.

ADA While we're on the subject of your "home in the city," what has "time" done to that marriage of yours?

WILLOUGHBY Made it parched and brittle.

ADA And ready to break?

WILLOUGHBY *(moving uncomfortably)* Break?

ADA Brittle marriages break, don't they?

WILLOUGHBY In Toronto? The centre of rectitude?

ADA There's no rectitude at Queen and University.

WILLOUGHBY Queen and University?

ADA The courts. The place of deeds and notes and… divorces.

WILLOUGHBY moves abruptly, then stands and fills his snifter with brandy. He staggers away from the table, then seems to feel the pain in his foot. He tries to shake it away and almost falls.

Sit yourself down, sir, and soothe the pain with brandy.

He nods obediently, sits quickly, and sips at the brandy.

WILLOUGHBY The minister mentioned your skills as a manager… but made no mention of your interest in matters legal.

ADA *(moving next to him, almost mockingly)* One doesn't reach my state of ripeness without learning a thing of two about the law along the way.

WILLOUGHBY Ripeness?

ADA Ripened by the sun of shining men.

WILLOUGHBY You can turn a phrase to flatter a man, by golly.

ADA I've learned to turn phrases and other things as well. But only for those who make the commitment of time. And, in a case like this, time that leads to the courts at Queen and University.

WILLOUGHBY I see you've managed to circle back to "time."

ADA Indeed.

WILLOUGHBY And we're ready for "time" to start tonight, are we?

ADA If a wink tells me "time" takes us to that famous corner.

He digs in his vest pocket, pulls out a monocle, squints as he inserts it in his eye, and looks at her bosom, slowly and carefully.

WILLOUGHBY A wink it is.

ADA I see you spy my anatomy, sir.

WILLOUGHBY A most pleasant sight.

ADA A sight reserved for the marriage bed, sir. Your "wink" was nothing more than the ogling of an old man.

WILLOUGHBY *(slapping the table, drunkenly)* Old it is, eh? I believe, my dear, that old is your trial, not mine.

ADA *(not playful now)* So insults already, is it? The right that comes with the deed? Is that capitalism?

WILLOUGHBY I just spoke to that son of yours about capitalism with our cigars.

ADA They do seem to go together, don't they now?

WILLOUGHBY A good cigar, madam, is the height of capitalism.

ADA So, it's "madam" now. Like the woman who washes your shirts.

WILLOUGHBY Where has this taken us?

ADA Where it seemed destined to go, Mr. Willoughby. I manage a resort, you wish a lodge, and, instead of negotiation, we get solicitation.

WILLOUGHBY Indeed, madam. We've moved from University and Queen to the depths of Cabbagetown where the painted women roam.

ADA I'm sorry sir, but you've just crossed my divide.

WILLOUGHBY The humour seemed to be your idea.

ADA When it was pleasant, yes; when it turned sour, no.

WILLOUGHBY And I turned it sour?

ADA *(pointing to the snifter)* Brandy is only sweet by the sip, sir. Any more sours the mind and sends it to the gutter.

WILLOUGHBY *(reaching for his cane, as if for a weapon)* I won't have this, no.

ADA Nor will I, sir. My father scratched this plot from the forest with his bare hands. He built this resort with my mother. We were forced to sell, but chose the buyer, believe it or not. The Paynes won our hearts with the deed. And now the deed has gone to someone who appears to be heartless indeed.

WILLOUGHBY *(rising with anger)* Cease and desist.

ADA *(laughing)* Sir, I will neither cease nor desist. Good night.

ADA leaves with a sense of triumph, her spine steeled, her step vigorous. WILLOUGHBY stays in his seat for a moment, as if absorbing the swift change in mood. He goes to pour more brandy, but the bottle is empty. He slips his flask from his pocket and pulls on it through the rest of the scene. He stands and begins to stagger around the dining area.

The lights dim, then a single spotlight shines on WILLOUGHBY.

WILLOUGHBY *Girl! Where is that girl!* I want brandy.

Oh, by the Jesus, I could buy and sell the whole lot of them in this godforsaken village, I could.

Merchants. Realtors. Owners of these pitiful resorts. I could have them all. *(drinking)*

I made my money, I did. I made my money in peace and I'll make my money in war. I'll make money with uniforms, and shovels, and carriages, and rifles, and cannons in this wonderful war to come, and I guarantee that I'd be able to make much, much more money in the wars that are sure to follow.

When these miserable country bumpkins go off to war, I'll whip their women in my factories to keep up with the demand for shells. Shells for

Hamburg, for Dresden, for Berlin. Why, my shells will kill more men than they dreamed of killing in all the wars before. *(drinking)*

Money! You bet I'll make money. I could make money over there now, too, if the fools could fix this bloody foot of mine. I'd be in that game, too, by God!

The damn British can talk a good game, they can, but they've got those unions and they can't beat the men and the women the way I can here. Oh, Canada. What a lovely place, it is. No laws. Politicians in my pocket. Money to make from coast to coast. *(drinking)*

I'd put my money in rockets next. Rockets will make the money in future wars, you watch. Rockets will fly high and alone and deliver their payload right in the middle of cities. Oh, I've read about rockets all right. I'm a dreamer that way. *(tries flask, but it is empty)*

Girl! What is that girl's name? Where is that little bitch? I need some brandy or this foot of mine will explode. I'd give her every damned dime in my pocket if she'd get her young ass up here with a bottle of brandy. *(He digs into his coat pockets, looking for something.)*

Where is that old bag of a woman?

What became of my papers? *(He pulls papers out of his breast pocket.)*

There they are. This is how I'll get that woman. Yes. I'll have the lawyer sign it over to her. I'll have him say she touched the strings of my heart. I'll have him say I didn't want this piece of property for my dream. I'll stick her with the taxes. That woman gets stuck with the taxes. That woman.

She's got her bosoms, she does, but she's got too many brains for her own good. But, oh my, my lawyer, he's a smart one, that lawyer. Yeah, I'll say, "That's it, let's stick her with the back taxes." Let's give her the deed and stick the broad with the taxes. *(He begins to laugh, then suddenly cramps and lurches forward as if to vomit.)*

Blackout.

SCENE FOUR

Spotlight shines upstage left.

LILA is back on the bench upstage left, waiting. She looks over her shoulder in anticipation from time to time. JOHNNY enters, wearing his uniform. He brightens as he sees her, but he too is nervous, conscious of what is behind them up at the lodge.

LILA I'm so happy we can steal these last few moments before midnight.

JOHNNY I think it's safe. Mother's gone to bed. Vera is out on the lawn somewhere. We're safe and alone now. Willoughby and the others have gone up to the lodge, I think.

LILA They were teasing me after washing up.

JOHNNY Teasing?

LILA They were ribbing me *(gently poking his ribs)* about you.

JOHNNY Me? I certainly hope it was about me and not about one of those handsome blokes in the village.

LILA They teased me about our little "chat" after dinner.

JOHNNY What did they say?

LILA Oh, you know, the things women say about other women who have chats with handsome men down by the lake.

JOHNNY You are a "ribber" all right, *(gently poking her)* young lady.

LILA *(looking pensively out on the water)* That's where *she* came from.

JOHNNY Who came from?

LILA Eve. From Adam's rib. *(another poke)*

JOHNNY Doesn't sound like much fun to me. Not as much fun as this *(He quickly kisses her.)*

LILA Oh my. Three times in one night.

JOHNNY Only three?

LILA *(getting up in mock indignation)* Why, John Payne, you are such a masher.

JOHNNY I can think of nothing I'd rather do for the rest of my life.

LILA Mash?

JOHNNY No, dear Li, mush.

JOHNNY jumps up and takes her in his arms. They kiss slowly and sweetly, then LILA pulls away. JOHNNY follows her a few feet from the bench.

LILA This has been the most wondrous night of my life.

JOHNNY I could easily say the same.

LILA Would you?

JOHNNY "This has been the most wondrous night of my life."

LILA There haven't been others; not nights, but other girls?

JOHNNY You know, dear Li, I've been far too serious all my life. I've read and studied and marched and trained, but haven't had a single night like this, ever.

LILA Oh, I just knew you would say that, Johnny.

JOHNNY Johnny?

LILA I'd like to call you that sometimes.

JOHNNY On romantic nights like this?

LILA Yes, dear, only on romantic nights like this.

JOHNNY And there will be many of them for us. Many wondrous nights.

TOM *(offstage)* John, are you down there?

JOHNNY What is it, Tommy?

TOM We need… we need to finish our business.

JOHNNY I'll be right there, Tommy.

LILA Business. What business?

JOHNNY Don't you worry, dear Li. Tommy and I have some final things to settle before—

LILA *(interrupting)* Before what?

JOHNNY Don't worry yourself, Li. This is men's business.

LILA Tommy is a boy, not a man.

TOM Are you coming, John?

JOHNNY I am.

JOHNNY pecks her on the cheek, then exits stage right. LILA sits down on the bench, pensively, as if she's going over the last few lines of the conversation.

LILA Boys, men, business? Oh, well. I guess he's right; it's not for me to worry.

LILA looks behind the bench and sees his guitar. She picks it up and begins to stroke the strings, trying to find the tune. She strums once or twice then and begins to sing.

"By the light of the silvery moon…
I want to spoon.
To my honey I'll croon love's tune.
Honey moon, keep a shinin' in June.
Your silvery beams will bring love dreams.
We'll be cuddling soon, by the silvery moon."

Blackout.

SCENE FIVE

Lights flashing, moonlight up centre stage. The sound of shells whirring, then exploding.

JOHNNY rises to one knee from a prone position. He wears a dirt-caked full-length woollen coat and a helmet, twisted askew on his head. He has his hands fiercely fixed over his ears. As the explosions recede and the lights continue to flash at a slower pace, he begins to speak with a mad, contorted expression frozen on his face.

JOHNNY It's the noise. The noise. The endless noise. *(pressing his ears tightly, then relaxing)*

In the militia they told us about blood on the battlefield, about broken limbs, about shots from snipers, but not about the noise. Never once did they talk about the noise.

Even in my dreams I hear horrendous shouts from the sky, brutal blasts in the trenches, and echoes, over and over and over, of explosions.

And when I wake there is that one sweet moment of stillness before dawn, before the sergeant and men stir, and then the hollering starts, here, on our side of the line, and soon, on their side of the line, and then the bursts of the bullets and the soaring screams of our shells overhead, and then the pounding in our own trenches with endless rounds of hot blasting metal. *(rising up, looking beyond, into the distance)*

And the smells. My God, the smells. My body stench mixing with the bodies of my men, with the dung of the donkeys, with the piss and shit of the men after a barrage of German guns. My food smells of wet wool. My water smells of lye. My own skin sickens me with the memory of the smell of the tanneries in Cabbagetown.

And there was gas that one night. The air bleached with its sharpness, my lungs stung with the bites of a billion bees. Why? Why didn't they tell us? Didn't they know? Didn't they care? *(holding helmet, ducks down suddenly)*

The sound of a shell approaching followed by a flash.

Oh, I earned the right to lead men in those summer camps with the militia. I deserved the stripes on my shoulders. I proudly wore the wool and the leather of my country in those heady days a year ago. I proudly stood to salute the majors and the generals and just as proudly took the salutes of the sergeants, corporals, and men.

I was ready.

I was trained and briefed and sent with my men to take our place in the line between the French and the sea, to hold firm against the Hun, to build a wall against their fury as strong as the steel we laid across our land.

But I didn't know about the absolute pitch black of the hours before dawn, the dead weary silence all along our line and theirs, the frightening expectation of when, just when, it would begin again: the hammering of hell, the thundering of the earth beneath my feet, the cratering from the skies above me, the endless echoing for miles around, and then, so many times, far too many times, the sudden shattering explosion that blasts apart the limbs and sinews and brains of the boys beside me.

When? When will it be me? Oh, how I wish Father were here, just to hear his name. *John. John. John.* Will I join you, Father? Will I? Will I die?

A thunderous explosion and then blackout.

SCENE SIX

Lights shine downstage left.

ROBERT *is alone on the dock. He seems intent on looking across the lake, towards the island.* TOM *enters, rushing down towards him. He has a piece of telegraph paper in his hand.*

TOM There you are.

ROBERT Yes, Tom, what is it?

TOM Mother asked me to find you.

ROBERT What is it, Tom?

TOM A telegram has come from the minister.

ROBERT *(grimly)* Is there word, Tom?

TOM There is, Robbie. *(scanning the telegraph)* Germany at war with Russia. When Russia invades Germany, the Germans will invade Belgium. There'll be a great war then. The minister says we'll be in by Tuesday, right after the king calls.

ROBERT It's so quick and ruthless. *(angrily)* A war called by bloody Mars, without rhyme or reason.

TOM I'm going.

ROBERT Tommy, please don't say that. You're just fifteen.

TOM I say it because I mean to do it. And I mean to do it soon.

ROBERT Tom, you've got to listen.

TOM What's there to listen for? The minister said it all in his telegram. The king will be calling and I'll be one of the first to answer the call.

ROBERT But Tom, they won't take someone as young as you.

TOM That's where you're wrong, Robbie. I'm using a dead man's name in this bit of business. The dead man is not too young to go. With some help from a friend, we got what we needed from the death certificate.

ROBERT Friend?

TOM A smart and brave man, he is.

ROBERT Was it John?

TOM John fixed it for me. He's a good man, John Payne. He's a real man and a friend. We're heading down to the city tomorrow and then—

ROBERT *(interrupting)* Tom, just be still and listen. This will be a slaughter. Men will ram into one another like crazed bucks on a rampage. And the result is going to be dreary death, mark my words.

TOM Well, Robbie, you mark mine. I'm not a slacker or a shirker or a coward. I believe in my king and I believe in my country. I'll be goin' before my mates because I'm a man who knows his way around. Yeah, that's right; a man, a real man, a man who ain't afraid of the Hun.

ROBERT He's not to fear, Tommy. He's to pity. We're all to pity now.

ADA *(offstage)* Did you find him?

TOM I did, Mother.

ADA Does he know?

ROBERT I got the news, Mother.

ADA Then come back up, Tommy. It's late for you.

TOM I will, Mother. *(to ROBERT)* I'll be as late as I want come Tuesday.

TOM turns without saying anything to his brother. ROBERT extends his telescope and holds it flat, looking for the island. He brings it down then.

ROBERT It's too dark to see the island.

(raising the telescope to the stars) But it's not too dark for the misery of Mars.

VERA enters from the dark, hears him, and comes behind him without him realizing it.

VERA Were you talking to someone?

ROBERT *(startled)* Why, no. I *(pause, embarrassed)* was just mumbling to myself.

VERA *(coming to his side)* Have you heard?

ROBERT Tommy came down with the telegraph.

VERA It's awful. So very awful.

ROBERT There may be ways to stop it.

VERA I'll try as hard as I can. We'll take to the streets on Tuesday and stay in the streets until we stop this war. Women will take this war away from the men. And you, Robbie?

ROBERT I'll go up to Algonquin. I'm sure the men will see the futility after a while. We'll organize in the camps and bring the men to Ottawa if we have to. Labour will unite.

VERA Oh, Robbie, there still is hope, isn't there?

ROBERT There's always hope where there's justice.

VERA And peace will follow?

ROBERT I believe so, Vera. I really do.

Blackout.

SCENE SEVEN

Spotlight centre stage.

TOM is at centre stage, standing at attention. He is wearing a uniform, as neat and clean-cut as the one JOHNNY wore in the early scenes. He breaks attention as he begins.

TOM We had our war, we did.

I followed Johnny on down to the city. We had to stay with Johnny's mum for a few days. And there was crying on the one hand with his mum, and fightin' on the other with his sister. She was fixing to go off to Europe, too, but she was lining up with all those spinster socialists, as Johnny got to calling them.

We finally moved on out of there. We took a train to Quebec and a truck to a field in the woods they call Valcartier.

It was all guts and glory in them early days at the camp. It was guts for breakfast. And glory for lunch. And guts again for dinner. We heard it all at Valcartier—from the minister, from the politicians, from the generals, all the way down the line.

And believe me, we ate up those guts and glory on that field in Quebec. *(begins to pace, nervously)*

Just like they all ate it up again at the cenotaph today.

But me, I kept lookin' at the names in shiny brass on that cold stone cairn. They were my mates, those names. Boys who went up on the ridge for rabbit. And into the woods for deer in the winter. Out on the lake for fishin' in the summer.

My mates. *(pacing)*

There were thousands of us in that camp at Valcartier. Thousands bunched together in the bowels of those boats on the cold Atlantic. And thousands in the cold rain on the Salisbury Plain in the west of England. And tens of thousands on the troop boats to France.

But, once we got there, the thousands began to shrink and shrivel by the day. And for what? *(pacing)*

They said all the words at the cenotaph today. Honour. Liberty. Freedom.

But they didn't talk about what it was like along the line in the mud of France. There were words for that, too.

> *Swinging the rifle up, beginning to mimic the shooting moves of the earlier "play" scene, punctuating the words with movements of the rifle.*

The never-ending *thunder* of shelling, the *screams* of the men up and down the line, the *wailing* of those poor souls left behind after the raids into no man's land. *Blood* and *bowels* and *rats* and *rags*. *Vomit* everywhere. And *mud* as deep and dense as the sloughs all along the steel near Rail's End. *(stopping the mimicking, beginning to pace again)*

And we were thousands… and then hundreds… and then dozens… and then just three or four.

On Vimy. Ypres. Passchendaele. And on places you never heard of before and will never hear of again. Places where the dead lie in the mud, buried by bombardment. *(pausing)*

Yeah, I know. I heard them say it again and again today. I heard them say it was worth the sacrifice because we're free. But, believe me, there's a price to pay.

They're dead in the fields of France. They're crippled in the hospitals of London. They're mad in the asylums of Canada. And, like me, they're also walking among you, men who were made into monsters. By God, I only hope we've become men of stuff strong enough to stop the next crop of lambs from lining up for the slaughter.

You know, she was sharp-tongued and nasty as a viper, that Vera Payne; but, there you have it, she got it right.

Johnny got it wrong. They found him, they did, out in no man's land, where his limbs looked like the bent branches of trees, not missing, no, just plain dead.

Now he's just a name in brass on a plaque on a cairn in the northern woods. Thirty-four names are on that plaque, all dead. Forty-nine men signed up for the battalion at the start; thirty-four names on the plaque. All dead.

And, across the Dominion, six hundred sixteen thousand signed up, and sixty thousand six hundred and sixty one names on plaques from coast to coast, all dead. *(pause, scans the audience)*

Not a bad collection plate for that old devil of death, Mr. War.

> *TOM stands and comes to attention and stays stiffly at attention throughout.*
>
> *"The Last Post" is played until the end.*
>
> *Blackout.*
>
> *Curtain.*
>
> *The end.*

STAFF ROOM

BY JOAN BURROWS

NOTES

"Write what you know," as the saying goes. After almost three decades in the classroom, Joan Burrows had accumulated enough hilarious adventures to fill more than one play. In *Staff Room*, set in a generic staff lounge peopled by teachers from any school, Joan (ever the good teacher) forces us to witness humans dealing with many issues—love, divorce, scandal, gossip, discrimination, and, of course, pompous administrators. This could be a play, however, about any workplace, not just about schools.

An early ninety-minute version of the play was adjudicated by Allan Stratton, whose enthusiasm spurred Joan to edit and rewrite what became a two-act play with fifteen scenes and fifty-five characters (which can be played by as few as eight actors). The Curtain Club, Joan's home theatre company, began celebrating their fiftieth anniversary in 2004 and decided to produce a season of revivals together with one original play—*Staff Room*.

Subsequently, Joan attended Theatre Ontario's summer courses in 2005 and 2006, where she continued to work with Allan Stratton on her second play, *The Photograph*, which received an ACT-CO Adjudicator's Award for Outstanding New Play. Her fourth play, *Willow Quartet*, won the Theatre Aurora Playwrights of Spring competition and is being produced by the Curtain Club as part of its 2011/2012 season.

Joan Burrows is a retired teacher of English and drama and has been an active member of the Curtain Club in Richmond Hill for over thirty years. In 2004, *Staff Room* won the Elsie for Outstanding Production in the Theatre Ontario Festival in Sault Ste. Marie. Since then it has been produced by Kanata Theatre, Theatre Guelph, and the Belleville Theatre Guild.

Staff Room was first produced in January 2004, at the Curtain Club, Richmond Hill, with the following cast and crew:

Actors:
Peter Shipston
Cam Lund
Shannon L. Hill
Brandon Moore
Victoria Curran
Lynda Muir
Carol Moore
Jonathan Kline

Director: Joan Burrows
Producers: Rob Mather, Wayne Milliner
Stage Manager: Sharon Dykstra
Set Designers: Darmeen Cheung, Matthew Devine
Lighting Designers: Rob Mather, Steve Meacher
Costume and Hair Designer: Suzanne Stoner
Sound Designer: Marina Leyderman

The production was chosen to represent ACT-CO (Association of Community Theatres for Central Ontario) at the Theatre Ontario Festival in Sault Ste. Marie, May 21, 2004.

CHARACTERS

Staff Room is designed as an ensemble piece. Although the set is constant (it can be any staff room in any school), the characters who pass through it see only the characters in their own scenes. Some scenes may overlap but the play is designed to allow eight or more actors of various ages and genders to play multiple roles. Costumes should be simple but varied enough to allow the audience to understand that each time the actors appear, they are playing different roles. The only recurring character is Stuart, who never sees or reacts to the other characters until the very last moment of the play.

Directors may cast more than eight actors to play the various roles, but the following pattern does allow for four males and four females to work as an ensemble within the framework of the play's structure. This is a suggested pattern only.

Male 1: STUART, JOHN, BOB, HENRY, STEVE, MARVIN, PAUL
Male 2: BROWNSTONE, ALLAN, ANDY, PETE, TOM, HAROLD, TJ (optional), BRUCE
Male 3: TED, MAC, JACK, JIMMY, JOE, JERRY, JEFF, MR. S.
Male 4: RICK, DENNIS, JIM, KARL, EMERY, WARREN, FRANK
Female 1: ALICE, MRS. C., SALLY, PAT, PAULINE, INGA
Female 2: ANNE, SHEILA, BARB, JAN, SYLVIA, SHARON
Female 3: MARG, SUE, PAMELA, THERESA, MRS. G., STELLA
Female 4: JANICE, MARGE, MISS AMES, LUCY, BRENDA, LACEY, MAXINE

ACT ONE

In the blackout, a school bell rings. Lights come up to find STUART wearing a lab coat and black framed glasses, holding a coffee pot that he is about to place in a coffee machine on the counter in a typical school staff room. The room is sparsely furnished with a dining table and some chairs on one side and a couch, chair, and coffee table on the other. There is a small kitchen area near the table and chairs with a counter, a small refrigerator, a sink, and a microwave. Various bulletin boards on the wall are full of paper, which no one seems to have paid much attention to. On the upstage wall is a series of mailboxes. There are four entrances into the room: upstage are the main door from the office and doors into the male and female washrooms; a swinging door is downstage left, which enters into the school cafeteria. STUART places the pot in the machine, checks his watch, and crosses into the cafeteria as BROWNSTONE's voice is heard offstage.

NEW TEACHER

BROWNSTONE *(offstage)* The staff room is right through this door.

He enters with JANICE, who is young and eager.

Why don't you wait in here, Miss James? I'll be just a few minutes. A bit of an emergency to take care of… uh… first week and all, always something, you know.

JANICE *(eagerly)* Thank you, Mr. Brownstone. Would you like to see my teaching reports from the faculty of education? I forgot to include them in the package with my resumé.

She tries to hand over papers from a folder.

BROWNSTONE I'll read them later when we have our interview. You did say that you were available to start teaching immediately?

JANICE Yes.

BROWNSTONE And why is that?

JANICE *(nervously)* There weren't any teaching positions in my subject area in Moncton so I decided I had to leave the province to find a job and my sister lives here and she suggested that I move here to find work and so I did and when I saw the ad in *The Globe and Mail* about the geography position at this school, I sent you my letter and here I am.

BROWNSTONE Of course. Of course. Well, let me just take care of a little problem first. Always seems to happen during the first week… desk shortages, timetable problems, lost students, that sort of thing. I'll come back for you in a few minutes. Just make yourself comfortable. There should be some coffee *(He looks at the counter.)* or there should be some shortly.

He exits quickly.

JANICE That's okay… I don't drink coffee.

She looks around the staff room, not really sure what she is allowed to look at. She walks to the couch and adjusts herself. She checks her reports before returning them to the folder. She sees the newspaper on the coffee table and opens it so that it completely covers her face. TED *and* ANNE *enter quickly and proceed to the counter.* TED *prepares four coffees while* ANNE *is busy stapling papers for a meeting.*

TED So apparently she lost it around 11:30 this morning. Jerry Brucklemeyer was next door. He had to leave his music class to go in and see what the commotion was all about. He found her running around the room waving scissors over her head and screaming, "Cut! Cut!" He managed to wrestle her to the floor and get the scissors from her, but by then she was whimpering and starting to curl into a fetal position so it was pretty easy. It seems she had that special education class working on some kind of media project, and the class must've gotten out of hand. Again. Or at least that's what Jerry thinks. He said the place was covered in newspapers and glue. One kid had been wrapped up so tight in paper and string he was thrashing around on the floor like a mummy trying to come to life.

ANNE My God. Was anyone hurt?

TED Are you kidding? I don't think the kids even noticed. We're talking about the *(shudders) whoo-whoo* room here. If there was a chandelier, those kids would be hanging from it. Remember last spring when Rosemary was away for those three weeks and we all had to take turns filling in? *Whooooo*—a scarier place is not found anywhere on this planet. Every time I got stuck with her class, I stood for the whole time with my back to the wall just trying to keep a lid on things. No wonder she went over the edge. I tell you, they were the longest teaching moments in my life. No, forget that. There wasn't any teaching going on. Just surviving. Me against fourteen wackos.

ANNE Were there only fourteen? It felt like forty-eight when I was in there. They were all over the place. This is pretty bad. It's only the first week. Usually Rosemary doesn't cave until Thanksgiving.

TED First week nothing. Rosemary has been stuck with that special class for seven years now and it keeps getting worse. Personally, I think she should've gotten out of it a few years ago when she was spending Tuesday afternoons tutoring three of those kids at the city reformatory. Nothing like teaching simple paragraph structure in a lock-up.

ANNE Wasn't that when she got on to the Valium?

TED No. The Valium came after the hostage incident in the girls' washroom. I'm pretty sure she's on Prozac now.

ANNE Maybe that's what happened this morning. Her meds got mixed up. Poor Rosemary.

TED Don't feel sorry for her. At least she's out of it for a while. All I'm worried about is that the rest of us are gonna get stuck covering her classes. This could take longer than last year. She left in a taxi straight for the hospital this time. It was pulling out just before we came in here.

ANNE *(crosses downstage to the window and then turns to the phone)* So, do you want me to call the other two to have our curriculum meeting in here? *(then realizes that someone is sitting beside it)* It's pretty quiet. Or we could head back to my classroom. It's free until lunch and then the Dungeons and Dragons nerds use it.

TED Are you kidding? Let's take our stuff to the book room on the third floor. Brownstone is gonna be on a rampage to find people to cover Rose's class, and I'm not just talking about today. We could get stuck for the whole semester if he isn't able to find someone to take it. You grab the folders and I'll take the coffee. *(He puts the four coffees on a tray.)* Let's take the emergency stairs behind the library. Check that the coast is clear before we head out.

ANNE *(going to the door)* Oh my God! He's heading this way.

TED Quick. Hide in the washrooms.

They each head for their own rooms, but at the last second TED *decides it will be safer if he is in the women's.* JANICE *lowers the paper. She looks worried.* MARG *enters the room from the washroom and crosses to the kitchen to pour two coffees that she places on the table.* BROWNSTONE *enters quickly from the office. He is all charm.*

BROWNSTONE So, Janice, I can see you now. How about stepping into my office and we can chat.

JANICE, *looking terrified, folds the paper and rises slowly, turning to look at the washroom door as she crosses to* BROWNSTONE. *He continues the conversation as he holds the door for her and they exit.*

I've been looking at your resumé and I see that you've taken part one of special education. That's very commendable. I'll tell you what I'm looking for. I've had a little situation arise that you might be able to…

ALICE *enters from the cafeteria carrying two sandwiches wrapped in Cellophane. She smiles at* MARG *and sits across from her at the table. They begin to try and unwrap the sandwiches as* ALLAN, *a slightly nervous teacher, enters with a file folder filled with various papers.*

MENOPAUSE MOMENTS

ALLAN Thanks for giving up part of your lunchtime to start looking at the mid-term exam. I have to submit it before Friday so we should make some decisions about what has to be on this thing. I've been collecting some essays that were in the newspapers and news magazines over the semester so maybe we should start by choosing the one you feel most comfortable with.

Throughout the scene he is trapped between the two women while they talk, eat, and scribble notes on paper being passed between the two of them.

ALICE Sure. I looked at some of these last week.

She grabs the folder from ALLAN's hands and begins distributing various papers among the three of them.

MARG Oh, dear. I forgot my glasses. I won't be able to read a thing without them. *(getting up to leave)*

ALICE *(pointing to ALICE's head)* You're wearing them, dear.

MARG God, I must do that ten times a day. *(pulling out an article)* What about this one? She's married to what's his name.

ALICE Who?

MARG Oh, you know. He had that column every weekend until he went into politics. You know. The one who looked like that actor who was in that adventure movie. What was it called? It was on TV a few nights ago. What was the name of it?

ALICE You mean the one set in Mexico? With that actress? Remember she was nominated for an Academy Award when she was a kid but she didn't win. A couple of years ago there was a drug scandal surrounding her or something. *(removing her sweater)* Is it hot in here or is it just me?

MARG *(looking at ALLAN who is wearing a heavy sweater)* Must be a flash, dear. Here, use these.

She hands a sheaf of essays from ALLAN's hand for ALICE to use as a fan. ALLAN looks on helplessly.

No. It wasn't a drug thing. Wasn't she under scrutiny for being anorexic? Remember she did that interview with Barbara Walters. She said she didn't have an eating disorder, she just kept forgetting to eat. How irritating was that? I mean, I have on occasion forgotten my phone number, my mother's maiden name, and my keys. But I've never forgotten to eat. You have to be a special kind of stupid to forget to eat. *(She chomps on her sandwich.)*

ALICE Maybe that's why she didn't win that Oscar. I like this section here. Good food imagery. We can ask a question on that. Speaking of which, I tried that recipe you gave me a few weeks ago.

MARG What recipe?

ALICE The one you said you used with your mother-in-law, with the soy milk.

MARG I don't have a mother-in-law. She died. What was in it?

ALICE Oh, I'm sorry. I thought it was you.

MARG It's okay. She's been dead for years. Thank goodness. So what was in it?

ALICE The chicken casserole thing with the soy milk. I was sure it was you. Maybe it was what's her name in math.

MARG Who?

ALICE The new one. She came over from Woodland Heights last year. You know, what's her name. She had the bone scan done a few months ago and came in here with all those calcium recipes. You were here, I'm sure. She said she was only going to cook with soy from now on and was out to lose twenty pounds.

MARG At her age? She can't lose that kind of weight at her age.

ALICE I know. My body and my fat are really good friends right now. It's hard to let go.

MARG Here, I've underlined twelve rhetorical devices that the kids should be able to identify. Let's use six or seven of them. You choose. I don't know about your class, but mine will find this pretty tough. Some of the words are more than two syllables.

ALICE This paragraph with the allusion will throw them. I doubt they even know who Julius Caesar was let alone the ides of March. That blouse is really sweet. Where did you get it?

MARG It was on sale in the mall. At what's its name. I stopped in the other night on the way home. I had to order a birthday cake for Jack for the weekend.

ALICE How old will he be?

MARG Fifty-five. I can't believe I'm married to a fifty-five-year-old. When did that happen?

ALICE I know what you mean. My son is going to be twenty-four next month and he's the youngest. I'm just glad his girlfriend is planning something, because I'll be too stressed with these exams to mark and reports cards to do it.

MARG I hear you. It's that time of year when you wake up screaming and you realize you weren't even asleep. The only thing that keeps me going is focusing on that retirement date I have posted over my desk. Three years, one month, six days, and… *(She looks at her watch.)*

ALICE Stop. I don't need the exact minute! Here, Allan, I've put down some higher-order thinking questions to go along with the recognition of the devices. You can choose the ones you want. My kids are gonna suffer no matter what. Marg thinks she's got the loser class this semester, but I'm the one with Charlie Hawkes sitting in for the third time. Next semester, you get him, okay, Allan?

ALLAN I…

MARG I've put some written response ideas for the second part of the exam. There are at least four to choose from. If you want to add some more, that's just fine. Oh God, look at the time. *(She stands.)* I have to set up the room for the Victorian tea party.

ALICE Who's your Jack the Ripper this year? *(also standing and preparing to leave)*

MARG Tony Margolis. He's out on bail, so I figured it was typecasting. Thanks, Allan, for organizing the exam this semester. Your ideas were great. *(She exits quickly through the main door.)*

ALLAN *(turning to look at her)* But I…

ALICE Yeah. Thanks, Allan. Let me know if you need help typing it up. *(She follows MARG.)*

ALLAN *(turning to look at her)* You're welcome.

Pause. He looks at the finished exam.

How do they do that?

He sits quietly and reads their notes.

PARENT INTERVIEW

RICK enters from the cafeteria with a bag of chips and crosses to the couch where he sits to scan the paper.

ALLAN How do they do that?

He collects the exam material, rises, and exits to the cafeteria. MAC enters from the men's washroom.

MAC Hey, you're still here? What are you doing?

RICK Rehearsal with the kids. I have some projects to mark that I don't want to lug home so I thought I'd stay another hour or so and try to knock off a few of them. Did you have a meeting or something?

MAC Not yet. Sheila arranged for Mrs. Cyprios to come in to see me. I've got Angela in my grade ten class and she's not doing that well, so Sheila thought it would be a good idea to bring the mother in. Before the shock of the report card hits her. *(looking at his watch)* She's supposed to be here any minute.

RICK *(looking at him)* Mrs. Cyprios?

MAC Yeah. Why? Have you met her?

RICK Oh, sure. I had Angela last year. Have you talked with the mother at all?

MAC No. I was working on the mid-terms and saw that Angela was failing, and last week she skipped my class twice. So I brought it to Sheila's attention. She said she would call the mother and ask her to come in. Have you met her? What was she like?

RICK Yeah. Well, I had the same problems with Angela last semester so I asked her to bring her mother in after school one day. *(looking around)* Man it was brutal.

MAC What do you mean?

RICK Her mother doesn't speak English.

MAC What?

RICK Angela's mother. She may have been here a few years, but her English is really poor. Every time she opened her mouth, I had no idea what she was saying to me. Sometimes I think she was asking me a question but I couldn't tell for sure. If I nodded "yes," she would cry and if I nodded "no," she beat her chest with her handkerchief. I don't really know if she even understood what the whole interview was about. By the time I called Angela into the room to translate for me, Mrs. Cyprios was sobbing on my shoulder, and I'm not sure what Angela was telling her, but she cried louder and louder. It was awful.

MAC Did you tell Sheila about it?

RICK I'm not going to tell the vice-principal that I made a mother cry during a parent interview. She hates me enough already.

MAC Well, Rick, you do have a reputation around here for causing trouble. Everything is a joke to you. Sheila still hasn't forgiven you for running in here with the firehose when she was blowing out the candles on her fiftieth birthday cake.

RICK *(shrugs)* The woman has no sense of humour. I wasn't about to tell her that I made Mrs. Cyprios cry. I just held her hand for a long time and kept smiling until she stopped bawling. Angela was glaring at me the whole time. Trust me. This will not be easy.

MAC Oh, great. What should I do? She's arriving any minute. I can't cancel.

RICK My advice? Speak really slowly and loudly. And smile a lot, even when you're telling her that her daughter's a loser. Maybe some charades will help.

MAC What do you mean?

RICK Acting things out. Gestures and stuff like that.

MAC I can't do that. I teach math not drama. *(pause)* Did you do that?

RICK No. But I probably should have. Look. Just try to get your point across as best you can. Whatever you do, don't let her speak. You'll never understand her.

SHEILA *(enters from the office)* Hello, Mr. MacAfee. *(with disdain)* Richard. *(with skepticism)* Working late?

She crosses to the coffee pot and pours a cup for herself.

MAC I'm meeting Mrs. Cyprios, remember? Will you be able to be in on the interview?

SHEILA Oh, that's right. Unfortunately, I have a truant student to deal with in my office. I may not be able to be with you, but do let me know how everything goes. I'll call her tomorrow as a follow-up. If she's arrived in the office, I'll send her in here.

She exits. They watch her go.

RICK Hey, maybe it's a good thing that Sheila's too busy to be with you. You don't want to look like an idiot in front of her, do you? *(MAC shakes his head.)* Well, listen, I better tackle those projects. Good luck, buddy.

MAC Sure. Thanks.

RICK crosses and pours himself a coffee. SHEILA ushers in a very plain-looking woman wearing a coat and headscarf and carrying a purse. RICK nods to MRS. CYPRIOS and turns to give MAC a thumbs-up before exiting.

SHEILA Here's Mrs. Cyprios, Mr. MacAfee. I'll leave the two of you in here to have a little talk.

She exits.

During the following dialogue, MAC should look generally terrified, speak a little too loudly and slowly, and use as many charades as possible to try to make his point. MRS. CYPRIOS should generally look totally confused at what he is doing and saying.

MAC HELLO, MRS. CYPRIOS. SO NICE OF YOU TO COME.

He hesitates, not knowing whether to shake hands and decides to do so but with great flourish.

WOULD YOU LIKE TO SIT DOWN?

He mimes sitting several times on the chair.

SIT... SIT... SIT DOWN. GOOD. GOOD. I WANTED TO SPEAK TO YOU... SPEAK...? TALK...

He mimes his mouth opening and closing.

TO YOU ABOUT ANGELA. SHE IS NOT DOING VERY WELL IN MY MATH CLASS.

Suddenly remembers to smile when delivering bad news.

SHE'S FAILING... BADLY... *(laughs)* SHE HASN'T PASSED ANY OF THE TESTS THAT WE HAVE HAD SO FAR...

MRS. CYPRIOS stares at him.

...PASSED ANY TESTS...

He creates a mime of himself as a teacher handing a test to Angela. Then he creates a bored, gum-chewing, hair-twirling Angela who, using her fingers to count, struggles with the test. She hands it to the teacher, and as the teacher, he mimes taking out a pen and marking big Xs on it, shaking his head and finally putting a zero at the top of the paper and then hands it to MRS. CYPRIOS. She hesitates, not sure what she is to do, but decides she should take the illusion. She stares at it, then at him and decides to hand it back to him. MAC did not anticipate this kind of participation. Now he is left holding an illusion that he doesn't know what to do with, so he crumples it up and throws it over his shoulder. MRS. CYPRIOS watches where it lands.

LAST WEEK ANGELA SKIPPED MY CLASS TWICE... TWO TIMES... SHE SKIPPED.

Stands and mimes skipping across the room, stops to see if she has recognized this, then begins skipping with an imaginary rope. MRS. CYPRIOS is now sitting very rigid, not taking her eyes off him.

I AM VERY CONCERNED ABOUT ANGELA.

MAC realizes he is frowning and immediately turns it into a big smile.

ANGELA NEEDS TO BE BETTER PREPARED FOR CLASS. SHE NEEDS... *(He points to his knees.)* NEEDS... NEEDS TO DO HER HOMEWORK EVERY NIGHT. DO YOU KNOW IF ANGELA IS DOING HER HOMEWORK?

MRS. CYPRIOS What?

MAC *(even louder)* HER HOMEWORK. HER MATH HOMEWORK. DOES SHE SIT DOWN AND DO HER MATH HOMEWORK EVERY NIGHT?

He disappears into the cafeteria and returns immediately doing his impression of Angela. He mimes coming into the house, going to the refrigerator, "Hi Mom," finding an apple, sitting at the table, opening a textbook, looking confused but taking out a pencil and scribbling on paper, etc.

DOES SHE DO THIS AT NIGHT?

He shows her his work but this time MRS. CYPRIOS *refuses to play his game. She is not letting go of her purse.*

MRS. CYPRIOS *(slowly as she opens her purse for a handkerchief)* I don't understand…

Panicking when he sees the handkerchief.

MAC BECAUSE, MRS. CYPRIOS, I AM PERFECTLY WILLING TO GIVE ANGELA SOME EXTRA HELP, BUT SHE DOESN'T COME AT LUNCHTIME FOR IT… LUNCHTIME… EXTRA HELP IS AVAILABLE AT LUNCH…

He continues his Angela impersonation. He opens a paper bag, unwraps a sandwich, making sure to take out the enormous wad of imaginary gum in his mouth before biting into it.

SHE WILL NOT DO WELL UNLESS SHE STARTS TO WORK AT IT… NOT DO WELL… WELL…

He begins to falter, running out of ideas.

(to himself) I don't know how to do "well." How the hell should I do "well"?

In desperation he reaches for MRS. CYPRIOS*'s hand to hold it consolingly. She screams and pulls her hand back sharply.*

MRS. CYPRIOS Mr. MacAfee!

MAC Yes?

MRS. CYPRIOS *(in perfect English)* Are you all right?

MAC What?

MRS. CYPRIOS *(taking off her headscarf)* Angela said you were a little high-strung, but you seem to be quite over the edge to me. Are you feeling okay?

MAC What…? Oh… I'm fine. I'm fine. It's just that… well, you see, I thought… that is… someone told me that…

SHEILA *(enters the staff room)* Well, Mrs. Cyprios, Have you been able to get some insight from Mr. MacAfee as to why Angela is performing so poorly?

MRS. CYPRIOS *(crossing immediately to her in order to get away from* MAC*)* I'll say.

SHEILA Good. Good. Well, why don't we adjourn to my office and continue the discussion. I can share Angela's attendance record with you and the number of lates she's accumulated this semester. It's not been looking good these past few months. We should be able to come up with a game plan with the three of us working together, don't you think?

MRS. CYPRIOS Does he have to come with us?

SHEILA Mr. MacAfee? Well, I just thought you would want to continue the interview with Mr. MacAfee as well.

MRS. CYPRIOS I know why my daughter isn't doing well in his class. He's an idiot.

SHEILA What?

MRS. CYPRIOS I don't know how or why you hire people like this, Mrs. Goetz, but no wonder Angela avoids his classes. I want her moved to another math class immediately.

MAC *(crossing to her)* Mrs. Cyprios, please…

MRS. CYPRIOS You stay away from me. Don't you come near me.

SHEILA *(pulling MAC aside)* Mr. MacAfee?

MAC Sheila… I mean, Mrs. Goetz… I can explain.

SHEILA I hope so. But first let me deal with this parent. *(turning)* Let's go to my office, Mrs. Cyprios, and discuss Angela, shall we? After all, she should be our first priority here. *(to MAC)* I'll deal with you later. *(She exits with MRS. CYPRIOS.)*

Stares after them. Then slowly turns in disbelief at what an idiot he has made of himself. He glares at the couch where RICK was sitting. JOHN enters from the main door with a stack of essays. He pours himself a coffee and sits at the table, takes out a pencil, and begins to mark the papers.

MAC I AM GOING TO KILL HIM!

He storms out of the staff room through the main door as ANDY, a caretaker, enters the staff room from the cafeteria, wheeling a large garbage bin trolley that contains various cleaners. He begins tidying up the room and continues doing so through the next conversation.

FATHERHOOD

JOHN Hello, Andy. Sorry to be in your way but I couldn't work in my room. The noise of the rugby game outside the window was just too much.

ANDY Not to worry, Mr. Harrison. At this time of the day, there's hardly anyone in the staff room, so it's a quiet place. I heard the kids outside, too. A very noisy game.

JOHN Yes. I think it's a semifinal or something. All I know is that most of them will be in class tomorrow showing off their war wounds. They seem to be very proud of whatever injuries they get from a rugby game.

ANDY It seems pretty brutal. Too much pushing and shoving. I don't really understand it. I try to watch sometimes, at the windows, when I'm cleaning the rooms on that side of the building. But I can't see the ball. They're always hiding it. It's not like soccer. Soccer I like. I can follow the soccer ball. *(pause)* Do you like soccer, Mr. Harrison?

JOHN Hm? Oh, yes. It's fine. My son plays it.

ANDY Do you go to watch him?

JOHN Sometimes, yes.

ANDY My son used to play. In the summers. In the evening. We always went to watch him. My wife and I and our daughter. We sat on a blanket and cheered him on.

JOHN Is he too old for it now? Or has he gone on to baseball or hockey?

ANDY Oh, no. My son… he was killed by a car two years ago.

JOHN *(pause)* I'm sorry, Andy. I didn't know. I…

ANDY It's okay, Mr. Harrison. Most people here don't know. He was hit one morning walking to school. It was early morning. He was going to school for a soccer practice and he crossed in the middle of the road. Not at the corner. I don't know why he did that. Maybe he was late. But he was never late for soccer practice. Maybe he did that every day and we just didn't know. You send your boy off to school but you don't think he's cutting corners. *(He shrugs.)* I don't know.

JOHN And he was hit. I'm so sorry, Andy. How old was he?

ANDY Fifteen. He'd just turned fifteen.

JOHN That must have been… must be terrible for your family.

ANDY My wife is… still very sad. Me? I used to work at Donny's school, but after the accident, my boss thought it would be better for me to take a transfer. My son's picture is on the wall there. He was on the junior soccer team that won the championship when he was in grade nine. They have pictures of all the winning teams on the wall outside their gymnasium. Donny is in the middle of his picture. He's holding up the soccer ball for the team. He's got the biggest smile.

JOHN It must've made you sad to have to look at it every day. I can understand why you would want a new school.

ANDY No, Mr. Harrison. I liked to look at the picture. It always made me feel good to see Donny smile so much. But my boss, I think it made him feel lousy whenever he caught me looking at it. I tried to tell him that it was all right, but he said I would be better here so he suggested a transfer. *(shrugs again)* Maybe he was right. This is a good school. The kids are friendly and most of the people here are nice, like you, Mr. Harrison. At least they don't look at me so sadly. You know me, I like to talk to the teachers when I come into their rooms at the end of the day. At my old school, they used to smile at me then leave when I came in to clean. I think I made them… uncomfortable.

JOHN I don't think the people here know about your son, Andy.

ANDY You know what, Mr. Harrison? I think it's better that way. I don't know why I told you. I guess the soccer game and your son playing it. Is he a good player, Mr. Harrison? Like my Donny?

JOHN Uh… no, actually. My son's not really a very good athlete. I… we sort of make him play on a community team during the spring and summer. We think it's important for him to have the soccer experience. Being on a team. Making new friends. Learning a little about the game. But he's not very good. No. He spends a lot of time sitting on the bench. He's only eight, though. He may come into himself yet.

ANDY Oh. When does he play again?

JOHN Actually, I think my wife said there was a game tonight.

ANDY And you're going to see it? With your wife?

JOHN Uh… well, I have these history essays to mark. I thought I could finish them up here this evening instead of doing them over the weekend.

ANDY Oh, your son plays again this weekend?

JOHN No… I don't know. He doesn't usually play on the weekend, no.

ANDY Oh, I see. *(pause)* Well, sorry to bother you, Mr. Harrison. You have to mark your work. Teachers and papers, eh? It'll probably take you a long time?

JOHN Some longer than others, Andy.

ANDY heads towards door. JOHN stands and crosses to him.

Andy… I'm sorry for what's happened to you. Thank you for telling me.

ANDY Mr. Harrison, you're a nice teacher. You're always ready to talk to me after school. Some aren't. But I think it would be better if you didn't tell the others about Donny. I don't want them to be… sad around me.

JOHN All right.

ANDY Good night, Mr. Harrison.

JOHN Good night, Andy.

ANDY exits the room. JOHN watches him leave then returns to his papers. SALLY, a school secretary, enters and crosses to the mailboxes where she puts a paper into a specific mailbox. She pours herself a coffee and then exits. JOHN puts down his pencil and crosses to the phone. He dials a number.

Hey, sport, how are you…? What are we having…? Great. Did Mom put on the extra cheese…? Well, save some for me, okay…? Of course, I'm coming home. Don't you have a big game tonight…? Yes, I'm coming… I love coming to your games, you know that… Well, I do… Sure we could. If I leave right now, we'll have time to practise your kicks before we go to the park… You just get that ball ready by the door… okay, son… Bye. *(He looks at the phone.)* Love you.

As he crosses back to the table to pick up his papers before exiting through the main door, JACK enters from the cafeteria with a plate of fries. He puts them on the table and then crosses to his mailbox where he retrieves a paper. He looks at the paper carefully as he crosses to pour himself a coffee. He shakes his head in disgust and then sits down at the table. Pushing his fries aside and taking out a red pen, he begins to mark the paper.

DIVORCE

JACK …Punctuation error… *(writing)* inconsistency with the use of the comma… This should be double-spaced, you moron…

SALLY enters from the office with a stack of papers that she begins putting into each mailbox.

… spelling… s.p. minus two, you schmuck… hah…! Sentence structure error… what a loser.

SALLY I don't think I've ever seen a teacher enjoy ripping apart a kid's paper as much as you seem to be doing. Who is it? Someone who just gave you a bad day or something?

JACK It's not a kid. It's my wife's lawyer… Ex-wife.

SALLY *(crossing to him)* What are you doing?

JACK I'm grading this letter he sent to me. He must've faxed it over this morning. It was in my mailbox.

SALLY You're what?

JACK Look at this piece of crap. I'm not responding to a letter that is obviously poorly constructed and badly written. I mean who does this guy think he's dealing with? Thomas R. Payne and Associates. Thomas U.R. Pain in the Ass is more like it.

SALLY Why are you correcting it?

JACK I'm going to fax it back to him. *(writing)* Tommy, not a very good first attempt at letter writing. Too many inconsistencies with the format and punctuation use. More attention needed in structuring sentences, see paragraph two. Spelling needs correcting. You are working at a Level Two. That's a C… minus. Re-submit.

SALLY Uh… Jack?

JACK What?

SALLY I know this separation has been kind of rough, but you're not going to send this letter back to her lawyer, are you?

JACK Sure I am. Why not? She's the one who wants the divorce. She can at least hire a lawyer who can spell. If I'm going to have another divorce decree, I at least want it spelled correctly. The first one was. At least, I think it was.

SALLY Jack, it's great that you can take out some of your frustration on the letter, but now let's just rip it up and toss it away. Let it go.

JACK No way. Old Tommy Payne is going to know who he's dealing with here.

He exits out the door and SALLY returns to filling the boxes.

SALLY He certainly is.

STUART enters from the cafeteria and crosses to the coffee. He goes to pour himself a cup but realizes the pot is empty. He looks around in annoyance and proceeds to make a new pot while muttering under his breath. When he is finished, he exits into the men's washroom as JACK re-enters holding the faxed letter in triumph. SALLY crosses to him.

So, you sent it?

JACK nods proudly and hands her the corrected letter. He crosses to the table and begins to enjoy his fries. SALLY looks at the letter and then crosses to him.

And what do you figure, Jackie boy? That little move will probably cost you an extra… five thousand dollars?

JACK suddenly realizes what he has done. His smile slowly fades into gloom and he pushes his fries aside as he rereads the letter. SALLY leans over, takes his plate, and exits through the main door. JACK sits for a few moments and then slowly begins banging his head on the table. This continues while BOB and DENNIS enter from the cafeteria. BOB is calculating something on his clipboard while he holds the door open for DENNIS, who is carrying a cash box and a box of red ribbons.

SECRETS

BOB Thanks for your help, Dennis. I had two kids who were supposed to show up at lunchtime to sell the rest of the ribbons, but you know kids. They either forgot or they found something more interesting to do.

DENNIS That's okay. I was on caf duty for the last twenty minutes anyway. It looks like you sold quite a few.

BOB Yeah. We may set a record at the rate we're going.

DENNIS Where should I put these boxes?

BOB Over on the coffee table is fine. I don't have a class next period so I can sit and count the money.

DENNIS crosses over to the couch area. JACK looks up from the table and realizes his fries have been taken. He exits through the main door and tosses his faxed letter into the garbage can on his way out.

DENNIS I can give you a hand, if you want.

BOB That's okay. It won't take me long.

DENNIS Well, if you need any other help with the assembly and such…

BOB Thanks, Dennis, but I think the red ribbon committee has everything taken care of. You should join next year. It would be good to have another male teacher helping out. Good for the students to see the role model. As you can imagine, I have all kinds of girls who are keen to help out, but it's hard to convince the guys to come on board.

DENNIS Yeah. Sure. I'll think about it. Well, I have some work to do, so I'll see you. I hope the assembly goes well. I know the kids in my homeroom are really looking forward to it and to the walk later in the afternoon.

BOB Are you walking with your class?

DENNIS Well, not everyone signed up, so I have to stay behind with the ones who aren't walking.

BOB How many are there?

DENNIS Oh, about seven or eight.

BOB You could ask Alma to take in your kids. She can't physically do the walk but she's offered to watch the kids who aren't going. Just make sure they have something to work on. She'll be happy to do it.

DENNIS Oh, I don't know.

BOB It would be good for your class to see you participating.

DENNIS I'll think about it. I'll have to see what work I could leave and if I even have time to prepare something. It's just easier to stay and do your own stuff, know what I mean?

BOB Sure. But think about it.

DENNIS crosses into the men's washroom as BOB crosses to the couch, opens the cash box, and begins counting the money. PETE Thornton enters from the office with papers he puts into various mailboxes.

PETE I got your message, Bob, that you wanted to see me, but I'm afraid I've had a busy morning.

BOB Oh, yes, sir. It was about Friday's assembly. At our planning meeting last month, the red ribbon committee agreed that the assembly would be for all the senior students, which would mean we'll need three hundred chairs in the gymnasium, but I received a note here from the caretaking staff that they were planning to set up one hundred and eighty.

He flips through some pages on his clipboard until he finds the one he is looking for. He shows it to PETE.

It seems to have been signed by you.

Still distributing papers and not looking at the paper held by BOB.

PETE That's right. We've decided that only the grade twelves should attend the assembly.

BOB Who's we?

PETE It was decided at the heads' meeting last night.

BOB But at our planning session, which you attended, it was agreed that the assembly should be for all the senior students, both the grade elevens and twelves.

PETE But after discussing the subject matter of the assembly, they reconsidered.

BOB The subject matter? The assembly is about AIDS awareness. Surely that's an issue pertinent to all the students, never mind just the seniors.

DENNIS enters from the washroom but realizes that it is an awkward time. He listens with the door slightly ajar. The others are unaware of him.

PETE When I brought the format of the assembly to the attention of the others, it was generally agreed that only the grade twelves should be subject to it.

BOB Subject to it? Three people who are living with the disease are coming in and talking to the kids.

PETE Exactly.

BOB Exactly what? Look, I don't understand what the administration finds so disturbing about these people coming in and sharing their stories. Hopefully it'll teach the kids.

PETE Exactly the point.

BOB I really don't understand. The schedule for the assembly is well organized.

PETE The schedule's not the problem.

BOB Then what? *(pause)* Is it the speakers? Don't worry, Pete. They've visited other schools. They're well aware of what it's like being in front of a teenage audience. They know what to expect.

PETE Two of your speakers are male while only one is a woman?

BOB Yes?

PETE Well, there is a… concern that the male speakers will be exemplifying a certain lifestyle, so to speak, which the students and, I might even add, some staff members may find… uncomfortable.

BOB What? Are you concerned that the men may be gay?

PETE Well, statistically speaking, that's the norm where AIDS is concerned, isn't it?

BOB Statistically speaking, AIDS is least prevalent among the lesbian population. Would you have preferred me to bring in some of these women to espouse their lifestyle as the safer choice for our young people today?

PETE I don't like, nor do I need, your tone, Bob. A decision has been made. Besides, it takes too long to haul out and put away an extra one hundred and twenty chairs. Our caretaking staff has enough to do.

BOB Do you mean to say that you would deny this information to our senior students because chairs are an issue? We could get the kids to help put the chairs away. They wouldn't mind. They've helped in the past. The whole school was allowed to come and see that hypnotist, for God's sake!

PETE It's too much work. The chairs are needed in the cafeteria for lunchtime anyway.

BOB Lunch won't be for another seventy-five minutes. I can get student volunteers to return all the chairs by then.

PETE And miss their period two class? I don't think so. The afternoon will be disruptive enough as it is with that walk. Look, the decision's final. The grade twelves can listen to the speakers and then return to their period two classes.

He finishes stuffing the mailboxes. BOB stares at him then returns to the coffee table to resume counting the money. PETE crosses to the door.

Bob, I commend your enthusiasm and the amount of time you've put into the campaign this year. But ever since you came to this school, this seems to be the only extracurricular activity in which you show any interest.

BOB I'm sorry?

PETE Well, I never see your name down as coaching any of the school teams, for example.

BOB I'm not athletic.

PETE Yes... well. Nice to see there's something you're good at then, isn't there?

He exits into the office. BOB *watches him go and then sees* DENNIS *in the doorway.*

BOB I suppose you heard most of that.

DENNIS I didn't think I should step into the middle of it.

BOB Why not? You could've helped me with the argument. *(pause)* Unless you happen to agree with the decision? You were at that heads' meeting. Why didn't you say anything to me at lunch?

DENNIS I thought you had been told.

BOB And you agreed? You think the grade elevens shouldn't be included?

DENNIS I think the whole school should be included but there was a vote and...

BOB The kids lost.

DENNIS Look, maybe I shouldn't be telling tales outside of the meeting but Pete spoke in favour of letting the elevens in on the assembly. He was just the messenger here today. It wasn't his decision.

BOB But how hard did he argue for it? *(*DENNIS *doesn't answer.)* Yeah. That's what I thought.

DENNIS *(another pause)* Are the speakers gay, Bob? Some of the kids were wondering, you know.

BOB One of the gentlemen is a forty-three-year-old father of two girls. He contracted HIV from a blood transfusion. The other is a thirty-two-year-old former drug user. He used one dirty needle too many. The young woman is twenty-three. She had unprotected sex. Maybe once but my guess, after having met her, is more than that. No, Dennis, none of the speakers are gay. That was the point of choosing them.

DENNIS Bob, you should be proud of your committee work here. Since you took it over, the red ribbon campaign has become the most popular fundraiser in the school. When Alma Hallon supervised it, she talked a couple of girls into going from room to room to sell a few ribbons. But you got the kids involved in those after-school movies, the car washes. You made it cool for the guys to start participating. They felt more comfortable about getting involved in the campaign without the stigma of being labelled...

BOB Gay?

DENNIS Yeah. It's really hard for kids. They're struggling enough with their sexuality without having to take on that issue. Especially the boys.

BOB What do you hear, Dennis? Do the kids think I'm gay because I head up this committee every year? Do the staff?

DENNIS What? Oh. I don't know. No. Why would they?

BOB Because I'm thirty-four years old. I'm single. If they drop into my classroom after school, chances are I'm marking with opera or classical music on in the background. I assume that's why most of the kids don't bother to come for extra help. They can't get past the fat woman singing. I can recite lines of poetry to my business class at will. I don't take part in the school's athletic program, as Pete Thornton so aptly pointed out. Thornton seems to think I'm gay, why shouldn't the rest of them?

DENNIS *(pause)* You're not gay.

BOB No, I'm not. I just happen to be the kind of guy who likes art and poetry and music. We grew up with it in our family, my brother and I. My brother died of AIDS five years ago. My brother was gay. He was also talented, creative, the funniest person I have ever known. But he was careless, reckless, and not very smart about some things.

DENNIS Does Thornton know about your brother?

BOB My brother is not Pete Thornton's business.

DENNIS But if he knew, maybe he'd understand why you take such an interest in the campaign. Maybe then he wouldn't treat you so... you know, implying that you're...

BOB And is that such a terrible thing for Pete to think about me? Listen, I'll let you in on a secret. I like the fact that Pete suspects that I'm gay. It makes him a little uncomfortable around me. He's usually very polite compared to how I've seen him treat some others around here. It works for me.

DENNIS But he shouldn't have made that last comment.

BOB No. He shouldn't have. If you had been in the room, he wouldn't have. And maybe, if he thinks about it later, he'll feel stupid about having said it.

DENNIS I doubt it.

BOB You're probably right. But as he said, the decision's been made, so I guess we'll have to hope that the grade twelves will pass on the information to the other kids. I know the elevens will be furious that they're not going to be part of the assembly. I'll just tell them that it wasn't my decision. Pete'll have to deal with them. It does bug me, though, that they're using the chairs as an excuse.

DENNIS Well, I'll make sure that others on staff know the real reason.

BOB You know what, Dennis? I think the ones who are interested will figure it out anyway. I would prefer that you don't say anything about what happened here today. Especially about my brother.

DENNIS Oh, sure. I won't say anything if you don't want me to. I'm pretty good at keeping secrets.

A pause as BOB *looks at him.*

BOB I know you are.

DENNIS *stares at him then turns suddenly and exits the room through the office door.* BOB *looks after him and then returns to counting the money, making notations on his clipboard.*

SINGLE

MARGE *and* SUE *enter from the washroom and quietly chat while they proceed to pour three coffees.* JIM *enters from the office and goes to his mailbox where he retrieves a deck of cards. He crosses to the couch area and sits at the coffee table. He begins shuffling his cards as* BOB *collects his money and boxes and exits out the main door.* TOM *enters from the cafeteria with a plate of fries. He crosses to the couch area and sits across from* JIM *who immediately begins dealing out a game of euchre and sharing the fries.*

BARB *enters from the office wearing her coat. She drops a bag of takeout onto the table.*

BARB Hi, women. Food's here.

She crosses into the women's washroom where she removes her coat.

MARGE Great. I'm starved. I kept looking at the clock all through the last period just drooling for these noodles.

She opens the package and places three takeout containers in front of their respective seats.

SUE *(searching in the refrigerator for hot sauce)* That's nothing. I kept wandering over to the window during my grade ten Italian class to see if she had left the parking lot yet to go get it. You can't imagine my excitement when I saw her car was gone.

JIM *(referring to the card game)* Pick it up.

TOM Are you sure?

JIM nods as TOM picks up the card and replaces it with one from his hand.

BARB *(returning)* Sorry. For some reason there was a lineup today. Did you get the hot sauce?

MARGE Right here. God, I don't know how you can pour that stuff on. I'd have heartburn all afternoon if I did that.

SUE She's single. Had more opportunities to develop a stomach for hot stuff.

BARB What are you talking about?

SUE Well, on average, how many times do you eat out during the week? And I'm not talking about McDonald's or Wendy's. I mean nice places with napkins and tablecloths.

BARB I don't know. Once or twice, I guess.

SUE And I'm presuming, in your fine-dining experience, you have acquired favourite Italian, Chinese, Indian restaurants, right?

JIM Aw, crap.

He picks up the cards and deals while TOM chuckles.

BARB Don't forget Thai.

SUE Exactly. Marge and I here, on the other hand, are thrilled that pizza arrives Friday night and we're not faced with yet another dinner to prepare in between chauffeuring the kids to wherever.

BARB Choices, ladies. Life is about choices. You've chosen domestic bliss. I haven't.

MARGE Bliss? Who said anything about bliss?

BARB You know what I mean. Along with all your grumbling about your kids and your husband and your in-laws, you have a family you go home to every night. I don't.

MARGE and SUE look at each other and shrug.

MARGE Trade ya!

They laugh as PAT, nicely coiffed and professionally dressed, enters from the cafeteria and hesitates by the door.

JIM Hearts.

TOM Are you sure? Hearts it is, then.

MARGE Hey, Pat. You here for lunch?

PAT I just thought I needed a break.

SUE You never come down for lunch. Here. Grab a seat. Do you want some Chinese?

PAT No. No thanks.

She sits in the empty chair.

SUE I don't know how you can stand working through your lunch periods. I go crazy if I don't get out of that classroom or workroom for half an hour or so.

PAT Oh, I don't mind. I can get some work done and it means taking less home. You know. By the time you get the kids organized and supper on and dishes… I'm usually too tired to do much at night these days.

MARGE I hear you. How old are your kids now?

PAT Jennifer is seventeen. And Patrick is fourteen.

MARGE Seventeen. Yikes. I thought you were going to say twelve. Where does the time go?

PAT I don't know.

Long pause as PAT *opens her yogourt and taps her spoon on the table. The other three women look at each other.*

JIM *(throwing his cards down)* Oh, man, how come you always have that bower?

TOM My deal. Say, did you get your carburetor looked at?

JIM Two hundred and eighteen smackers.

TOM Ouch. Next time go see my cousin. His garage is downtown, but it's worth it.

JIM Pick it up.

SUE So, Pat. What's new with you? We never get to chat much.

PAT Oh, nothing much.

SUE How's Jack?

PAT He's fine… he's… fine. *(another pause)* Actually we had this… argument last night. Well, not really, but sort of. I guess we were just both tired. You know.

SUE Sure. That happens. *(pause)* Are you all right?

PAT Oh, sure. I was just upset. You know. I didn't sleep well and then he left this morning before we could say anything. It's just…

SUE What?

PAT It's just that we seem to be doing that a lot lately. Getting upset. Not talking.

MARGE *(pause)* Was it about money? My fights with Charlie are always about money. Usually. Sometimes it's about his mother, but usually it's about money. He doesn't think I should spend it. And the more he yells, the more decorating I do. It helps.

PAT No. No. Money's never usually an issue for us. I don't know. It's just lately it seems that we can't do anything right. Neither of us. We seem to be constantly disappointing each other. I do or say something that infuriates him and then he does something that just drives me crazy. And last night, it just seemed to escalate to a place we've never… We said some things that were really… awful… And then he… he… oh this is terrible. I shouldn't be telling you this stuff.

SUE *(pause)* Pat, did he hit you?

PAT Oh, no. Nothing like that. No. I don't want you to think that happened. He would never. I mean… It's just that he said… something really hurtful to me. Oh, I know he didn't mean it and I…

Looking at the women, realizing that they have stopped eating.

This is really pathetic. I shouldn't be talking to you about this. You shouldn't have to listen to me go on about a stupid fight. I'm spoiling your lunch. You probably really looked forward to it.

MARGE Are you kidding? We can do this any time. I'm glad you're here. We all are, aren't we girls?

Nods of agreement from the others. Really awkward silence at the table as they continue eating.

TOM *(teasing)* What's this game called again?

JIM Shut up and deal.

BARB *(a pause, and without looking at the others)* If nothing else, it's made me really glad I'm single.

MARGE *(looking at her)* Barb!

BARB *(realizing she said that out loud)* Uh… well, it has.

PAT *(starts to laugh)* You're right. She's right.

BARB I just mean that I don't ever have to bring stuff like that to work, that's all.

PAT You're absolutely right. *(still laughing)* That's the best thing you could've said. It must sound terrible to you. It isn't. It's usually… It's just… I don't know why I'm laughing. But I feel a whole lot better. Thanks for that perspective.

BARB Sure.

SUE You know, Pat, you should make a point of eating with us more often. We talk about all sorts of things at this table. Solve everyone's problems. Don't we, girls? It would do you good to come down and bounce off a little steam about Jack. Hell, I do it about Donald all the time.

MARGE Every day! *(SUE looks at her.)* Well, you do.

PAT Maybe I'll do that.

MARGE We take turns buying noodles for each other on Friday. Kind of celebrates the end of the week, you know? Barb has second period free so she phones in the order and then drives over to pick it up at 11:45.

PAT Tell you what. Count me in for next Friday, Barb. I'm buying.

BARB Sure.

PAT And I promise to be in a much better mood.

SUE Pat, your mood doesn't matter. Just come for lunch.

PAT smiles and exits the room through the main door. The three women look at each other.

Wow!

BARB Yeah.

SUE I always thought her life was perfect. I mean every day she looks absolutely fabulous. I feel like a wet dishrag next to her. There's never a hair out of place, manicured nails, smart clothes. I always wanted to be her when I grew up.

MARGE You're older than she is.

SUE Exactly. Who knew that we already had so much in common?

MARGE You two?

SUE She's married to a Donald!

The women grin as they begin clearing the table.

TOM Euchred! Ha!

JIM *(gathering cards)* I can't believe it. Two days in a row. What's the count?

TOM *(taking out a paper and writing)* Seventy-two to sixty-eight. I'm on a roll.

MARGE *(as the men leave the room)* Good game, boys?

TOM As always. How about you, good lunch?

MARGE Great.

TOM exits into the washroom.

JIM *(to BARB as he sees her about to throw away the cartons)* Aren't you going to finish that?

BARB *(looking at him and then the cartons)* It's all yours, big guy. It may be cold. You may want to nuke it.

JIM Nah. I'll take it to the workroom and have it after next period.

He pours the Chinese food onto the plate of fries and hands the empty container back to BARB. He leaves through the main door. BARB looks at the empty container and then at the others. They start to clean up the table.

MARGE So, anybody got any big plans for the weekend?

BARB My friend Claire is dragging me to a singles' dance tomorrow night, but I don't think I'll go.

SUE Oh? Afraid you won't meet anyone?

BARB No. I'm afraid I will.

She exits into the washroom. The two women look at each other and laugh as they head out the door. MARGE exits while SUE checks her mailbox, discarding every memo into the garbage pail. She exits as JIMMY backs in from the cafeteria with a box in his hands. He looks around the room and at his box and then returns to open the swinging door.

HORMONES

JIMMY *(calling)* Where should I put the box of masks, Miss Ames?

MISS AMES *(from offstage)* See if there's room on the staff-room table, Jimmy. I'll be right in to sort them out. Henry, maybe you could carry in these two boxes for me?

HENRY *(from offstage)* Sure, Miss Ames.

JIMMY carries his box to the table while HENRY, also a teenage boy, enters from the cafeteria, carrying two boxes, which he places on the other side. The two boys look at each other for a second and then high-five each other across the table.

JIMMY Yes!

HENRY Do you believe this? We get to spend the rest of the afternoon with Miss Ames. Alone.

JIMMY Yes!

HENRY I just saw Bobby Turnbull coming into the cafeteria with the rest of the glee club and when he saw me helping her, boy, was he green with envy!

JIMMY Yes!

HENRY I wonder what she wants us to do with this stuff?

JIMMY Yes!

HENRY What?

JIMMY Who cares? I'll do whatever Miss Ames wants me to do with this stuff. How long do you think we can make this last?

HENRY I don't know, but I'm sure going to work as slow as I can at whatever it is she needs me to do.

JIMMY Yeah… Did you smell her hair today?

HENRY I purposely went over to her to ask her about these boxes. Are you sure it was her hair? I thought it was her neck. What is that?

JIMMY *(recalling his sniff)* Cinnamon?

HENRY *(sniffing)* Peaches?

JIM Sex!

The boys giggle with glee as MISS AMES, *a pretty teacher in a short skirt and high heels, struggles in from the cafeteria, balancing more boxes. The boys immediately rush to help her.*

MISS AMES Oh, thank you, gentlemen, so much. I am so sorry. I didn't realize that the glee club would be needing the cafeteria for their rehearsal this afternoon. I thought we could use the tables in there to go through the boxes and decide what masks we should use for the display.

JIMMY That's okay, miss. It's pretty quiet in here. We could spread them out on this table.

MISS AMES I'm afraid we may need more room than this. I would hate to get everything out and then have some staff members come in and want to use the room. I'll tell you what. Why don't we just go out into the large hallway outside the office and spread them out there? Classes won't let out for another hour, so it should be fairly quiet.

JIMMY You mean, where all the guys'll see us? Great idea. I mean, lots of room and everything.

MISS AMES Good. I really appreciate you boys giving some of your time this afternoon to help me. You did such a wonderful job on your masks in class that I thought you should have some input as to how they should be displayed.

HENRY Oh, no problem, Miss Ames. I really want to help you.

JIMMY Me too.

MISS AMES I can always count on you two, always so co-operative. Listen, to show my appreciation, I'll tell you what I'll do for both of you.

The boys look at each other.

JIMMY *(dreamily)* What's that, Miss Ames?

MISS AMES *(looking through her purse)* I'm going to buy drinks for all of us. Why don't you look through the boxes and choose the masks that you think should go on display in their first stages and which ones the class should paint for a final product. Be careful, because I'm not sure if all the papier mâché is dry yet. Some of them may still be a little wet.

As she exits into the cafeteria, she drops some coins and the boys get in position to watch her bend over to pick them up.

JIMMY Man… She could get me more than a soft drink!

HENRY I know what you mean!

JIMMY What were you thinking when she said she was going to do something for us?

HENRY *(looking at JIMMY)* The same thing you were. *(staring at the door)* Why can't all our teachers be like Miss Ames?

JIMMY *(staring at the door)* Yeah. How old do you think she is?

HENRY Old enough!

They punch each other.

JIMMY No, I'm serious. I mean, she can't be that much older than us. This is her first year teaching. She probably went to university for four years, so if she graduated when she was eighteen…

HENRY I bet she graduated when she was a lot younger. She's really smart… let's say sixteen.

JIMMY Okay… so that would mean she's about twenty… That's not that old. I mean, my mom's forty-three, that's old.

HENRY Like I said… old enough!

The boys are snickering as MISS AMES enters carrying three cans of Coke.

MISS AMES Are they hard yet?

HENRY *(gasping)* What?

MISS AMES The masks? Are they dry enough to put up and paint?

HENRY *(recovering)* Oh, sure. I think so. *(looking at JIMMY)* Don't you think they're hard, Jimmy?

JIMMY Oh, yeah, sure. Where do you want to hang them, Miss Ames?

MISS AMES I thought we could start at the top of the large wall outside the art room. I've asked a caretaker to bring us a ladder.

JIMMY *(suddenly realizing something)* Gee, Miss Ames. Henry and I can't climb ladders.

HENRY Huh?

JIMMY We've got vertigo.

HENRY Huh?

JIMMY We found out last year in gym class. We couldn't climb that rope thing. Every time we looked down, we fell off of it. Didn't we, Henry?

HENRY I don't...

JIMMY *(interrupting)* But I could hold the ladder for you and hand you the masks. Are you afraid of heights, Miss Ames?

MISS AMES No. Ladders don't bother me at all. And what can Henry do?

HENRY *(in rapture)* I can watch... uh, the display. I can watch that the display is going up right.

MISS AMES Well, we certainly are a team, aren't we, boys. All right. Grab some of the boxes and let's get the masks organized in the hallway first.

As she collects some boxes and exits out the office door, the boys watch her.

JIMMY A whole afternoon of looking up at Miss Ames on a ladder. Are you ready for this?

HENRY You bet!

The boys open their cans, which explode. They look at each other in shock and then scurry to clean up their mess before getting caught. They grab the boxes and run out of the room. Blackout.

Interval.

ACT TWO

SCHOOL DANCE

A throbbing bass is heard coming from beyond the cafeteria door of the staff room. HAROLD, an older teacher, enters from the men's washroom with a newspaper. He crosses to the couch and sits down to continue reading. JAN, middle-aged and somewhat frazzled looking, enters the room from the cafeteria. Every time the door opens, the bass and music blare through.

She crosses to the phone and dials, nodding to HAROLD who ignores her.

JAN It's me… where's your father…? How come…? Okay… Let me talk to your sister… Well, get her out of there and tell her to come to the phone right now… Hi, Danny. Yes, it's Mommy… In a few hours, dear… Tell him I told him to stop doing that to you… Don't hang up, Danny… I need to speak to… Danny…? Dammit!

As she is redialling, LUCY, young and new to teaching, enters, music blaring as the door opens.

LUCY Oh, sorry, I thought this was my break.

LUCY crosses to the bulletin board to check the schedule.

JAN It is, dear. I just ran in to make a quick call home… Busy? How can it be busy? I just called there. *(redialing)* I bet Jessie is trying to call the school when she realized Danny hung up on me. Is anyone in the office to transfer the call? In case the phone rings?

LUCY Gee, I don't know. I could go look.

She starts for the office door and tries to open it.

It's locked. I guess for security.

JAN Still busy. Never mind. I'll go back to the dance and call again when it's my break. *(standing)* Who's off with you? *(looking at HAROLD)* Oh, Harold's in already. Okay, see you in fifteen.

She exits and music blares as the door opens.

LUCY *(looking at HAROLD who is engrossed in the paper)* So? Any problems on your shift, Harold?

He doesn't respond but turns to the next page. LUCY looks uncomfortable with his snub.

Sorry. Didn't mean to disturb…

She crosses to the counter and pours herself a coffee.

STEVE *(bursts in the door holding his hand)* Ice! Ice! I need ice. Quick.

LUCY What? What happened? *(crossing to him)*

STEVE I was dancing with Tanya Soloway and Suzie Casey when I flung my hand behind my back and banged it on the pop machine.

LUCY You were dancing? Are we allowed to dance with the kids?

STEVE Sure. Why not? I mean, they asked me and I didn't want to look like a stuffed shirt. Just because we teach 'em doesn't mean we can't show 'em what we can do on the dance floor.

He demonstrates his moves and accidentally hits his hand again.

Oh my God, my little finger is really swelling.

LUCY Does it hurt? Can you move it?

STEVE *(trying)* Ow! Isn't there any ice in this fridge?

LUCY *(crossing and opening the refrigerator)* I don't see any. Maybe over in the phys. ed. office.

STEVE Good idea. *(He starts to go.)* I don't have a key for it. Do you?

LUCY No. Maybe Harold does.

They look at him but he is now dozing quietly with the paper fallen across his chest.

I don't think so.

STEVE Shit. Who's on duty tonight? Who would have one?

He crosses to the schedule.

Isn't there an administrator here? Oh great, Richard! He hates me. I can just see him rolling his eyes if I tell him what happened. I'm not asking him for a key. Looks like I'm going to have to tough it out. Ow!

LUCY Why don't you soak it in cold water or something. Here I'll wrap some cold paper towels around it. That might help.

They are busy in the kitchen area when JAN comes running back in.

JAN Sorry. I just wanted to check on my kids. I walked by the office and I can hear the phone ringing, but no one's in there to answer it. They're home alone. This will only take a second and I'll go back and finish my shift. *(dialing)*

STEVE Say, you don't have any Aspirin or Midol in your purse, do you?

LUCY Sorry. No.

As JAN *talks on the phone,* LUCY *begins to wrap* STEVE*'s hand in an inordinate amount of paper towels.*

JAN Jessie… I know. I know. Don't give the phone to him. Is Dad home yet…? Jeez. Did you order pizza…? Did you have enough money…? All right, I'll pay you back when I get home… What forty-eight dollars…? Oh, last week, yeah, right… Okay, okay, I'll pay you all of it when I get home… I don't know if I have it in my purse… I'll write you a cheque… All right, I'll stop at the bank… What's happening…? Tell him to stop… Put him on the phone right now… I told you… Danny…? Yes, sweetie, it's Mommy… In a few hours… Put Markie on the phone, Danny, Mommy needs to speak to him… don't hang up, Danny, just pass the phone to Mar… Danny…? Danny…? *(slamming the phone down)* Goddammit, that kid is stupid! *(looking at* STEVE*'s overwrapped hand)* What happened to you?

LUCY He was dancing with the students and he hit his hand on the pop machine.

JAN Oh, is that what they were all laughing about?

STEVE Laughing? Who was laughing?

JAN I don't know. I saw Suzie Casey and a bunch of her boyfriends doing this wild dance where they were flinging their arms all over the place. *(She demonstrates.)* I thought it was some new rap thing, but I guess they were just imitating you.

STEVE It's nothing to laugh at. I think I broke my hand.

LUCY And you're in that staff-student hockey game next week.

STEVE Well, it'll probably be better for that.

KARL*, middle-aged, enters and slams the door with his back to it.*

KARL I know I'm early from my shift, but please don't send me back out there. I can't stand it any longer. How can they call that music? It's banging. That's all. Very loud banging.

JAN You're showing your age, Karl.

KARL Age? Age has got nothing to do with it. And the way they dance. It's disgusting. Shouldn't we be doing something about the way they're dancing? I mean, my God.

LUCY What do you mean?

KARL They're rubbing up against each other, constantly. And they're going up and down each other's bodies. Sometimes in groups. How can they do that?

JAN They don't have our backs, Karl. That's how they can do it.

LUCY I think the dance is going really well. I mean, I haven't chaperoned one before, but the kids seem to be really having fun. Everyone's just having a good time. No one's drinking or throwing up in the bathrooms. That used to happen all the time at my school dances when I was in high school.

Realizing that they are looking at her.

Not to me. Just in general, I mean. They're just having good clean fun out there.

PAMELA enters the room quickly.

PAMELA *(in shock)* I just caught two kids having sex in the stairwell.

KARL What?

PAMELA Two students. In the stairwell. They were having sex. Well sort of.

JAN What do you mean *sort of?* What are you talking about?

PAMELA I decided to take a quick hallway tour just to get out of that noise for a few minutes. So, I thought I'd go upstairs and check along the science wing just to make sure no one was up there and when I turned the corner of the stairs, there they were. Doing it.

KARL Lying down? On the steps?

PAMELA No. Well, he was up against the wall in the corner and she was…

KARL What? She was what?

PAMELA *(loud whisper)* On her knees.

LUCY Oh my God!

JAN What did you say?

PAMELA I shouted at them. "Stop. Right now." And then I said, "Put that away!"

JAN What?

PAMELA "Put that away." I didn't know what else to say. It was such a shock to see it… them.

JAN "Put that away?"

She starts to laugh. The others try not to but succumb.

PAMELA It's not funny. It's terrible. Right in the stairwell.

STEVE Who was it?

PAMELA You're never going to believe this but… wait, I don't think I should say.

STEVE Why not?

PAMELA Well, you'll feel differently about them if you know who they are. I know I do already.

STEVE Oh, come on, Pam, we're going to find out eventually. The kids'll talk. Especially after what you said to them. That's got to be a classic. It'll be around the whole school by noon on Monday.

PAMELA Well, let it. I'm not saying another word.

KARL Where are the two kids now? Back at the dance?

PAMELA No. I made them come with me until I found Richard. I told him what happened, and he escorted them out the door. I think he's going to deal with them on Monday morning.

STEVE Well, that'll be an interesting weekend for them. Wondering when they should tell Mom and Pop. *(He looks at LUCY.)* So how was the dance, dear? Did you have fun? Bring home any extra money?

LUCY Steve, that's awful.

STEVE Listen, if it's who I think it is, this isn't the first time the stairwell has been used for profit. Right, Pamela?

PAMELA *(looking at him)* I'm not saying anything.

STEVE You don't have to.

LUCY So… are all the school dances this exciting? I'm not sure I want to volunteer for the next one.

STEVE They're fine. Just stay out of the stairwells.

JAN *(pointing to STEVE)* And off the dance floor.

PAMELA Hey, if we're all in here, who's on duty?

KARL Jeez. What time is it? *(crossing to the schedule)* According to Richard's official schedule, Jan and I have ten more minutes of break. Everyone else hit the trenches.

PAMELA salutes before heading off into battle.

JAN I'm going to get an Aspirin from my purse. Anyone else?

KARL's hand goes up. She heads towards the washroom.

STEVE Me too. I think I'll try to find Richard and get that phys. ed. key. I'll tell him I broke my hand while I was chasing a couple of kids out of a stairwell. I was leaning in to yell at them when the door closed on it. What do you think?

JAN It's your lie. You can only hope he hasn't seen Suzie Casey dance yet. *(She imitates him.)* I can't believe you were dancing with the kids. You never learn, do you, Steve?

STEVE What're you talking about?

JAN The ski trip? Two years ago? How is that knee anyway?

He looks at her and exits into the cafeteria. She exits into the washroom.

KARL *(looking at* HAROLD *before heading into the washroom)* You're up, buddy.

LUCY *(waiting for* HAROLD *at the door)* Harold, it's our shift.

No answer.

Harold?

She comes over and leans into him.

Harold?

She looks nervously around the room then shakes his shoulder slightly, whispering.

Harold? Mr. Peterson?

He wakes up suddenly, scaring her.

Sorry, Harold. But it's our shift.

He looks at her.

We have to go back out again. It's our turn.

He slowly sits up and proceeds to take earplugs out of his ears.

HAROLD What? Sorry, Lucy, I can't hear a damn thing with these in.

LUCY It's our shift, Harold. I would've let you snooze, but Richard may have come in and seen you. I didn't want him to catch you sleeping.

HAROLD Oh, that's fine, Lucy, dear. That's fine.

She crosses to the door and music blares through. He gets up and begins to put in his earplugs again.

So, how is your first dance going? I bet you're enjoying yourself. I suppose you actually like this loud music, too.

LUCY *(yelling over music)* I don't mind it, Harold. But I'll let you in on a little secret: I don't recognize most of the songs the DJ is playing. Does that mean I'm getting old?

HAROLD *(yelling back)* You, Lucy? Never. You know, even with these things in, I can still hear that beat. How about it, Lucy? Care to dance an old man to his supervisory duty?

She grins and as they exit to the cafeteria gyrating to the beat, JOE *enters from the main door. He is dressed in a track suit, has a whistle around his neck, and carries a clipboard. He crosses to the mailboxes and reads a message in his box. He grimaces and crosses to the phone, looks up the number from his clipboard, and begins dialing.*

COACH

JOE Hi, Paul. It's Joe. I have the basketball scores from our games here last night… Oh? Am I the last to call in…? Well, that's the problem with being the convenor, Paul, you always have to wait for someone, eh…? Okay, I guess. No incidents, if that's what you mean. We have staff sitting in the bleachers now… Yes, all through the games… Usually four or five, depending on who can volunteer… Last night? Uh… three, why…? When were you talking to her…? Look, I told her last night that I'd be calling in the scores to you today. She didn't have to waste her time doing it. What does she think? I'll call in the wrong numbers or something…? She won… All right. She killed us. What? She thinks she's doing me a favour letting you know ahead of time before I call in the scores to you…? I don't have a problem phoning you these scores, okay? It does not bruise my ego to tell you that my guys were beaten by her team… I thought she phoned the score in to you already… That's right, Paul… Are you laughing…? You better not be laughing at me, Paul. My guys worked damn hard. They deserve a little better than your laughter… No, I don't have a problem saying that my team lost to hers… All right, lost badly to her… What can I say…? I thought the officiating was a little one-sided… Well, they seemed distracted for one thing… No, not my guys, you idiot, the officials. They seemed a little terrified of her. She never stopped screaming at them the whole game. They were calling everything on my guys… He fouled out… I know he's my best player, but she managed to get him fouled out… Before halftime… Yeah, tough break is right… No, I don't think she out-coached me. Maybe she has more to draw on, what about that…? Okay, so her school is smaller, but maybe she gets more gym time for practices? How about that, eh…? We meet them again next Monday… I hope so. It couldn't get worse, right…? Oh yeah? Thanks for your sensitivity, Paul. I hope you choke on your whistle! Well, I'd like to see you coach against your wife!

He hangs up the phone and storms out of the room through the main door, turning off the lights in the room. SYLVIA, *a teenage girl, enters cautiously from the cafeteria wearing an iPod with the headset around her neck. As soon as she sees the coast is clear, she shuts off her headset and the music subsides. She hurries over to the main door and waves in her friend,* BRENDA. BRENDA *enters carrying the latest teen magazine, which she hugs to her chest.* SYLVIA *is obviously the leader of this escapade, while* BRENDA *is her nervous follower.* SYLVIA *switches on the lights with bravado, frightening* BRENDA.

FANS

BRENDA *(looking around the room and whispering)* Are you sure this is going to work?

SYLVIA Look, no one is here, right? No one is going to be in this room at this time.

BRENDA How do you know? Have you ever been in here before?

SYLVIA *(lying)* Sure. Lots of times. Look, they all went home hours ago. We can use the phone to call long-distance and no one will ever know. They'll think it's some teacher with relatives in England.

BRENDA *(suddenly seeing the washrooms and still whispering)* What about the washrooms? Maybe someone is in the bathroom.

SYLVIA So let's check.

She immediately heads to the women's.

BRENDA *(still whispering)* Wait a sec. I'm not checking the men's bathroom.

SYLVIA Why not? You're the one who's paranoid that someone's here.

BRENDA Look, it's bad enough to be caught in the staff room with no supervision, but I'm not going in there to find some male teacher peeing into a urinal. What if he turns around or something? Ooooh!

SYLVIA Fine. I'll check the men's. You check the women's.

BRENDA *(starts for the door of the washroom)* Wait a second. What if someone is in here? Oh my God! What if it's old lady Porter? What am I gonna say? You know how she's always leaving class to run to the bathroom.

SYLVIA Porter is not in the bathroom.

BRENDA How do you know?

SYLVIA Because she wasn't even in school today, dorkus!

BRENDA Oh. Yeah.

SYLVIA Now go on. We haven't got all night, you know. I told my mom to pick us up at 6:30.

They enter the washrooms. BRENDA runs out immediately, expecting to find SYLVIA. She waits, growing more concerned with each passing second. Finally she crosses to the men's door.

BRENDA *(whisper)* Sylvia? *(pause, a little louder)* Syl? Are you okay?

She opens the door a little.

Sylvia? Are you still in here?

SYLVIA Yeah.

BRENDA What are you doing?

SYLVIA I'm having a pee.

BRENDA What? Are you crazy? You're in the men's washroom for God's sake.

SYLVIA So? I had to go. It always happens whenever I see toilets.

BRENDA Oh my God. Sylvia, hurry up. Someone could come in at any second.

SYLVIA Oh, will you relax.

A toilet flushes. BRENDA quakes at the sound. SYLVIA emerges wiping her hands on a paper towel.

Man, what a worry wart.

She tosses it into the garbage.

If I had known you were going to be this paranoid, I would've asked Terry to do this with me. She's way cool.

She grabs the magazine from BRENDA.

BRENDA Sorry. But now that we're actually in here, it's kind of scary. What if we get caught?

SYLVIA We get caught. *(looking at the magazine)* Isn't he just so gorgeous?

BRENDA But Mr. Stevenson will kill us. He might even expel us.

SYLVIA For what? Using the phone? *(crossing to the cafeteria door)* Look, if anyone comes in, we'll just say that we had to call our parents but neither of us had a quarter to use the pay phone in the caf. So we thought it wouldn't hurt anyone if we used the phone in the staff room because we knew no one would be in here on the phone at this time of the day, right?

BRENDA All right… But what if we get yelled at for being in the staff room? We really shouldn't be in here without a teacher. They have stuff in here that we're not supposed to see.

SYLVIA What kind of stuff?

BRENDA I don't know. Tests and stuff. We could be caught and everyone will think we were trying to steal exams or something.

SYLVIA Look around, Brenda, and see if you can see anything important in this room that's worth taking. I bet the microwave doesn't even work.

She pushes BRENDA to the main door.

Look, you keep your head outside the door just in case someone heads this way, and I'll dial the number.

She pulls a piece of paper out of her bra and props open the magazine so she can look at the picture while she dials.

BRENDA But I get to talk, too, right?

SYLVIA Yeah. Yeah. But first let's check we have the right number. Are you sure this is going to work?

BRENDA I swear. This is the number my cousin lifted from the phone records at the Hyatt. He's certain it's good because it was called in three times on the same day… the fifteenth, and one call was returned.

SYLVIA Okay. Here goes.

She begins to dial a long series of numbers, checking the paper as she does.

…Oh my God… it's ringing.

BRENDA lets out a squeal then remembers to keep her head outside the door.

Hello?

Suddenly remembering to sound older.

Yes, hello. Good afternoon. Or good evening. *(to BRENDA)* What time of day is it over there right now?

BRENDA I think it's six hours ahead… or maybe it's six hours behind… I don't know.

SYLVIA *(into phone)* Yes. Sorry. I'm calling from across the Atlantic. From Toronto actually and I'm not sure what time it is there right now… Is it really? Oh, I'm sorry… Well, yes, to whom am I speaking…? Me? Well my name is Sylvia French and I'm calling on behalf of the Linley and the Lying Bastards fan club here at my high school. Would Linley be available…? Oh. But this is the correct number, isn't it…? Uh… He gave it to me when he was playing a concert here on the fifteenth and he told me to call him any time to ask him some… Yes… He did, too…! I told you… Who are you…? His mother? *(to BRENDA)* Oh My God, I'm talking to Linley's mother.

BRENDA Let me. Let me talk. It's my turn.

She runs over to the phone and attempts to grab it from SYLVIA.

SYLVIA Are you crazy? She'll hang up if you don't let go.

The girls struggle with the phone until SYLVIA eventually gains control.

Yes… Hello…? Hello…? Yes, I'm still here, Mrs.… I mean, I think there's some kind of interference on the line or something.

She finally succumbs to letting BRENDA listen in on the conversation.

So Linley isn't there right now, is that right…? The tour…? Oh, right. Right. I just thought he would be home by now. This is his home number, right? I mean I know he's a Lying Bastard and everything but I hope he didn't give me the wrong number… It is?

The girls are joyous, making silent screams to each other.

Oh sure, I understand. *(BRENDA is pointing to herself.)* Uh… Listen, would you mind if my fr… my vice-president in the fan club speaks to you… Here…

She hands the phone to BRENDA, who is suddenly frozen with her mouth open listening intently.

…What's she saying…? Is she saying anything…? Brenda?

BRENDA Thank you… Yes, I understand… Certainly… Yes, goodbye.

She hangs up the phone. She turns slowly to face SYLVIA.

I just talked to Linley's—of Linley and the Lying Bastards—mother!

SYLVIA I know. So did I.

They scream.

What did she say?

BRENDA What?

SYLVIA His mother? What did she say to you? You said you understood something. What?

BRENDA Oh. She said never to call that number again. She said she doesn't know how we got it but now it would have to be disconnected, and we were never to try and call Linley again.

SYLVIA You mean, she didn't believe that he gave it to me?

BRENDA I don't think so. No. She sounded sort of… mean. Poor Linley *(looking at the magazine picture)* He has a mean mother. One more thing we have in common.

SYLVIA *(looking at the paper)* I'm going to keep this forever, right next to my pictures of the concert.

BRENDA And I'm going to cut out this picture and put it with mine.

They head for the door.

Sylvia?

SYLVIA What?

BRENDA Thanks for letting me come with you. This was the best day of my life.

SYLVIA Yeah.

They hug each other. SYLVIA *puts the iPod on her head as* BRENDA *peers out the door to see if the hallway is clear. She gives the okay and the two of them dance out of the room screaming "Lying, Lying Bastards! That's what we are!"* STUART *enters from the cafeteria and crosses to the coffee machine. Again it is empty. He is furious as he prepares another pot. As he exits into the cafeteria,* JERRY *enters when the door swings back in. He crosses to his mailbox and is reading some papers when* MARVIN *enters from the main door.*

BETRAYAL

MARVIN Hey, what's going on in Halliwell's office?

JERRY What do you mean?

MARVIN Closed doors all afternoon. I saw Archie McConnel and June Berman go in there around one o'clock. I was in the office photocopying for period three. I said hi to Archie, but he didn't even look at me.

JERRY Oh.

JERRY *crosses to pour himself a coffee.*

MARVIN Doris mouthed "Walter" to me and nodded to the office door but she couldn't say anything. I doubt she knows what it's about anyway. Do you know if Walter's in there?

JERRY How would I know?

MARVIN You teach right beside him. Was he in his classroom after lunch?

JERRY *(angrily)* I don't check to see if Walter is in his classroom every period.

MARVIN Okay. Just thought if he was in trouble, you'd know about it, that's all.

JERRY Why should I know about it?

MARVIN Because you're friends with the guy.

JERRY I'm friends with a lot of people on this staff. You're friends with him, do you know why he's in the office?

MARVIN No.

JERRY Well, don't assume I know everything that Walter does.

The next three lines are said at the same time.

MARVIN Hey, what's going on?

JERRY You shouldn't go around making assumptions about people.

MARVIN You know something, don't you?

THERESA enters from the cafeteria into the middle of their argument.

THERESA Hey. Hey. What's wrong?

MARVIN Walter Dunlop is in the office with the big union reps. They've been in there all afternoon.

THERESA Why?

MARVIN I don't know but I think Jerry does. I was just asking him, that's all.

THERESA Jerry…? Do you know what's going on?

JERRY I… I'm not sure.

THERESA Is Walter in trouble…? Was there a fight in his class or something…? Did you hear any yelling from his classroom this morning?

JERRY No… nothing like that.

MARVIN Then what? Look, if Walter's in trouble, we have to be able to help him.

JERRY Don't be too sure about that.

MARVIN What? What are you talking about? It's Walter, for Christ's sake, of course we're gonna help him. My God, we were just up at his cottage last Friday night for the poker game. *(pause)* Is he sick or something?

JERRY *(looks at them)* Look, I don't know why he's in with the union. Honestly, I don't… it's just that a few days ago when I was off sick, that weirdo supply teacher… Cannon, you know, the guy who carries the knapsack around all day. Well, he filled in for me and he left me a report of what happened during the day. He said that he overheard some of the girls whispering in my period three class about Walter… well, not specifically about Walter, at least he didn't mention his name in particular, just that they were talking about the art teacher who takes the photographs.

MARVIN What photographs?

JERRY Walter takes photos of some of the students… portraits. He has them on a bulletin board in his classroom and then gives them to the kids at the end of the semester.

THERESA Yeah. I've seen them. He told me that when he asks some kids to volunteer to be live models each year, he offers to do portraits of them. Kind of like a thank you for sitting still for the whole period while the art classes sketch them. It's really hard for some of these kids to do that. The portraits are along the side wall in his room. They're really good. Really professional looking. I think the kids sort of view it as somewhat prestigious to be chosen for Mr. Dunlop's wall.

MARVIN So? Did some kid not like their photo or something?

JERRY Look, this is really… *(He is uncomfortable about continuing.)* The note I got from Cannon suggested that the girls were talking about… other photos.

THERESA What other photos?

JERRY Cannon heard the girls whispering about… nude photographs.

THERESA and MARVIN speak at the same time.

THERESA What?

MARVIN Are you crazy?

JERRY I know. I know. I don't believe it either.

MARVIN Did you talk to the girls?

JERRY No. I don't even know which girls they are. Cannon didn't write down their names. He wouldn't even know them.

THERESA Did you go to the office with this? Did Cannon?

JERRY No. I don't know. I'm not going in there with a half-baked rumour like this about Walter before I even get a chance to find out what it's about. I was hoping Cannon would be back in the school yesterday or today but he hasn't been in.

MARVIN Well, this is crazy. This is really stupid. Walter would not be taking nude photographs of students. This is really sick. That they would say something like that about him is just…

THERESA *(interrupting)* Who's in your third-period class, Jerry?

MARVIN What do you mean? You don't believe it, do you?

THERESA I'm just asking. What girls are in that class?

JERRY That's the thing. It's the best senior class I've ever had. There aren't any kids that I would suspect of being malicious… Mary Holmes, Patty King, Tracy Spenser…

THERESA Tracy?

JERRY Yeah. Why?

THERESA I play bridge with her mother on Tuesday nights. She was telling me in the fall that Walter Dunlop had asked Tracy if she would be interested posing for him for the student models. We talked about it one evening over cards. I said I thought it would be a good idea for Tracy. She's so shy and quiet. It would really improve her self-esteem. I told her mother about the portraits Walter did and that Tracy would get a really good photograph of herself. Her mother said Tracy felt uncomfortable about doing it but she was going to urge her to get the photos done. *(slowly)* I never really asked her if she did them. I just assumed she had.

JERRY *(pause, looking at them)* I saw Mrs. Spenser in the office this morning.

THERESA What?

JERRY I was here early. I had band practice at 7:30 and I saw Halliwell take her into his office

THERESA Was Tracy with her?

JERRY No. I don't think so. But Tracy wasn't in my period three class just now.

They look at each other.

MARVIN Look, that doesn't mean anything. It could just be a coincidence. Isn't the mother the head of the parents' council or something?

THERESA She was. Last year. *(to JERRY)* What are you going to do?

JERRY I don't know.

THERESA Do you still have Cannon's report?

JERRY It's in my bookbag, in the workroom.

MARVIN Wait a minute. You can't just walk in there and hand over something like that without finding out all the details. This is Walter we're talking about. Christ, we've been teaching with Walter forever. Jerry, he's one of your friends.

JERRY I know that. He's one of yours, too.

THERESA Jerry, you know Walter better than any of us. I mean you've been to his home. You and your wife have vacationed with him and Lois. Did you… did you ever think… have you ever seen… I mean, I've seen his portraits. They're beautiful.

JERRY *(pause)* He doesn't take them here, you know. He takes them in his home. In his studio. I've seen his studio… but I've never seen anything like what we're talking about. Ever.

MARVIN Me either. My God, he's got two daughters of his own, for heaven's sake.

THERESA *(looking from one to the other)* This guy Cannon, can you get his home number from the office?

JERRY Probably. Doris must have it.

THERESA I think you better call him.

MARVIN What?

THERESA Call him, Jerry. You have to.

JERRY looks at them and then leaves the room. MARVIN and THERESA stare at each other, neither one knowing what to say.

MARVIN I'm sorry. But I can't believe this is true. I've worked too long with the man. Jerry better be careful. This could blow up in his face. Yours too, for that matter.

THERESA I know.

MARVIN turns and exits out the main door.

She sits at the table, with her hands folded in front of her, looking straight ahead. She whispers.

Son of a bitch!

SCAR WASH

PAULINE Rockwood, a female teacher, casually dressed and wearing a baseball cap, comes hurriedly into the staff room from the cafeteria. She looks around the room then crosses quickly into the men's room. She returns to the staff room immediately.

PAULINE Dammit!

She crosses back to the cafeteria and exits. THERESA gets up from the table and exits into the women's washroom. PAULINE re-enters from the cafeteria and holds open the door for LACEY, a teenage girl carrying large posters and markers, and EMERY, a teenage boy who follows behind with various-sized buckets with rags falling out of them.

Production note: the character of TJ can be played by a third person acting as a teenager dressed in a large moose costume. This character says nothing during the scene but can be physically reacting to what is happening around him/her. The suggested animal is a moose but if another animal costume is more readily available, feel free to insert it instead. If it is too difficult to costume this character, he/she can be excluded from the scene.

Just dump all that stuff in the middle of the floor for now. Thanks for coming so early to help get the car wash organized. We can wait in here until the others start to show up.

LACEY Where's Mr. Millstone, miss? Have you seen him yet?

EMERY Yeah. He has the key to the water tap. We can't even get the hoses connected until he turns on the outside water for us.

PAULINE I thought Mr. Millstone might be in here but he's obviously running a few minutes late. Why don't you check the signs to see if the information is correct before we post them outside?

LACEY We did that already, Miss Rockwood.

PAULINE *(impatiently)* Do it again. *(more sweetly)* Remember last year, someone had written car *warsh*.

EMERY That was TJ, Miss Rockwood. Lacey wouldn't let him near the markers this year except to colour in the letters.

LACEY grabs a marker from TJ's hand.

PAULINE All right, then. Why don't you decide where you want to put each one so there's no arguing when we go outside?

The students huddle on the floor looking at the various posters while PAULINE crosses downstage to look out the window.

LACEY I think mine should go on the pole right on Main Street.

EMERY Why?

LACEY Because it's the most colourful. People will really see it and follow the directions to the car wash.

EMERY People will come to the car wash because TJ will be out there dressed as the school mascot. It's gonna be pretty hard to ignore a six-foot moose jumping up and down. He'll draw a lot more attention than your stupid poster.

LACEY The poster will help.

EMERY Let's put all the posters on the main pole. It's not going to do any good to hang them where we're doing the car wash.

LACEY Why not?

EMERY Because people will already know they're at a car wash. And besides, remember last year? The posters got so soaked that all the ink started to run. We couldn't even read them after an hour.

LACEY I remember. What did yours end up saying? Oh, yeah. Instead of School Fund Raiser for History Books and Soccer Equipment, it had melted into Cool Fun for Hooker.

The students snicker.

EMERY Yeah. No wonder it was a record year for the car wash. Hey, Miss Rockwood, what do you think we'll make this year?

PAULINE *(distracted)* What?

EMERY How much do you think we'll make this year? Ballpark figure.

PAULINE walks upstage from the window.

PAULINE I really don't know, Emery. Obviously we won't make anything if we can't even get the water turned on. I doubt you kids will last long hauling buckets of water from the school to the parking lot.

She crosses to look in the cafeteria once again.

EMERY Oh, I'm sure Mr. Millstone'll be here soon. He's just late as usual. He probably just slept in, being Saturday and all. Maybe he forgot to set his alarm this morning.

PAULINE *(under her breath)* Oh, his alarm was set all right.

EMERY Huh?

PAULINE *(turning her attention to them on the floor)* Uh, Emery, I'm sure you're right. Lacey, the car wash is five dollars not five hundred. You forgot to put the decimal point in here. We'll never get any takers at that rate. Are you sure you checked all your posters carefully?

LACEY *(grabbing a marker from TJ's hand and correcting her mistake)* Sorry, miss.

JEFF Millstone walks in from the cafeteria. He is wearing sunglasses and looks a little worse for wear. He cringes when he sees PAULINE.

EMERY Hey, sir. About time. Do you have your late slip from the office? *(The others laugh.)*

JEFF Very funny, Emery.

He looks around for coffee.

Any coffee on?

PAULINE No. Why would there be coffee? Haven't you been up long enough to have two or three cups? I've been up for quite a while, myself.

JEFF I just woke up. I didn't want to stop for some and be any later than I already was. I just thought that you might have put some on for me.

She crosses to him, away from the students, who continue to fix their posters, fold rags, and joke among themselves.

PAULINE I was busy. I've been here for over an hour already helping the kids finish their posters and organize the buckets, sponges, rags. All the things we're going to need for the car wash, the fundraiser we're supposed to be doing together as the teachers in charge of the student council.

JEFF All right. All right. I'm here now. Lay off, will ya?

PAULINE Where have you been?

JEFF I told you last night. Petey needed help with that engine. We ended up taking the whole thing apart. By the time we got it all back in place, it was three in the morning. I didn't want to drive home and wake you up. So I crashed on Pete's couch.

PAULINE Too tired or too drunk?

JEFF I had a few beers. A few. Guys do that when they're taking apart engines.

PAULINE A few beers. And how many shots of tequila?

JEFF *(looking at her)* Pete did more than me. I had one… or two.

PAULINE Or ten. You reek of cigarettes.

JEFF It's Pete. I was working beside him bending over the hood of the car. You know he's had trouble quitting.

PAULINE He's never tried. *(sniffing his coat)* Hey, that's more than cigarettes I smell!

JEFF That was Pete, not me. He was getting pretty stressed out about that engine. He just needed time to mellow out before rebuilding the exhaust system.

PAULINE I bet.

JEFF Look. I'm sorry. Okay? I had no intention of staying late. It was just supposed to be a few hours working on the motor and a couple of beers. The time just went by. That's all.

PAULINE Every time you get together with Pete the time just goes by, and you usually end up stinking drunk and passed out somewhere. You know how I feel about him.

JEFF Yeah, I know how you feel about him. But he's my friend and he's been my friend since high school.

PAULINE But he's a rotten influence on you. You…

JEFF What? I what?

PAULINE Never mind. We have this same argument every time you come home from his place. It's tiring. And lately, you seem to be spending more and more time there.

JEFF Maybe there's a reason for that.

PAULINE What do you mean?

JEFF *(pause)* He's having a lot of car trouble.

PAULINE glares at him and JEFF crosses to the other side of the students. He bends down to look at their work.

Great job, guys. I think these are better than last year's.

LACEY Thanks, sir. Mine is going on the main pole.

EMERY They all are.

JEFF Well, they're all really good. Did you do them this morning?

LACEY No, sir. We started them last night. At the meeting you missed.

JEFF Oh. Right. I had another appointment.

LACEY That's what Miss Rockwood said.

JEFF She explained that I had to be somewhere else?

LACEY Oh, sure. Something about priorities and how the student council and some other things had to take a back seat.

JEFF *(looks at* PAULINE*)* Well, sometimes that happens, kids. You know.

EMERY Oh, sure, Mr. Millstone. But Miss Rockwood helped us get these started last night. We worked on them in partners. She stayed until after six o'clock.

PAULINE I wasn't in a rush to go anywhere. Not even home.

JEFF I bet.

PAULINE And they did a great job. I guess that's what commitment to a task or, more specifically, to a partner can accomplish, right kids?

JEFF Commitment to your partner is certainly important, kids. But I think another lesson here is not to mistake commitment with neediness.

PAULINE What do you mean by that, Mr. Millstone?

JEFF Well, sometimes it's important to understand the difference between when your partner is committed to doing a poster as opposed to needing your partner to do a poster… all the time.

PAULINE But that's what partners do in a project. They fulfill each other's needs.

JEFF Trying to fill someone's constant needs can get really exhausting.

PAULINE Well, maybe the neediness to complete the project, Mr. Millstone, wouldn't be there if there was even the slightest indication that one of the partners was interested in the project in the first place.

By now the students are looking back and forth as if at a tennis game.

JEFF But, Miss Rockwood, commitment doesn't necessarily mean that the partners have to be spending every single minute of every weekend working on the same assignment. Sometimes there are other projects that need to be taken care of.

PAULINE Ah, but Mr. Millstone, that's where the prioritizing comes in, doesn't it? What project deserves the most time and attention? Which one will mean the most in the long-run? That's what separates the men from the boys.

JEFF All men begin as boys, Miss Rockwood.

PAULINE And some choose to remain so.

JEFF Do not!

PAULINE Do too!

JEFF Am not!

PAULINE Are too!

They suddenly realize that the students have been listening to every word.

Uh… we need to get this car wash started. Do you have the key for the outside faucets, Mr. Millstone?

JEFF Huh…? Oh, yeah. It's in my pocket.

He crosses to her, looking in vain for the key in his jacket pocket.

Or I may have left it on the workbench. I remember I took it out so I wouldn't lose it. I guess I forgot to put it back.

PAULINE *(hissing to him)* Are too!

EMERY Maybe we can find one of the janitors, Mr. Millstone. He should have a key, shouldn't he?

JEFF Good idea, Emery. I'll go find one. They must be around somewhere.

PAULINE I'll go with you.

She follows him to the cafeteria door.

JEFF It's okay. I can find a janitor by myself.

PAULINE Oh, I insist.

He grimaces as she marches out behind him. MRS. G *enters from the cafeteria when the door swings back in. She crosses to the kitchen area and retrieves a punch bowl and ladle that she begins to wipe down. The kids look at each other.*

EMERY Well, looks like we're in for another one.

LACEY Yeah.

EMERY You know, I really like Mr. Millstone and I think Miss Rockwood is great. I just wish they would like each other more, know what I mean?

LACEY Exactly. For two people who live together, all they do is fight all the time.

EMERY They live together? But they're not even married. When are they gonna do that?

LACEY Maybe that's the problem. Don't you remember what we went through last year at the school fair when Miss Rockwood was hinting that they should start living together? She volunteered to sit in the water chair and Mr. Millstone must've paid out more than fifty bucks to throw the ball to hit that lever thing. That chair collapsed a dozen times. He was getting pretty good towards the end.

EMERY And she was looking like a drowned rat. Or what about the pie-throwing contest?

They all shudder in memory.

He should've known she hasn't coached the girls' softball team for nothing for the last three years. *(imitating her perfect throw)* Wow! What an arm! Mr. Millstone swallowed so much shaving cream that day, he started growing a beard for a few months. Oh, well. Let's make the best of it. If we keep them separated for most of the morning, maybe they'll end up leaving together by the afternoon.

LACEY *(looking out the window)* Too late.

EMERY What do you mean?

LACEY I guess they found a janitor to turn on the faucets.

They all look out the window and grimace.

EMERY Ooh! I bet that's cold… What are the chances he has a change of clothes in his car?

LACEY About the same as hers.

The students pick up their posters and pails, shaking their heads and grumbling about how to stop the water fight while exiting out the cafeteria door. SHARON *enters from the main door. She is wearing a pretty summer dress and carrying a purse.* MRS. G *turns and sees her.*

REUNION

MRS. G Sharon. Sharon Harrison. Well, my goodness. Look at you. How long has it been?

SHARON Gloria. How are you?

They embrace awkwardly.

It's been about ten… eleven years, I guess. And you look… exactly the same.

MRS. G Oh, Sharon. Always the diplomat. I was so thrilled to get your response to the party. There's so many of the old staff coming back. Harry will be thrilled to see you. There's going to be such a crowd that, actually, it's down in the gymnasium. Did you not see the balloons leading you down the stairs?

SHARON I surely did, Gloria. But just thought I'd come in here and freshen up first. Wanted to see the old staff room again. See all the changes. After all these years. *(She looks around.)* It looks exactly the same.

They laugh.

MRS. G Well, some things, Sharon. Some things. But how are you? How's that new school treating you?

SHARON Fine. It's not so new anymore.

MRS. G And look at you. Two babies and you still look as slim as ever. I guess that's where phys. ed. teachers have it over French teachers, eh?

SHARON Three.

MRS. G What?

SHARON I had three babies.

MRS. G Oh? Oh, yes. Well. Listen, we'll just have to catch up, so why don't you go freshen up and I'll head on down to the party? There's always some who want to leave early, and I haven't even got the punch ready yet. I'll see you down there.

She exits through the cafeteria with the punch bowl.

SHARON Sure, Gloria. See you.

She looks around the room once more then exits into the women's washroom. WARREN *enters the room. He is casually but neatly dressed and sports sunglasses on his head. He looks around the room and shakes his head in recognition. He walks over to the mailboxes and checks to see who has his now. He groans "Still here!" at one name in particular. He looks around to see if he is totally alone, then pulls out the mail from the principal's box. As he is thumbing through it,* SHARON *returns from the washroom and watches him.*

Anything interesting, Mr. Fraser?

WARREN *(startled)* Jesus Chr— Sharon.

SHARON Hello, Warren.

WARREN Hi. You scared me half to death there. I thought I was alone. *(stuffs the material back into the box)*

SHARON Still snooping in the mailboxes, I see. Is this a practice you've continued or is it just something about being here that brings out this inquisitive nature of yours?

WARREN Actually, it's harder at Hillside. The mailboxes and photocopiers are in the same room. There's always someone at the photocopier.

SHARON But you still manage.

WARREN I still manage. *(pause)* It's good to see you. I wasn't sure if you would make it back or not.

SHARON It's Harry's retirement. I had to come back for Harry. He hired me. You, too.

WARREN Yeah. I wasn't sure who would show up for this. I just hoped there would be someone I knew. Someone to talk to besides Gloria G. I saw her name on her mailbox. Isn't there a mandatory age for retirement?

SHARON *(laughs)* I gather she's still "parleying."

WARREN Does the government know that the single most viable threat to bilingualism is right here in this building?

SHARON laughs again. Awkward pause.

SHARON So… how've you been? I heard you married a few years back.

WARREN Yeah… and the divorce is final in August.

SHARON What? Oh no, Warren, I'm sorry. I didn't know that.

WARREN No? I thought that bit of news would have filtered through the gossip channel by now.

SHARON I haven't been at work for most of this year. I was off on a pregnancy leave.

WARREN Another one? Oh. Congratulations. So this was your…?

SHARON Third.

WARREN Three kids. Wow. So everything's great with you and Dan.

SHARON Dave.

WARREN What? Oh, sorry, Dave. Yeah right, Dave. Old Dave must be really happy. You both must be.

SHARON Sure… Things are a little rough at the moment. He lost his job three months ago. Downsizing. He didn't really see it coming, so it's been kind of tough. The new baby and all. Some guys are great at the Mr. Mom thing and…

WARREN Some men define themselves by their work. I gather Dave needs more definition than folded laundry and a clean kitchen floor.

SHARON Something like that. The pregnancy wasn't really planned. Just kind of happened. So, it's been a year of surprises.

WARREN You got pregnant by accident? Excuse me, Ms. Physical Education, but aren't you the one who teaches the health unit on birth control to sixteen-year-olds? I seem to recall a few practice lessons from you on how to put on and wear a condom.

SHARON That was a long time ago, Warren.

WARREN And what? That simple procedure doesn't work anymore? It worked for us. It worked for us for almost two years.

She looks away from him.

Okay, sorry. What's past is… But, Sharon, let's face it, I never knew you to have an unplanned moment in your life. Unless, of course, you want to count that July first weekend eleven years ago when you told me you were going to spend a week with your sister in Calgary. Just to see the Stampede, you said. And one week became a month. The month became a summer. You ended up driving back across the prairies with Dan—sorry, Dave, who moved in with you just after you decided to take that transfer to Cedar View High. The next thing I knew you were married that Thanksgiving. Behaviour which all seemed pretty spontaneous to me. Speaking as the one left behind here. It felt like I had been hit with a ton of bricks.

SHARON A ton of bricks? That's funny. How about if I had tossed you one brick at a time?

WARREN What are you talking about?

SHARON The bricks, Warren. The bricks that kept hitting me every time I passed these mailboxes. Oh, you taught me well, you know. "Check out Harry's box whenever you can, just to see what's coming our way." "Nothing like being prepared when the blue memos strike." You used to pride yourself on knowing who was in deep shit or which kid was going to get the boot because of the notes left in Harry's box.

WARREN I still don't understand what you're getting at.

SHARON Do you remember the day we received the memo about Gloria G. getting the headship of the moderns department? I mean, that one came out of left field, didn't it? None of us saw that coming. I remember it was the end of the day and I was standing here reading the blue-papered memo and anticipating what snide comment you would make about it. I looked in your mailbox to see if you had picked yours up yet. The blue memo was still there, but so was one of those pink phone messages. One of those while-you-were-out messages that the secretaries used to put in our boxes for us. Before we had voice mail. I know I should never have looked at your pink slip but, hey, I learned from the master. I simply put my hand inside, pulled it out as if it belonged to me, stood here, and read it. The phone call came at 2:10. You couldn't possibly have come to the phone because that was when you had your grade twelve history class. The one you complained about all the time. Of course, I would know this, but apparently Liz didn't. The message, as I recall, was actually very succinct: *Liz will be ready at six!* Ready? Ready for what? Maybe she's your dental hygienist, I thought. But a dentist doesn't phone to say, "I'll be ready for you." Dentists are never ready for you. So who was she? I returned the message to your mailbox and went over and sat on the couch. Almost immediately you came into the staff room. The giveaway, Warren, was not that you didn't mention Liz's message to me or that you said you had to head home to start in on the bundle of essays under your arm. The giveaway was that you didn't comment on Gloria's promotion. Nothing. You just tucked everything under your arm, pink slip included, and walked out of the building. I stood and watched you from the window as you drove out of the parking lot. Too distracted to make a Warren Fraser comment. I phoned you three times that night but, of course, you didn't answer. That's when I started my own mailbox mission. Not randomly as I'd seen you do. Just yours. And through the rest of May and June, once or twice a week Liz would throw another brick at us. "Call her at work." "Call her at home." "Reservations at seven." But you never once owned up about her to me. I became very good at suggesting dates with you when I knew you were already going to be with Liz. It was almost delicious watching you squirm out of them. If it didn't hurt so much. Then my sister invited me out west. And the rest, as you would say, is history.

WARREN *(long pause)* You knew about her.

SHARON I knew.

WARREN You knew and you didn't say anything. Why didn't you say anything?

SHARON I didn't know what to say... without sounding so angry. So jealous. I had to come in here every day and face you knowing you had been... I felt... stupid. Or rather I felt that you thought I was. I was young. We both were.

WARREN Liz was someone... it just sort of happened. She wasn't... important.

SHARON I think I knew that all along. That's what made it worse.

WARREN You were important. I just didn't know how much until you didn't come back. *(pause)* I didn't know that... If I had known... I should have stopped it. I should have told you.

SHARON But you didn't.

WARREN You should have... said something.

SHARON But I couldn't. And so now here we are. Eleven years later. At Harry's retirement, who, I'm sure, is being paraded all over the gymnasium floor by Gloria. I think he could use some rescuing.

WARREN Sharon…

He moves towards her.

She backs away.

SHARON I think you should go down first. If we walk in together, Gloria will have a field day.

WARREN pauses then walks to the door.

WARREN There'll be a mob of people downstairs. We probably won't get a chance to talk to each other there.

SHARON I think we already have.

He looks at her before standing and crossing to the door.

WARREN See ya, Sharon.

SHARON Bye, Warren.

He exits. SHARON watches the door for a few seconds then crosses to the telephone. She dials a number.

Hi, sweetheart… Just calling to see if you were home yet. So, how did you do…? Third? Wow, Angela, that's great. How many were in your swim meet…? A ribbon? So how many is that now…? And did you get there on time…? Why…? Where did you leave it…? Didn't we have this talk last night about being more organized to help Daddy out…? What is he doing now…? Yes, if he's close by… Hi, I've just arrived… I haven't even seen Harry yet… I'll be home as soon as I can, Dave, but I can't leave until Harry gives his speech… I don't know… All right… All right… I don't know. I haven't been downstairs yet. Old friends, I guess… just lots of old friends… I'll try… Bye.

She hangs up the phone and sits quietly for a few moments. Suddenly the staff-room door bursts open and two men stagger in, one holding up the other. The first man, PAUL, leads the second one, BRUCE, into the men's washroom. SHARON exits through the office door as PAUL backs out of the washroom door. MAXINE enters from the women's washroom and bumps into PAUL.

GRADUATION

MAXINE Hey… sorry.

PAUL Oh my God.

MAXINE What's wrong, Paul? Shouldn't you be in the cafeteria getting the graduates organized? Inga will have your head if she finds you're not doing what she assigned you to do. You know what a Hitler she is about this night. "Ve vill start on time. Ve vill finish on time. No one vill disrupt my graduation ceremony. No one." *(looks at him and realizes he isn't laughing)* Paul, I was doing Inga. You usually love it when the school secretary imitates the vice-principal. Paul, why are you staring at the bathroom door?

PAUL It's Bruce Jameson.

MAXINE Who's Bruce Jameson?

PAUL Bruce Jameson. From the board office. He's here to give out the senior diplomas and deliver the opening speech tonight. The greetings from the board speech.

MAXINE So, he's in the bathroom? Why are you staring at it?

PAUL I phoned him a few days ago to confirm that he would be attending the ceremony. I told him that a few of us would be getting together for dinner beforehand and if it was more convenient for him, he could meet us at the Trough at five o'clock. Everything seemed to be going well and then suddenly he turned really pale and said he felt sick. He couldn't even drive over here. I had to bring him in my car. I was driving with one hand on the wheel and the other pushing his head out the passenger window. He was throwing up all along Main Street. It was awful.

MAXINE What's wrong with him?

PAUL I'm not sure, but it could have been the six Scotches with beer chasers he drank.

MAXINE What? Are you crazy? Why did you let him drink so much?

PAUL It was happy hour! It was two-for-one prices. How was I supposed to know the guy was a lush? I thought maybe he was just nervous about having to give a speech or something. Maybe he's heard about Inga Herrmann before. I know I belted back a few thinking about her. She's a maniac about the graduation ceremony. She's going to kill me. He's the newest member to the board. She hasn't met him yet and told me to take special care of him at dinner. She's going to absolutely, positively torture me with every fibre of her vice-principal's being if I don't get him in shape for the ceremony.

INGA Herrmann slams open the cafeteria door. She is wearing a convocation gown and carrying a clipboard. She blows on the whistle around her neck. There is sound of a crowd coming from the cafeteria. This sound should occur each time the cafeteria door opens.

INGA Hartford! I'm looking for you, Hartford! You are supposed to be in the cafeteria organizing the graduates and award winners. You're not there, Hartford. I see you in here. Why are you in here instead of there?

PAUL I—

INGA In there, Hartford. Follow me. Now.

PAUL hurries to the cafeteria door and follows INGA inside, returning immediately to whisper to MAXINE.

PAUL Don't leave this room. Watch that door. I'll be right back.

MAXINE turns slowly to look at the door. She tentatively opens it and calls in.

MAXINE Uh… Mr. Jameson? *(no response)* Are you all right, Mr. Jameson? Do you need some assistance?

There is a loud groan from the room.

Oh.

She looks around for help but sees none is there. Just then, Mr. Slodovonik, the night janitor, enters with his trolley and broom.

Oh, thank God. Listen. I really need your help. There's a man, a very important man, in the men's room. He's sick and he needs some help. I'm not sure what condition he's in so I don't think I should go in there, so could you please go in to see if we should call an ambulance or something?

She opens the door for the caretaker who stands looking at her.

His name is Bruce Jameson. Quickly.

MR. S *(in broken English)* Hello. How you are?

MAXINE Hello. Didn't you hear what I just explained to you? This could be life and death here.

MR. S I am fine. Too.

He smiles at her.

MAXINE Oh no. *(slowly)* Do you speak any English? English?

MR. S Yes. Hello. How you are. I am fine. Too. *(pointing to the cart)* Broom.

He smiles at his accomplishments. MAXINE is shaking her head when PAUL suddenly sticks his head out from the cafeteria door.

PAUL Has Jameson come out yet?

MAXINE *(crossing to him)* No. Get back in here and go see how he is. I can't go in there. What if he's sitting on the john or something?

PAUL I will in a sec. Adolph's on a bit of a rampage in here. *(pleading)* Please, don't leave, in case he comes out.

INGA *(from the cafeteria)* Hartford!

PAUL Gotta go!

MAXINE looks after him helplessly as STELLA Simpson enters the staff room.

STELLA Oh, Miss Boyd, I'm so glad someone is here. Mrs. Herrmann said I should be able to find extra trays in here for the food after the ceremony. The parents' association has been really generous this year. We seem to be overflowing with baked goods. I guess it helped that I handed out some suggested recipes at our last meeting. The fudge brownies are just pouring in.

MAXINE *(obviously distracted)* There may be some over in the kitchen. I don't know.

STELLA Are you all right? Is something wrong?

MAXINE Oh. A little situation has developed and I'm not sure what to do about it.

STELLA Maybe I can help. I haven't been the president of the parents' association for the past four years for nothing. I'm really good at emergencies. What is it?

MAXINE I don't really think I should involve you in this, Mrs. Simpson. You're dealing with the cookies. And Inga, Mrs. Herrmann, goes berserk when people don't do exactly what they're told.

STELLA Nonsense. I can multi-task. I'm a homemaker.

MAXINE Well, here goes. You see, there's a very sick man in the men's washroom.

She looks at the washroom door.

STELLA A pervert?

MAXINE No. No. A man from the board office. He was supposed to give out diplomas tonight but he went for supper and we think he may have had a few too many… raw shrimp. Mr. Hartford brought him here, and he's been groaning in the bathroom, and we don't know whether to call an ambulance or clean him up and push him up on stage anyway because Inga expects him to be on stage in exactly…

INGA *(opens cafeteria door and whistles)* Fifteen minutes to processional! Mrs. Simpson? What are you doing in here?

STELLA Just getting the trays, Mrs. Herrman. Remember?

INGA Right. Carry on.

She exits.

STELLA First of all, someone needs to check on this man immediately.

She looks at the janitor, who is preoccupied with dusting.

MAXINE I tried that already. Don't go there.

PAUL enters quickly from the cafeteria.

PAUL Okay, she's gone to check on the awards table. What's happening?

He jumps when he sees STELLA.

MAXINE He's still in there. You better see what's happening.

PAUL Right.

STELLA I'll go with you.

They look at her.

I nurse part-time. Nothing will shock me.

PAUL and STELLA exit into the men's washroom. MAXINE follows and stares at the door. FRANK, the sleazy photocopier repairman, enters the room. He is casually dressed with his shirt sleeves rolled up and chewing bubble gum.

FRANK Hey, doll, if I had known you were that desperate, I would've tried harder to talk you into that date this afternoon.

MAXINE Not you again. I thought you fixed that photocopier hours ago and slithered away from here.

FRANK I had to go back to pick up a bigger part… for the machine, sweetheart, not for me. It won't take me long to install it.

MAXINE *(under her breath)* I bet.

FRANK And when I finish, how about you and me gettin' together for that little drink I talked to you about over your desk this afternoon.

MAXINE I'm sorry but I don't know of any place in the area that serves pond scum.

FRANK I love that you're a challenge. You think about it while I put that piece in place. *(creepily)* I know exactly where to put it.

He exits into the office.

MAXINE *(disgustedly)* Oooohhhh!

PAUL enters from the men's room.

PAUL Well, I'm dead meat now.

MAXINE What's happened?

PAUL Old Jameson is hugging the toilet bowl. He refuses to part with it. There's no way he's going up on that stage. Inga is going to hang me out to dry. She's going to blame me for taking him to the Trough for dinner and getting him drunk. I'm going to be transferred to the farthest region of this board, where they spend their lunch hours square dancing and pig calling. I am so dead.

MAXINE There must be something we can do. Where's Mrs. Simpson?

PAUL She's still in there. She seems to think we should let nature take its course for a while and transport him when it seems a little… safer. She's pouring water down him so he doesn't get dehydrated. She managed to get his jacket and tie off him so he's not a complete mess.

MAXINE That's it!

PAUL What?

MAXINE You said that Inga has never met Mr. Jameson, right?

PAUL Yeah. He's new. Some bigwig superintendent hired from Ottawa or London or somewhere. Why? I don't get it.

MAXINE Look, all you have to do is get someone into his jacket and tie and pretend to be Jameson.

PAUL What?

MAXINE Come on. You must have a friend in the area who would come over and do this favour for you. Think.

PAUL *(checking his watch)* In twelve minutes, I don't think so. *(suddenly seeing the janitor)* Hey, what about him?

He immediately runs over and grabs the janitor by the shoulders and rushes him into the men's room, explaining to him what he needs.

MAXINE *(calling out)* No, not him. He won't do. You don't understand.

INGA *(enters from the cafeteria door and blows her whistle)* Ten minutes until processional. Where's Hartford? He's left his post. Did he come in here?

MAXINE *(guarding the men's door)* Why, no. I haven't seen him, Inga.

INGA *(checking her clipboard)* He's supposed to be on his triple-check of the graduates to see that they are in an alpha line. I want them to be in perfect alpha order.

MAXINE I'm sure he's in there somewhere, Inga. There are so many kids you probably just missed him.

INGA *(exiting into cafeteria)* Hartford!

FRANK enters from the office wearing a suit jacket and adjusting his tie.

FRANK Hey, shouldn't you have your coat on by now? Too busy daydreaming about our date, eh?

He blows a large bubble.

MAXINE Oh will you dry up. Read my lips, machine man: it ain't happening. No drink. No date. Nothing.

She bursts his bubble.

Nada.

FRANK But are you sure?

PAUL and the janitor enter from the men's room holding BRUCE Jameson between them. He is completely dishevelled and somewhat groggy. The janitor remains totally confused throughout the rest of the scene, not really understanding why he has been dressed in different clothes but willing to co-operate with anyone. He is dressed in BRUCE's jacket and tie but the jacket is hugely oversized for the man and the tie clashes with his blue work shirt. STELLA follows behind them.

STELLA Just lay him out on the couch. He's exhausted from all that retching. He needs to rest for a while.

PAUL *(struggling to put BRUCE down)* There we go, Bruce. You can lie here. Don't worry about going up on the stage. It's all taken care of. I'll just get Mr.... what's your name again...? Mr.... Never mind. This man will fill in for you and everything will be fine.

MAXINE Paul. This guy can't fill in for Mr. Jameson.

As he pulls the janitor across to the cafeteria door.

PAUL Look, Maxine, I don't have time to argue with you now. I've got seven minutes to get this guy to the front of the processional line, explain to him that he has to pretend to be from the school board, and offer greetings and shake some hands of some teenagers. It's a cinch.

MAXINE *(urgently)* Paul!

PAUL *(exasperated)* What?

MAXINE What's this man's name?

PAUL I don't know. We haven't had the time to make a proper acquaintance for God's sake.

MAXINE I think you'd better talk to him—now!

PAUL Sorry, Mr.... I'm sorry but I didn't get your name in there. *(shaking hands)* Hello.

MR. S Hello. How you are.

PAUL Pardon?

MR. S I am fine. Too. *(pointing to his cart)* Broom.

PAUL *(looking at MAXINE and falling to his knees)* Aaaahhh! I was so close, Maxine. I was almost there. I almost managed to pull this off. Inga Herrmann is going to have my head on a platter. She is going to absolutely, positively—

INGA enters from the cafeteria and catches PAUL on his knees.

INGA Five minutes to processional. Places everybody. Mr. Hartford, what are you doing down there?

Everyone looks at PAUL as he struggles with what he will say.

FRANK *(with complete charm)* I believe he's doing me a favour, madam. My name is Jameson, Bruce Jameson. I'm the representative from the board office who will be speaking this evening. My contact lens fell out and this fine young man has helped me retrieve it. I wouldn't be able to read my speech otherwise.

INGA Well, fine. Get up now, Hartford. Get Mr. Jameson in line and then get in there to lead the procession down the hall. Make sure you take a garbage can along with you to collect gum from any chewing graduate. No one chews on my stage! Including you, Jameson!

He mimes swallowing and then she exits. "Pomp and Circumstance" is heard from beyond the door.

PAUL *(shaking FRANK's hand)* Wow. Thanks, man. Are you sure you're okay with this? I can't thank you enough. Whatever you want, you got it.

FRANK I want a date with her *(pointing to MAXINE)* at the end of this gig.

MAXINE What? Are you crazy? No way. Uh-uh!

FRANK *(starting to leave)* Have it your way. And to think that your little problem was almost solved.

PAUL Wait. Maxine. Please. Do it for me.

MAXINE You can't expect me to go out with this creep!

PAUL *(begging)* Yeah. I can. Please, Maxine. For me. *(pointing to the cafeteria)* She hates me. She'll make my life miserable. You know I can't square dance.

INGA *(from the cafeteria)* Two minutes, Hartford!

STELLA I really think you should, dear.

MAXINE What?

STELLA It's just one date, after all.

Everyone stares at MAXINE, hoping she will say yes. Even the janitor senses the tension and looks pleadingly at her.

MAXINE Oh… all right.

Everyone is relieved at the decision, including the janitor who joins in on the congratulations.

(to PAUL) You owe me big time for this!

PAUL *(as he exits into the cafeteria with FRANK)* You got it. Come on, buddy, I'll show you where to go. Do you think you'll be able to talk for a few minutes at the beginning about the importance of education and all that crap?

FRANK Not really, but I could give you ten minutes on how to install the new XS-400 Multicopier. *(turning to MAXINE before he exits)* See you later, doll face.

MAXINE glares after him.

STELLA Don't worry about him, dear. Things will be fine.

MAXINE You don't know him, Mrs. Simpson. He's such a snake. He makes my skin crawl.

STELLA I recognize his kind. That's why I've decided to go along on your date with you.

MAXINE What?

STELLA Besides being a homemaker, nurse, and president of the parents' group, I'm also an excellent chaperone, and it looks as if you're going to need one.

MAXINE *(hugging her)* Thanks so much, Mrs. Simpson.

STELLA Besides, I think I could use a stiff drink after tonight. And the snake can buy. Now, how about helping me arrange the baked goods? The other mothers are probably wondering what happened to me.

They exit into the office. A large groaning sigh comes from the couch. The janitor looks over and remembers the man he carried from the washroom. He goes over and looks at him.

MR. S Hello. How you are.

No response. He looks at his new jacket and tie and at the man again. He shrugs his shoulders and pushes his cart into the cafeteria. There is a moment of silence and then STUART sticks his head into the door from the office. He looks around carefully and then enters. He is carrying a small bag and a newspaper. He goes to the kitchen area and checks the coffee. It is empty. He smiles, walks over to the table, sits down, and slowly opens his bag. He carefully takes out a large recognizable coffee cup from Tim Hortons, Second Cup, Starbucks—whatever—and proceeds to slowly lift the lid. He puts his feet up, opens the paper on the table in front of him, and sighs. He is about to lift the cup to his lips and enjoy his first morning sip of coffee when a loud moan comes from the couch. STUART freezes. Then more horribly loud and inexplicable groans come from the couch as BRUCE Jameson wakes up to find himself in a place he can't remember and missing his clothes. He struggles to his feet, turns and sees STUART. He staggers to the table, eyes fixed on the large coffee. STUART stares at him.

BRUCE Black?

STUART looks at his coffee, then at him, then slowly slides the coffee over to the stranger. BRUCE picks up the coffee and heads for the door as STUART stares out at the audience.

Blackout.

The end.

A YEAR IN EDNA'S KITCHEN

BY SANDY CONRAD

MUSIC AND LYRICS BY IAN BURBIDGE AND SANDY CONRAD

NOTES

In 2003, the Kincardine Theatre Guild mounted a new play by Sandy Conrad titled *A Year In Edna's Kitchen*. Ian Burbidge wrote original music and songs for interludes. Though a fictional story, the play is set in the context of one of the most unnecessary rural tragedies in recent Canadian history. In May 2000, an outbreak of E. coli polluted the water supply in Walkerton, Ontario, killing at least seven people. Contamination from farm runoff was eventually identified as the reason why two thousand five hundred people became ill. Sandy Conrad and Ian Burbidge live near Paisley, Ontario, very close to Walkerton.

Sandy Conrad is a high-school English teacher and originally wrote *A Year in Edna's Kitchen* as a school production for Chesley District High School where she taught. The idea caught the attention of Anne Chislett at the Blyth Festival and Sandy was asked to do a complete rewrite, working with dramaturge Suzanne Turnbull. That version had a public reading at the Blyth Festival. When the Kincardine Theatre Guild asked Sandy and Ian to submit the play for their 2002/2003 season, Sandy wrote a third draft of the play.

A Year in Edna's Kitchen was presented at the 2003 Western Ontario Drama League festival hosted by Galt Little Theatre. One festival veteran turned to his companion at the end of the curtain call and was heard to say "Yup. That's a keeper," and it clearly was. A few years later, Elora Community Theatre mounted a second production of this play, delighting sold-out houses for two weeks.

This version of *A Year In Edna's Kitchen* premiered at the Kincardine Theatre Guild in Kincardine, Ontario, during their 2002/2003 season with the following cast and crew:

Edna	Gloria Durrant
Jack	Rob Millar
Gina	Sarah Millar
Jeff	Scott Mullenix
Carol	Saoirse Cameron
Grandpa	Jim Peddie
Ruth	Linda Mielke
Linda	Shirley Bieman
Wilf	Ken Inglis
Joe	Bob Richards

Producer: Stacey Millar, Reg Daze
Director: Sandy Conrad
Music Director: Ian Burbidge
Stage Manager: Caroline Gorski
Lighting Design: William McLaughlin
Sound: Tom Humphrey, Justin Boucher, Mike Walsh
Costumes: Leise Peddle, Trish Richards
Piano / Voice: Ian Burbidge
Fiddle: Chris Lazarenko
Guitar: Margaret Wysman
Mandolin / Guitar: Tim Bellamy
Bass: Lou Tusz

A Year In Edna's Kitchen was developed with the assistance of the Blyth Festival's Roulston Roy New Play Development Fund, 1998.

CHARACTERS

CAROL Weber
EDNA Cameron
GINA Cameron
GRANDPA Henry Weber
JACK Cameron
JEFF Cameron
JOE
LINDA
MUSICIAN
RUTH Bender
WILF

NOTES

Information in square brackets [ ] is a local reference, and any theatre doing a performance of this play is invited to substitute their own local references and place names.

ACT ONE

SCENE ONE

The MUSICIAN *and* CHORUS *sing "A Farmer's Life" between the following three vignettes.*

VIGNETTE ONE

MUSICIAN Stones on the wagon, seeds in the ground
Equal parts of sun and rain.
Finally get a harvest worth bragging about,
Then the price goes down the drain,
And you start all over again.

A bright, fresh day in late August, 7:30 p.m. The hockey moms, JOE, JACK, *and* WILF *are at the horse track.*

WILF Get a good price for your cattle this year?

JACK Well, [Montgomery] *(local car dealership)* won't be selling me a new truck this fall, but I should be able to heat the house for the winter. How 'bout you?

WILF Same old, same old. One step forward, twenty steps back. You'd have to be selling air conditioners or swimming pools to be getting rich this summer.

JACK Least you've still got your looks, Wilf.

WILF Damn straight. Looks and brains. And my brains are telling me that I've spent too many years sweatin like a pig and prayin for rain.

JACK Comes with the job.

WILF Comes with the old job, Jack. Have you ever been in one of those hog barns they have down country? One man can run the whole operation.

JACK Hog barn?

WILF Seems that farming is changing and we're getting left in the dust.

JACK I just never thought of a hog barn as a farm.

WILF Why not? A pig's a pig. Maybe we're all just gettin too used to losin money instead of makin it.

JACK How much money do they make?

WILF A lot, Jack. A lot!

MUSICIAN & CHORUS

It's a farmer's life,
And it gets in the blood,
The way the eyes can read the sky
And with a tractor and plow
Write stories in the mud,
But if just one year it would all go as planned
From January to December,
Then that would be some kind of year,
Now that would be a year to remember.

VIGNETTE TWO

A hot and humid day, late August, 10:30 a.m. EDNA and CAROL are exchanging recipes and vegetables in the kitchen.

EDNA Here's the one for salsa *(handing CAROL a recipe)* and this one's for chocolate cake.

CAROL And once again… we put zucchini in cake because…?

EDNA Moistness… healthier… and… it uses them up.

CAROL Got it. And they can't tell it's in there, right?

EDNA You are catching on!

CAROL *(indicating two bushels of corn on the cob)* You really don't mind taking this corn. Aren't you all sick of it?

EDNA I'm freezing it. If my calculations are right, I won't have to buy corn again till May… as long as we only eat it twice a week.

CAROL But it's not that expensive…

EDNA Store-bought doesn't taste the same. I can always tell when it's the real thing.

CAROL I just want to get a job. Planning lessons and marking papers will seem like a holiday after this summer. Gardening is a nightmare. Everything gets ripe at the same time.

EDNA It just seems that way. This was your first time with a garden. You've got the knack. Remember your strawberry crop. Mom never had one like that all the years she lived there.

CAROL Don't remind me. I haven't even been able to eat strawberry ice cream since the jam-making marathon.

EDNA Next year you'll be doing pickles.

CAROL No. Never. I'm not even going to grow cucumbers next summer.

EDNA You're too good at it. You'll see. Come February, you'll be ordering your seeds like the rest of us.

MUSICIAN & HOCKEY MOMS

Cows gaining weight every time you turn around
The price is at an all-time high
You're thinking 'bout the furniture that you could replace
But he's got that look in his eye
And there's a new field tractor to buy.

VIGNETTE THREE

A cool day in late August, 11:30 a.m. LINDA *and* RUTH *are at an outdoor market.* GINA *is selling apples.*

LINDA *(to* GINA*)* Hey slugger. When're you going back to school?

GINA Not till Monday.

RUTH Nice hitting this weekend. What an arm.

GINA *(hamming it up)* I was home-run queen of the tournament.

LINDA Now that's something to admire. Would you believe that my daughter wants to run for Queen of the Furrow?

RUTH Thank goodness I had three sons. I couldn't do all that girl stuff.

LINDA I can't either. How did I get such a… a "girl" for a daughter? She hates baseball and loves clothes. *(to* GINA*)* Will you please take her shopping in London next weekend?

GINA Can't. I'll be here. You could bring her down right after school on Thursday and we could hit all the malls.

LINDA No, she wants a whole weekend in stores. Yuck! Maybe I can get her grandmother to take her.

GINA Sorry, but we're getting ready for the fall fairs and Pumpkinfest.

RUTH Now, your mom promised she wouldn't enter her jam this year. It's my turn for the red ribbon. She promised.

GINA I honestly don't know what Mom is entering, but I'm sure she'll leave you one victory in the jam competition. I'm entering our hay and… um… squash.

LINDA How is that pet pumpkin of yours anyway? Big enough to live in yet?

GINA Never mind. You'll have to wait and see like everybody else.

MUSICIAN & CHORUS

You're a farmer's wife
And it gets in the blood,
The way the eyes can read the sky
And with water and seed
Write stories in mud,
But if just one year it would all go as planned
From January to December,
Well that would be some kind of year,
Now, that would be a year to remember.

SCENE TWO

In the kitchen, about 8:30 a.m. Breakfast is out but the dishes aren't done.

GINA enters from upstairs looking like she just got out of bed.

GINA Where's Dad?

She pours herself a coffee. EDNA sits at the table looking over bills with piles of papers around her.

EDNA He and Grandpa went into town early to get a battery for the truck. Jim Anderson's coming at 11:00 to pick up the cattle.

GINA The market's not very good.

EDNA No… I don't know if we're going to cover the cost of the feed. We had to buy hay this year, and you can see for yourself how much corn we're likely going to take off that field.

GINA Why doesn't it rain anymore? It's like the thirties. More coffee?

EDNA Thanks. So, tell me about your week. Did they initiate you or anything?

GINA Hardly. Most of what I heard is how hard the course is and how there are no decent jobs in Canada. They predict that a bunch of us will fail by January.

EDNA When's the last time you even came close to failing anything?

GINA I didn't say I was going to fail.

EDNA Meet any nice people?

GINA Look, I know my college is costing money.

EDNA That's not something you should be worried about. After all the work you've done here, we probably owe you… even after we pay for college.

JEFF appears in pyjamas from upstairs.

JEFF Look who's here.

GINA Look who's up!

JEFF It's Saturday. A lot of guys my age won't be seeing the sun this morning. But not me—I am under strict orders to be out of bed by the time Dad gets home… whenever that is.

GINA Why don't you just get up at the same time every morning? It would be better for your body.

JEFF Ahhh… it's an alien. *(shaking* GINA*)* What have you done with my father? Let him out right now. I know he's in there.

GINA Quit it… I'm in training to be a nurse. I'll be passing on everything I can to improve your health. I see fibre in your future.

JEFF I don't believe in fibre.

GINA That's rational.

JEFF If I don't believe in it, it doesn't exist. Right? If a tree falls in the forest does it make a noise?

GINA If you fell in the forest, would I care?

JEFF *(taking his coffee over to the computer)* Still resorting to insults… too bad. I thought higher education might have sharpened your wits.

EDNA Don't get comfortable there, Jeff. Your dad wants you ready and waiting—and that means dressed.

JEFF "Don't get comfortable"—if I had a dime every time I heard that… I'll just check our email and one website… okay?

EDNA Do they have classifieds on the Internet?

JEFF They have everything on the Net. What do you want to buy?

EDNA I don't want to buy anything. I'm looking for a job.

GINA What?

JEFF Why?

EDNA Don't look at me like that. It's not that big a deal.

GINA But you've always been at home. What are you qualified for?

EDNA Thank you, Gina. I don't think I'm "qualified" for anything, but I do have a high-school diploma. I just need to bring some money into this family for a while.

JEFF Why? Are we poor all of a sudden?

EDNA According to this *(holding up a statement)* we are.

GINA We're not poor. We own a farm.

EDNA We owe the bank, even after all these years.

GINA The farm is paid for.

EDNA Not if we re-mortgage it to buy another one.

JEFF The farm for Jeff you mean?

EDNA I'd bet Gina's tuition that that's where your dad and mine are right now.

GINA When did this get decided?

EDNA Well, it's just talk at this point.

GINA Why doesn't Jeff buy his own farm?

JEFF Ya, why doesn't he?

EDNA Why don't you have this conversation with your father? You haven't answered my question—are there job postings on that thing?

JEFF Probably lots, but not for around here. I think I just found a site for people who need help getting a date, though. Interested, Gina?

GINA What are you asking me for? I've got a boyfriend. You're the one who went to the prom last spring with a bunch of guys.

JEFF And girls! We just didn't go as couples.

EDNA Are there any nice-looking boys in your class?

GINA I don't know… yes… I guess… some. I'm not exactly looking!

JEFF You should be. Barry Gold is strictly high-school material.

GINA Is the dateless brother giving relationship advice to his popular sister?

EDNA Wouldn't it be fun to date someone new for a change?

JEFF A guy who knows words with more than two syllables?

GINA Mom, what kind of advice is that? Drop a guy I care about just for a "change"?

EDNA I hate to see you get tied down.

GINA You don't like Barry?

EDNA He's fine—

GINA But?

EDNA You've been going out with him since you were in grade ten.

GINA And when did you start going out with Dad?

EDNA I don't think you should be modelling yourself after me. *(indicating her table mess)* How glamorous and exciting is this? Forty years old and looking for my first job.

GINA I didn't say I was trying to be you. All I'm saying is that I have a nice boyfriend already.

EDNA Fine.

JEFF Mom, I think your best bet is the local papers.

EDNA I've been watching for something… there's not much out there.

JACK and GRANDPA Henry enter.

GINA Hi Dad. Hi Grandpa. Coffee?

GINA gets coffee for JACK and GRANDPA.

GRANDPA Look who's home! Double-double.

GINA I remember.

JACK Got in a bit late last night. Thought you'd still be sleeping.

JEFF Maybe you should go from business to business and fill out applications.

JACK Your mother doesn't need to apply for anything. That plan is dead in the water, Edna. Are you ready to get to the barn?

EDNA We need money.

JACK Not necessary. I know how I can make some. Henry and I popped over to Mike's this morning. You know he's putting up a hog barn.

EDNA He was thinking about it.

JACK No, he's doing it. He's got the applications filled in and ready to go. I think that's the way for us to go, too.

EDNA What?

GRANDPA Guaranteed price for five years! A one-man operation. You could make ninety thousand bucks the first year… and pay off the barn in five.

GINA I thought you didn't approve of factory farms, Dad?

JACK I don't approve of losing money every year either, or market prices that screw me out of a decent living, or NAFTA… I'm tired of working for nothing.

EDNA This is a big switch from buying another farm down the road.

JACK Well, Henry wanted me to talk to your brother and see what I thought.

EDNA Dad wanted you to?

GRANDPA I'd help him run it till Jeff finishes school.

GINA Are you going to put the barn up here? Our neighbours will hate us.

JACK First of all, you don't say anything to the neighbours till I've got the approval. And secondly, it's my business what I do with my land. I thought of all people you would appreciate this idea. You're the one who's always talking about farmers staying up with the times. What's more efficient than two thousand hogs in one barn looked after by one man?

GINA Did you say two thousand?

JEFF That is a lot of manure.

JACK It's all liquid. You keep it in the lagoon and spread it once, maybe twice a year.

EDNA And keep your windows shut for about a week. You mean to tell me that we're going to be living beside an open sewer? When will I hang out my laundry?

JACK We'd be making enough money for you to use the dryer.

EDNA I don't want to. I like the way it smells when it's been hanging outside.

JACK I'm not arguing about laundry. Do you want to work at Tim Hortons? Is it a bad thing to have cash rolling in for a change? Jeff, are you ready? Jim's going to be here any minute.

GINA I'll be right out.

JACK No rush. Why don't you explain to your mother how much she'd be able to buy if we were business people instead of poor farmers? You better be right behind us.

JACK and GRANDPA exit.

JEFF Poor? I never knew we were poor before!

GINA Do you have any clue what this farm is worth?

JEFF *(getting his rubber boots on)* Oh ya… I know what it's worth.

GINA I don't like Dad's idea, Mom… those people with the contracts… they don't just give money away.

EDNA Well, you won't have to worry about it—you won't be living here to smell it. And what would be wrong with me working at Tim Hortons?

GINA *(pulling on rubber boots also)* Oh right, I keep forgetting that I'm not allowed to care about the farm anymore because I'm an "educated" city girl.

EDNA Which is a lot more than I had at your age.

GINA Please, spare me. I've heard it a million times.

EDNA Have you? *(as GINA exits)* I don't think you've even "heard" it once!

SCENE THREE

Rain at supper hour late in September. CAROL, RUTH, and LINDA are at hockey registration night in the local elementary school gym. RUTH is already in line with her application and chequebook out.

MUSICIAN & CHORUS

It just might be your ticket to big money and fame
It just might be the best ride of your life.
You'll be king of the castle,
They'll all know your name,
If you're fast on your feet
At the hockey game.
Sometimes it's the moment when the blade hits the ice
Or the sound of the buzzer after goal number two,
A rush of good feeling,
A natural high.
It's everything right, and it's not always easy
But for now, it's your life.

LINDA *(entering in a wet raincoat)* Whatever happened to in-between weather? Now it's either hot and dry, or cold and wet. Don't we get fall anymore?

RUTH Why didn't we have this rain two months ago? I don't like to water the garden, but if I hadn't, our corn would still be this high. *(shows LINDA that the corn would be up to her knees)*

LINDA I would've just been watering weeds. I can't keep up and I don't really want to. It's Ray who wants the garden, but he can't spare the boys for an hour to do some weeding.

RUTH Doesn't Jane help?

LINDA You mean Queen of the Furrow Jane. Hardly. It's not worth the fight. But I told her she better have a job by next summer. *(beat)* How long is this gonna take? I didn't thaw anything for supper.

RUTH It won't be long.

LINDA Sometimes I wish I'd had triplets, and they could all play on the same team. Now I've got Shawn and Eric to taxi around—different games and different practice times. How did you do it with three?

RUTH I never minded. Sitting in a car, then sitting in an arena drinking hot chocolate and Baileys was a lot more exciting than cleaning out stalls. Now Teddy can drive so I just have Tyler and Tom to get around.

LINDA Tyler's playing again. I thought—

RUTH Tyler is thirteen, not old enough to decide what he's going to do in his free time. I'd rather be watching him play hockey than worrying about what he's doing with his so-called friends in town.

LINDA Eric will be happy to see him back.

RUTH If he'd just try a little harder, the coach wouldn't have to hound him all the time.

LINDA Jack's been pretty fair with the boys. The ones who show up for the practices always get played. I like that.

RUTH Tyler says that Jack "gets on his case."

LINDA Jack? If anything, he doesn't push the boys hard enough. I would not let them get away with half the stuff he does.

RUTH I think you mentioned that to him.

LINDA Yes… and I'm not sure he appreciated it.

RUTH Well, not when you yelled it three times during the game. He seemed a little put out.

LINDA That's putting it mildly. Hey… I call it as I see it.

RUTH Speaking of Camerons, isn't that Jack's sister-in-law?

LINDA It sure is.

Calling out to CAROL *who's walking by with her briefcase, umbrella, and raincoat.*

Carol. Hi. We were just talking about your brother-in-law.

CAROL Really. Why?

LINDA He was our sons' hockey coach last year. Have you met Ruth Bender? Ruth, this is Carol Weber.

CAROL I think we met at one of my showers. Nice to see you again.

RUTH Nice to see you again. You know, we actually like Jack just fine, but he'd never guess.

CAROL I forgot that he coaches hockey.

RUTH How could you forget? You married into a hockey family. Your Mike was quite a local star for a few years.

CAROL Really, that doesn't surprise me at all.

Awkward silence.

LINDA You're here late.

CAROL Oh… this is pretty typical. I got this maternity-leave grade eight class at the last minute, and I don't feel like I'll ever catch up. My bulletin boards are an embarrassment.

RUTH I'm sure you'll be fine. Who's pregnant?

CAROL Ellen Cooper… I think that's her name.

RUTH *(to LINDA)* Oh, Frank Johnston's wife… they live out on the Sixth Concession. She kept her own name. I always wonder why they do that.

CAROL Oh… I… guess they just like it.

LINDA Sad for the kids to have different names from the mother though.

CAROL Yes… I guess.

RUTH Mike coaching this year?

CAROL No, he's got a few "irons in the fire" so to speak. Too busy. He wants us to curl together.

LINDA You'll love it. Ray and I will see you there, and Thursdays are ladies' nights.

CAROL No… no… can't do it. Baseball was great; beer fund was excellent. But I can't give up a school night.

RUTH You need to get out in the winter or the weeks really drag.

CAROL Well, the job is full-time, so… I don't think this winter's going to drag much. Thanks anyway.

LINDA At least come and see a few games with us. We'll teach you how to be a good hockey mother.

RUTH Oh, something I should know?

CAROL What? Me… NO. Not yet.

RUTH Never too soon, dear.

LINDA *(indicating the registration desk)* Ruth, it's your turn.

RUTH Right… well, it was nice to meet you again. Hope to see you in the arena. *(exits)*

LINDA You'll get used to Ruth. She likes to organize everybody. She and I keep these coaches in line. They're all afraid of us.

CAROL I can believe it.

LINDA You gotta show them who's boss, right.

CAROL I guess. There seems to be a lot of that going around.

SCENE FOUR

A very cold but sunny Saturday morning on Thanksgiving weekend. EDNA's peeling apples in the kitchen, JEFF's organizing his music and trumpet, getting ready to depart.

EDNA You'll be here for supper?

JEFF Probably not. The rehearsal's over at four, but I think we're going to see *The Sixth Sense* in [Owen Sound].

EDNA Did you tell your teacher you have your own church to go to on Thanksgiving?

JEFF I almost never go. I didn't think it would be a big deal.

EDNA It's a family day. Gina's home. We're all going, even your dad.

JEFF Gina's home every weekend. I'd be more excited if she actually stayed in London.

EDNA She will. You know your sister… doesn't like to let anybody down, and she seems to have a lot of commitments here. Eventually she'll make the transition.

JEFF If you say so.

EDNA She doesn't like change, never has.

JEFF *(sneaking some cut-up apples)* Aren't we having pumpkin pie?

EDNA Both. Apple's Mike and Grandpa's favourite.

JEFF I wish Mike and Carol weren't coming.

EDNA How can you say that? Mike's my only brother.

JEFF They're brutal together… They're either ignoring each other or arguing. I hate that.

EDNA Couples shouldn't fight in public. Mike knows better than that.

JEFF Well he's giving as good as he gets.

EDNA The first year of marriage is tough, especially for Carol. She's new to the area, new job.

JEFF Ya, she gave up a lot.

EDNA She knew what she was getting into… not that I blame her. But she did make the choice. *(beat)* It's better if we don't get involved. The less we know, the less embarrassed we'll all be when it blows over.

JEFF Why is it we're "family" whenever there's a special occasion, but strangers when it comes to feelings or "personal issues"?

EDNA It's called respect. We respect privacy. Where do you come up with these questions anyway?

JEFF I have a lot of time to think when I'm plowing. I can't read… can't hear my Walkman. I have to have something to occupy my mind.

EDNA Your dad thinks you read too much.

JEFF Ya… 'cause he doesn't like reading. It would be okay if I was busy playing hockey or euchre like him.

EDNA He works hard; don't take that away from him. Farms are a lot of work all the time, and some of it is quite boring.

JEFF I know. Jeez… why do you think you have to tell me that?

EDNA I'm just being realistic about things.

JEFF You're forty now—you don't have a choice.

EDNA Jeff!

JEFF Sorry. I know farming is a lot of work, okay. I'll be ready when I have to be. I'll never read another book unless it has animals on the cover, and I will learn to play hockey, baseball, and pool for rainy days. I will drink Canadian beer and learn the names of all the hockey players on my new favourite team. I will wear my John Deere hat and I'll never, ever, ever talk about classical music or my emotions to another living soul. Happy?

EDNA Are you?

JACK and GRANDPA enter with Tim Hortons doughnuts.

JACK Would you believe I stood in line for twenty minutes for these? Help yourselves. You know I'm not a patient man.

JEFF No argument here.

GRANDPA [Port Elgin] is just as busy as it was last weekend for Pumpkinfest. *(Port Elgin has an antique show and fall fair event the first weekend of October. This location could be changed as long as there's an event of a similar nature at this time.)*

EDNA What did you buy doughnuts for? I've been baking all morning. I've got three dozen butter tarts cooling right now on the back porch.

JACK Don't worry. These will be gone by lunch. What can I say—your men were hungry and we were so far from home.

GRANDPA Where're these tarts?

EDNA You can't have one. You have to eat doughnuts.

She goes to get him a tart.

JEFF My ride's here. See you guys later. See you tomorrow, Grandpa.

GRANDPA Yup. Safe trip.

JEFF Bye Mom. Hope you have a good day. *(exits)*

EDNA *(entering the kitchen again and calling after JEFF)* Bye.

JACK What's he doin with the trumpet?

EDNA Rehearsal. Some of the kids in the school band are playing at the Anglican church in [Owen Sound].

GRANDPA Fancy. Our little church not good enough?

EDNA He likes to play as much as he can.

GRANDPA Might as well get it out of his system. Mike used to have ideas about playing guitar in a band, but I haven't seen that guitar since he got my farm.

EDNA That's right. He never plays anymore. Poor Mike.

JACK Poor Mike. Far from it.

EDNA I just meant "poor" in that things aren't going so smoothly for him. I didn't mean poor in money. Is that all you think about anymore?

JACK Oh, I'm sorry. Maybe I should take a holiday and let the farm look after itself. You can answer the door when the bankers call. I'll be in our hot tub drinking champagne.

EDNA *(combination of teasing and sarcasm, not an attempt to escalate the conflict)* Shame on me. I keep forgetting that you are single-handedly keeping us out of the poorhouse.

JACK You're welcome. Maybe it's time to show her the contract, Henry? Let Edna see the numbers for herself.

GRANDPA Wait till you see this, Edna… what a deal.

EDNA You have the contract, Jack? When were you going to tell me?

JACK Nothing's signed. We just met with Mike this morning to look over the details.

EDNA You said before that we'd have to borrow almost a million dollars for the barn. And now you've gone ahead with it? When were you going to tell me?

JACK Well, I guess I'm telling you now.

GRANDPA I'm goin to help out with the loan… I've got a bit saved.

EDNA Dad, I thought you retired from farming. Why are you getting into this?

JACK Edna! It's very generous of your dad to be helping us out like this. I sure as hell appreciate it.

EDNA Oh… yes… I know it's generous, but it's a lot to take in all at once. That's a lot of money.

JACK You have to borrow money to make money. It's the only way I'm goin to get out from under…

GRANDPA Least it's a safe investment. We're thinkin wiener hogs here and Mike'll have the finishing barns.

JACK I'll go over the contracts with you if you like.

EDNA I don't have time today. I have four loads of laundry on the line, haven't started the cleaning. I have to get the turkey ready. We are having seven people here for lunch tomorrow right after church.

JACK Where's Gina? Can't she help?

EDNA She's helping the Golds pick apples all day.

JACK Tell you what. We'll get out of your hair and have lunch in town. That's one less thing you'll have to do today.

EDNA You're sure it's not too much trouble.

JACK I heard that *(kissing her)* and I love you, too. You are the perfect wife and I am a lucky, lucky man. See you later. Start counting your chickens.

EDNA You mean pigs, don't you?

JACK Only a couple thousand.

EDNA Great.

JACK Bye dear. Let's go, Henry.

EDNA See you tomorrow, Dad.

GRANDPA I might be back for supper if that's okay.

EDNA Of course. See you then. *(as JACK and GRANDPA leave)* No trouble at all.

SCENE FIVE

MUSICIAN & HOCKEY MOMS

You don't have to be old to be an old boy,
A budding youth will ripen soon enough,
It don't take many years
As long as they've been spent right round here,
No, you don't have to be old to be an old boy.
You don't have to be old to be an old boy,
You'll fit right into this community,
No, age is not a factor
As long as you can drive a tractor,
You don't have to be old to be an old boy.
Just stop your truck in the middle of the road,
Chat with a neighbour in the other lane,
Roll down your window and take your time
'Cause that feller right behind you's less important
Than dicussin if it is or it ain't gonna rain.
You don't have to be old to be an old boy,
There's overalls for every size and shape
As long as your favourite places to shop
Are Canadian Tire and your local co-op
Then you don't have to be old to be an old boy.
No, you don't have to be old to be an old boy,
Just go to church on Sunday for an hour
And if that's the only time that you are seen
Not wearing a cap advertising a machine
Well, you don't have to be old to be an old boy.
Course, you can't be an old boy,
If I don't know your old man
And you can't be an old boy, if your car comes from Japan
And if you sip on café latte or you munch on escargot
Then I guess I got to tell you just in case you didn't know,
That you won't be an old boy, even when you're an old, old man.
'Cause you don't have to be old to be an old boy
Just to see things as you know they really are,
You don't need to see the light
When what you've always believed is still what's right.
We know it's not that your mind is closed,
You just haven't liked the changes that you've heard proposed
And you don't need to be told
That you don't have to be old
To be an old boy!

JACK, GRANDPA, WILF, and JOE are at a local auction. It's a cold, gloomy day in November, about 1:00 p.m. They're leaning against a fence watching machinery being auctioned off. WILF is eating pie and the others are sipping coffee out of Styrofoam cups.

JACK How's the pie, Wilf?

WILF Dandy. The ladies have outdone themselves.

JOE Must be good. That's your second piece.

WILF I didn't know you were countin. You're almost as bad as Louise. I have to eat my raisin pie when I get the chance.

GRANDPA I'm partial to apple with a slice of really old cheddar.

JOE No… nothing beats Eleanor's rhubarb and custard.

The men all agree that rhubarb is indeed a fine pie except for JACK, who's paying more attention to the auction.

JACK This is making me sick. That baler went for next to nothing. He's gettin sweet dick all for his machinery.

WILF Who bales hay anymore? *(looking pointedly at JOE)*

JACK Are they auctioning the farm, too?

JOE Yup. No one in the family wants it. Son's a dentist.

WILF *(to JACK)* I heard you were looking to buy this place.

JACK Crossed my mind at one time.

WILF But now you're thinking about going into hog farming.

JACK Now how did you get wind of that?

WILF Somebody must've mentioned it.

JACK *(looking meaningfully at GRANDPA)* Somebody's supposed to keep a lid on it.

GRANDPA It's nothing to be ashamed of.

JOE Do what you like, but do not call it a hog farm. These things don't run like any farm I ever heard of.

WILF This is from the man who still bales his hay and puts it in the barn one bale at a time.

JOE It works fine, always has.

WILF There's no fouler place on this earth than the top of a haymow in ninety-five degree heat. I take whatever technology makes the job easier.

JACK You don't like the idea of a pig barn, Joe?

JOE I don't.

WILF He didn't like the idea of indoor plumbing either, Jack. Eleanor had to put her foot down.

JOE I like owning my barn, my land, my feed, my animals, and telling the bank and the government to go to hell when I get the chance.

JACK So you haven't got concerns about this "environmental hazard" some people are talking about?

JOE My environment is my farm, and you're three concessions away from me. And I don't raise pigs.

GRANDPA Have you noticed how clean these operations look from the road? Most of the time you wouldn't even know they were there. Maybe I should take my daughter-in-law for a tour of the real thing… she could see for herself how good the conditions are. She seems to have it in her head that farms are pretty green places with clean barns where animals live till they die peacefully of old age.

JOE From the city?

GRANDPA Yup.

JACK She's sure got a lot of opinions, that's for sure. And if she doesn't have an opinion about something, she gets on the Internet till she finds one.

JOE There's nothing that burns my ass so much as a city person thinkin they have any business telling me what I can do on my farm. Damn that makes me mad.

WILF Remember that game farm I wanted to start on my back hundred acres? Neighbour started a petition and got it blocked. They won't even let me hunt near them and I sold them the damn property.

JOE Your own fault, Wilf. You fought for that severance and sold it for top dollar. Can't have your pie and eat it, too.

GRANDPA You can't see the future. When someone moves in beside you, you never know what kind of trouble they'll make.

WILF Well, keep your heads, boys, 'cause I think there might be some trouble blowing your way over these barns. They won't even consider allowing them over near [Chesley]. Knew a fella who applied for a permit… got turned down flat.

JOE Wilf, when the hell do you get any farmin done? You're so damn busy collecting every rumour and piece of gossip between [Lake Huron and Hanover].

WILF Gotta have your ears open, and your mind workin; otherwise, you're left in the dirt.

GRANDPA Well, I guess we'll find out who our friends are.

WILF Don't worry. You got a lot of friends in this community. I'll be puttin in a good word every chance I get.

JOE Now that's gotta put everybody's mind at ease.

JACK You can never have too many friends. I think I've seen enough of this… Henry, what say we mosey on out of here. Rain's not gonna hold off much longer.

WILF Heard they're calling for snow by supper.

GRANDPA Jeff comin home with us?

JACK Ya, he's in the house… wants to buy a set of books. Apparently Harold collected some writer that Jeff likes.

GRANDPA Harold read books?

JACK Go figure. You think you know someone…

GRANDPA Well, I'll be damned.

SCENE SIX

EDNA and CAROL are in the kitchen doing Christmas baking. It's a Friday evening, 7:30 p.m., in early December; snowing heavily, but not stormy.

CAROL *(chopping candied pineapple)* Here's two cups of pineapple.

EDNA Don't forget, we're doubling the recipe.

CAROL Right. I was wondering why I had extra of everything. Mmmm… I can smell that now.

EDNA Gingerbread. When the kids were little they used to help me decorate them. They didn't look "pretty" but it was such a nice thing to do together.

CAROL Mom and I did a gingerbread house every year.

EDNA People complain about how busy the season is, but if it weren't for all these little traditions, Christmas would be gone before I got a chance to enjoy it.

CAROL This *(indicating the baking mess)* is a nice change from school work. I can't wait till the holidays. I can't even take weekends off… it's the job that never ends.

EDNA Look, I could finish this cake.

CAROL Oh no… This is a pleasure, really. It's nice here.

EDNA Is Mike home?

CAROL No, he's helping Jack with the team tonight… shooting drills or something.

EDNA Jack is not enjoying the team so much this year… the kids aren't coming out to the practices.

CAROL That would be frustrating. *(looking at the recipe again)* You know, I always thought fruitcakes sounded so healthy. They're basically sugar.

EDNA And brandy.

CAROL Yes!

EDNA They're delicious though. You've got your wedding cake in the freezer, don't you?

CAROL Ya… I'd never heard of that before, and now I've met women with cake from like twelve years ago. What if we never have kids? Then when do we eat the cake?

EDNA Oh, you'll have kids.

CAROL Not soon.

EDNA There's no rush. When you're ready.

CAROL You haven't seen Mike and I together lately, have you?

EDNA I see you all the time.

CAROL When do you see us at the same time?

EDNA I hadn't noticed.

CAROL Remember Thanksgiving?

EDNA You're too hard on yourself. Rough times pass… especially the first year stuff.

CAROL We got married more than a year ago. You know the expression—the honeymoon is over?

EDNA Uh huh. *(nodding)*

CAROL It's so over.

EDNA Just work through the problems… one at a time.

CAROL How do you and Jack deal with conflict?

EDNA Conflict? I don't know… we don't really have any.

CAROL You never get mad or disagree with Jack?

EDNA Well, of course I do.

CAROL That's conflict, Edna.

EDNA No, conflict is fighting, and we don't fight. I can't remember the last argument we had.

CAROL You must be a saint. I haven't noticed that Jack is the easiest guy in the world to get along with.

EDNA I'm NOT a saint… my mom… she was. She never complained.

CAROL So I hear. I wish I'd known her. If only I'd met Mike a year sooner. Sounds like she had a great life though… everyone just worships her memory.

EDNA She did… for the most part. She… she was… she made the best of things.

CAROL There is a difference between making "the best of things" and having a good life.

EDNA Well, even saints don't get everything they want. You have to compromise.

CAROL Edna, is this your way of telling me to back off and let Mike build the hog barn?

EDNA I didn't say that.

CAROL Because I'm not backing off. I'm supposed to be his partner. It is unforgivable that he went ahead with this without discussing it with me first.

EDNA Oh my goodness… it's just what men do. I'm sure it never crossed his mind that you would be interested.

CAROL Well, I am. I expect to be consulted when he's making a major decision about our home and our livelihood.

EDNA But it's Mike's farm.

CAROL Yes… but when he married me it became our farm. When he borrows the money for the barn it becomes our debt. Like it or not, Edna, I expect to have my say!

EDNA But Jack says the debt will be paid off in five years.

CAROL Oh yes… I've heard about all this money we're going to make. But what about the liability? What if we have a leak like those barns in [Ashfield Township]?

EDNA That's one example. You've been listening to a lot of propaganda against the barns.

CAROL Propaganda? Is that what Jack calls it? Do you know when I started listening to the "propaganda," Edna? When one of my colleagues at school handed me a petition trying to stop all factory farming in this township. "Thanks for destroying the quality of life in our community," she said. "I hope you'll be very happy with the cash you sold out for."

EDNA Who? Jack says people don't even have the facts.

CAROL It seems to me that people do have some facts that are scaring them.

EDNA So this woman really upset you. That was awful.

CAROL Yes… no… What's awful is the risk to the land and the water that this kind of intensive farming poses.

EDNA Jack says that you can't take one bad example and use it to build a whole case against the operations. You can do it properly. The tanks don't have to leak. Jack would never cut corners.

CAROL "Jack says. Jack says." Am I talking to Jack, Edna? Are you one and same… do you think exactly alike?

EDNA I was just trying to explain. You need to listen, too! I am trying to help you understand how the guys are thinking.

CAROL So, you're on their side.

EDNA I'm Jack's wife.

CAROL Oh… that's right. And you never have conflict with your husband.

EDNA I understand why he's doing it.

CAROL But it's not right.

EDNA But it doesn't have to be wrong… it all depends on how you look at it.

CAROL I can't give in… I know you want me to. Have you and Jack read those articles I left you?

Do you want another North Carolina here in [Bruce County]?

EDNA Yes, we read them. Jack… I keep telling you though, it doesn't have to be dangerous. The government has regulations… the township has regulations. It can be done properly.

CAROL You can have a nice big bonfire in your backyard, too, Edna. You can burn brush or just sit around and watch the flames. But houses burn down… and barns burn down and that's not something anybody plans for. Fire is fire and it will always be dangerous. These barns are dangerous.

EDNA I'm not sure you're really fighting over the hog barn issue at all. I think you're fighting for power.

CAROL Call it what you want… there may be "underlying issues" but we are fighting over the hog barn.

EDNA Is it worth a marriage?

CAROL Maybe I don't think my marriage is worth anything if I have no power in it.

EDNA But Mike has to have power, too. You can't both win.

CAROL I know. I know… I hate this. I didn't see it coming.

Car lights in the driveway.

EDNA That must be Barry and Gina. Let's not discuss this in front of them.

CAROL I'm sorry I spoiled your evening. Please understand that I am acting out of deep principles.

EDNA I know you are. But you should know that Mike loves you and wouldn't do anything to risk your safety or your home.

CAROL I understand that…

GINA enters with a large suitcase and gift bags from Christmas shopping.

EDNA Hi, hon. How are the roads?

GINA They're fine if you're careful. Hi "Aunt" Carol.

CAROL Hello "niece." Nice to see you.

EDNA Barry not coming in?

GINA He's whipped. I made him shop all afternoon.

EDNA And he was probably up at five milking cows.

GINA Poor baby.

CAROL What did you buy?

GINA Everything. I'm done.

CAROL No… Say it isn't so. I haven't even started.

GINA I am a very organized woman, remember.

CAROL Rub it in.

GINA Anyone up for a rye and Coke?

CAROL shakes her head.

EDNA I'll get you one.

GINA I'll do it.

GINA looks in the oven at the cookies.

Gingerbread men! Can I decorate?

EDNA Maybe tomorrow… unless you have a lot of studying to do.

GINA School's over.

EDNA This early. Don't you have exams?

GINA I'm done.

EDNA Oh, I wanted to come down next Friday and stay over.

GINA I didn't know. Why didn't you come last weekend?

EDNA I had to work at the craft show. I'm disappointed. I guess I'll have to come for the January sales.

GINA Ya… sure…

CAROL So, did you have a big party to celebrate this week?

GINA Well… we had a party for two girls who dropped out of the course.

EDNA What! That's awful!

GINA Not really. They're fine with it… they just changed their minds. They looked happier than I've seen them all year.

EDNA What a waste. Will they get their money back?

GINA Who cares? If they were miserable, the money wasn't really their first concern.

EDNA They're just throwing it all away—money and career.

GINA They changed their minds, Mom. It's their business, not yours.

CAROL *(sensing a subtext)* Probably better they quit now than waste any more time or money. It can be so hard figuring out what to do with your life when you're eighteen.

GINA No kidding. Are you sure I can't get you guys a drink?

EDNA You drank that fast.

CAROL Not for me. I think I should go home.

EDNA Thanks for the help with the cakes. I hope I wasn't giving you too much advice along with my recipe.

CAROL I'm sure it's a good recipe… obviously it's worked for you all these years.

EDNA Those old recipes can stand the test of time.

GINA Lighten up, ladies! It's only a fruitcake. I don't even like it.

EDNA That's right. You only like gumdrop cake.

GINA Yes I do.

CAROL Gumdrop cake, another healthy Christmas treat.

EDNA We'll make it sometime.

CAROL I hope so… I really do.

EDNA We will…

GINA Are you guys sure I can't get you a drink?

CAROL I'm gone… I just hope I can get in the lane. It's really coming down.

GINA Okay, bye "Aunt."

CAROL Bye "niece."

EDNA Safe drive. Give my love to my brother.

CAROL Ya… ya. Night. *(exits)*

MUSICIAN & FULL CHORUS

(chorus) It's a fine line between helping and hurting
Caring and cursing
Holding on and holding back
When to scream
And when to whisper
And when to say nothing at all
When to bend and when to straighten
And when… to let it fall.
I'd give my life to see you happy
You may not believe that now
I know you're doubtful and full of fear
And what you're not saying, I just don't hear.

Repeat chorus.

Your love means everything to me
But I feel a stronger call
You seem so sure of yourself, so clear
But what I'm not saying, you just won't hear.
The lines on our face make us family
The lines that we speak make us friends
But family and friends aren't forever
If silence just dries up your heart in the end.

Repeat chorus.

SCENE SEVEN

A cold but clear night sometime between Christmas and New Year's, 7:00 p.m. The women are sipping coffee and Baileys from travel mugs, Thermoses, and Styrofoam cups while watching a hockey game.

RUTH A DustBuster!

LINDA Yup. After sixteen years and three children, he still hasn't figured it out. GET THE LEAD OUT, BOYS. LET'S SEE SOME HUSTLE!

CAROL *(surprised by the yell)* Maybe he doesn't fully value your feminine side.

LINDA Oh no, he's tried that route. Last year my gift was a day at the spa. DID YOU SEE THAT, REF? COME ON… EYES OPEN… STAY AWAKE.

CAROL I would have loved that.

LINDA I've never been so bored in my life.

RUTH It's a lot of money and you have nothing to show for it at the end of the day! *(beat)* Why aren't they passing? PASS THE PUCK AROUND, BOYS. PASS IT.

CAROL You didn't enjoy the massage?

LINDA No. All I could think while I was lying there was what a waste of time this was… and what exactly was Ray thinking when he decided I might enjoy this!

CAROL So even after all these years, he still doesn't understand you.

LINDA I'm not that hard to figure out… a combination of practical and… oh… nice, I guess. A DustBuster is practical, but it… well… it sucks as a Christmas present.

CAROL Literally!

They all laugh at the pun.

LINDA Anyone need a refill?

Both CAROL and RUTH hold out their mugs while LINDA pours Baileys from a Thermos.

RUTH This has got to be my last one. I'm driving three kids home tonight.

LINDA Look at that… the kid's offside and the ref hasn't called it. OPEN YOUR EYES, REF. DO YOUR JOB!

CAROL Can they hear you?

LINDA I hope so.

CAROL Do they get mad?

RUTH Who cares? TYLER, GET TO THE NET. MOVE IN! Didn't you ever see Mike play?

CAROL I did, but I don't remember the yelling from the stands. I do remember the fights though. That's why I stopped going.

LINDA Oh… we've seen some fights. Look at Eric. What's wrong with him? It's like he's allergic to the puck.

CAROL He is the sweetest kid. He's very well-behaved on the playground.

LINDA Sweet! Maybe I shouldn't feed him before the games. That might make him a little meaner.

CAROL You're kidding!

LINDA Ya… but look at him. He's got no edge. Watch Ruth's Tyler… now there's a kid with an edge.

RUTH More like a chip… a big one on his scrawny shoulders.

LINDA I like attitude in a kid. Shows they've got spirit.

CAROL You wouldn't like it if you had a class full of them.

RUTH SHOOT OR PASS, BOYS. COACH—GET OFF YOUR BUTT AND DO SOMETHING.

LINDA You and Mike got plans for the big New Year's celebration?

CAROL I don't know yet… I will just be glad when it's 2000 and all this hype about the millennium is over. *(beat)* Hey… that guy just knocked Eric into the boards and he doesn't even have the puck.

LINDA That boy should have gotten a penalty for that. REF… YOU WORKIN FOR THE OTHER TEAM NOW? HOW MUCH ARE THEY PAYING YOU?

CAROL That's so unfair.

RUTH I took some cash out of the bank and hid it in a safe spot. And I've stocked up on all the basics. Our family could eat for two weeks if chaos strikes.

LINDA Even milk?

RUTH I froze fourteen bags.

CAROL It's not really the millennium anyways—2001 is really the beginning of a new century.

LINDA Oh… I hate that argument. 1999 becomes 2000. Might not be *logical* but that's the big deal—nineteen something is gone forever.

RUTH I would not be on a plane that night for all the money in the world. NO… BLOCK IT! DEFENCE… GET ON IT… HUSTLE!

LINDA That was close. Boy that Harper kid is good in goal.

RUTH Why can't Tyler try that hard? He could be so good… of all of his brothers he's got the most natural ability.

LINDA He is good.

CAROL I think that kid just tripped Eric with his stick. What a jerk! Isn't that illegal?

LINDA There's no goal yet… the kids are getting punchy. It's not illegal if the ref doesn't call it.

CAROL Why didn't he see it? Isn't that what he's paid for? Ref… Come on. REF… ARE YOU BLIND? CALL THE PENALTY.

RUTH No… Looking the other way I guess.

CAROL YOU SUCK, REF. YOU SUCK THE BIG ONE!

MUSICIAN & OLD BOYS

It's breakfast at four a.m. and supper at ten
It's road trips and hours of homework not done
Bone-tired exhaustion
You think with your feet
You're ready to fight
And it's not always easy but for now
It's your life
At the hockey game
At the hockey game.

SCENE EIGHT

In the kitchen in late January. A Monday morning, 8:00 a.m. JEFF is alone, his binder and chemistry textbook open on the table, flipping through his notes and sipping coffee. A winter storm is in progress. The radio is on to [FM 102] announcing highway closures. It announces that any exams to be written today will be written tomorrow. With relief JEFF turns off the radio and closes the books. He goes to turn on the computer when GINA enters under layers of winter clothes.

GINA You're up. Turn on the radio.

JEFF I just turned it off. Highway's closed. My school's not even open.

GINA The highway's closed?

JEFF From [Owen Sound to Amberley].

GINA Yes! Get off the Internet. I want to call Barry.

JEFF Don't think so.

GINA Come on.

JEFF No, I just got on. I'm sure he'll be over later.

GINA I want to talk to him before Mom and Dad come in. Please…

JEFF Crap… fine. Why aren't you in London? Technically, you don't even live here anymore.

GINA Really, then "technically" you should have been up at 5:30 helping to carry water to the barn. You owe me!

JEFF No way… it's your choice. You're free to NOT be here.

GINA *(grabbing the phone and dialing)* You don't own the place yet, so shut up about me being here. You're worse than Mom. *(indicating phone)* Busy… damn.

JEFF *(grabbing a book and flaking out on the couch or easy chair)* You will not see me around here on weekends when I'm in university. I'm going to enjoy my four years of freedom… away from the home farm!

GINA I'll look forward to that. In fact… I live for that day.

JEFF Me too!

GINA *(having tried the phone again)* I wonder if Barry's on the Internet.

JEFF Do you actually love him that much or is it just the sex?

GINA Thinking about my sex life again, are you? You really need to get a girlfriend… this obsession with me is so unhealthy.

JEFF I just asked you a question, Gina. It's not a therapy session.

GINA Therapy is exactly what you need.

JEFF I'd rather have the sex. *(looks at GINA and realizes potential for confusion)* NOT with you!

GINA Good to know. *(dialing again)* Come on, Barry. Shoot, here come Mom and Dad.

JEFF What's the big secret?

GINA Nothing. Shut up. *(JEFF responds with a "what-did-I-do-now" gesture.)*

EDNA and JACK enter in winter clothes. EDNA takes off her boots, but not her coat, hat, or scarf. She gets bacon and eggs out of the fridge, winter clothes come off gradually as she gets breakfast underway. JACK has an armload of wood.

JACK Jeff, set this around the stove so it dries out. *(as JEFF takes the wood)* Pipes were frozen this morning… could have used some help.

JEFF I was up till two studying!

EDNA Gina, turn the radio on.

JEFF Don't bother. The highway's closed. My exam's tomorrow.

EDNA Oh no… How are we going to get you home, honey? Will you be penalized for missing classes?

GINA No.

EDNA But it's the first day of second term. Don't worry, we'll have you on the road the second the highway's open. Get all your stuff down here and be ready to go.

GINA Barry will take me back when it's safe.

JEFF How come all the other college people went back three weeks ago?

GINA I don't know. How am I supposed to know? Do I have a calendar with all the other college schedules in my head?

JEFF I don't know. Do you?

JACK Ah… it's nice to hear this intelligent conversation between my educated kids. Jeff, get dressed. I want you to plow the lane.

JEFF Why? It's just going to blow in again. They're not even plowing the highway.

JACK Just do it. It'll be worse if we leave it.

EDNA We want to be ready to go as soon as we can.

JEFF leaves in a huff to get dressed.

GINA Forget it! I'm not going back, so leave it.

JACK Don't snap at your mother.

GINA Why are you ignoring what I say?

EDNA Maybe I just think it's important to be in class. Maybe I wouldn't take my education for granted.

GINA Maybe you should be getting one then!

JACK Gina!

GINA What if I don't want to go back today?

EDNA You don't have to go if it's not safe. There's no reason to be such a witch about it.

GINA Really… what if everything I want is right here?

EDNA What are you talking about? You need to let go of this life.

GINA Why?

EDNA Because you have a very exciting future.

JACK Gina… just get packed and ready to go.

JEFF returns and starts slowly dressing for outside.

GINA No. *(pause)* I'm not going back, EVER! I dropped out of the course two months ago. Barry and I are going to get married.

JEFF *(suddenly in a hurry)* Tractor and snowplow here I come. See you in about four hours. *(exits dragging clothes behind him)*

JACK What? Now you tell us?

GINA I was afraid to. I knew Mom would be upset.

JACK You should've talked to us before you dropped out.

GINA What good would that have done? Nobody listens to me. I'll pay you the money back.

JACK I'm not worried about the money.

GINA Mom, please tell me what you're thinking.

EDNA I don't think so. I don't think it matters to you at all.

GINA Yes… it does.

EDNA No… You've destroyed something today… how will I ever respect you again?

JACK Oh for cryin out loud, Edna, don't blow this out of proportion. She's just gettin married. *(to GINA)* Are you pregnant?

GINA NO!

JACK *(to EDNA)* See… not the end of the world. Our daughter's comin home and we're gainin a son-in-law.

EDNA It is the end of the world. I've lost a daughter today.

JACK Edna!

GINA Mom…

EDNA Breakfast is ready.

JACK Ignore her, Gina… when she gets like this, you can't have a conversation with her.

EDNA Don't talk about me as if I weren't in the room.

JACK Then talk to your daughter—she's in the room, too.

EDNA *(pause)* How many eggs would you like, Gina?

GINA I'm not hungry. *(pause)* I can go live at the Golds' till Barry and I find our own place.

EDNA Whatever you think. I wouldn't want to interfere.

JACK You live here as long as you like. Edna…

EDNA I'm not interfering… did you hear that, Jack? She can do what she likes!

GINA I think it's better if I go… soon.

EDNA How many eggs?

JACK and GINA look at EDNA who is ignoring both of them. GINA suppresses a sob and runs upstairs. JACK sits down at the table in disgust. EDNA quietly wipes the tears from her eyes with the dishtowel.

End of Act One.

ACT TWO

SCENE NINE

Three vignettes around song.

MUSICIAN & CHORUS

Short days, long nights, fall back in October,
It can feel like you never see the sun.
Make plans, break plans, don't count on anything,
A storm could easily close the roads before the day is done.
It can be a cold mean season,
Make you forget the reason
For living in a country locked up in snow and ice,
Crushed beneath the weight of threatening skies,
All around you the world is grey and white.

VIGNETTE ONE

Valentine's dance. CAROL *and* LINDA *meet in a washroom.*

CAROL So the rumours aren't true—you do have legs.

LINDA Ray says I clean up "real good."

CAROL You do!

LINDA It's so uncomfortable. I hate these pantyhose. I had to shave my legs. *(indicating dress shoes with a heel)* And who can walk normally in these things?

CAROL You get used to them.

LINDA Why would you bother? *(showing* CAROL *her watch)* Oh, look. A Valentine's gift.

CAROL Wow… he's back to trying the feminine approach.

LINDA Sort of—he bought me a watch and jumper cables for my car. He's covering all the bases.

CAROL I like Ray.

LINDA I think I'll keep him.

CAROL Good idea.

LINDA *(awkward pause)* How about you… gonna keep Mike?

CAROL You mean is Mike going to keep me?

LINDA Well… I hate to say anything. I have heard you're not too popular with the family.

CAROL No… not too popular.

LINDA If I were you, I woulda kept my mouth shut and just worked on my husband in private.

CAROL I'll remember that next time.

LINDA You know I'm not saying that you shouldn't have your say… but getting into it with the whole family… wow… you just don't do that.

CAROL Mike got us into it. It wasn't a private issue between us in the first place.

LINDA Don't get upset. I'm not the enemy.

CAROL Right now… I wish I had done things differently. Things are very uncomfortable with Jack and Edna. But I feel the hog barns are wrong.

LINDA Well, you are what you are… the guy married you for better or worse.

CAROL I'm that bad?

LINDA No… you're just a bit different than the women he grew up with. Edna's mom was a sweetheart and Edna… she's as nice as they come. Mike was surrounded by… um… you know… pleasant… non-aggressive women.

CAROL I never thought of myself as aggressive till I moved here. And you know what, I'm pretty sure that if I went a couple rounds with Ruth Bender, it's me who would lose.

LINDA *(laughing)* Never cross that woman! Even I wouldn't try that!

CAROL *(pause)* I think I might be getting somewhere with Mike anyway… he's starting to listen.

LINDA Really?

CAROL He's not finding as many excuses to leave in the evenings at least.

LINDA Are you using any other "weapons"… like… making him sleep on the couch?

CAROL Linda!

LINDA Hey, all's fair in love and war.

CAROL Maybe… but that would be punishing me, too!

LINDA Ooo… I like your style.

CAROL It's too soon to celebrate… but… I have hope… perhaps next year I'll get jumper cables, too.

LINDA I wish you luck.

MUSICIAN & CHORUS

It can be a cold mean season,
Make you forget the reason
For living in a country locked up in snow and ice,
Crushed beneath the weight of threatening skies,
Everyone will have a story
Of the storm they can't forget,
Of snow so deep and wind so cold,
A squall so long, to hear it told, they hadn't warmed up yet.

VIGNETTE TWO

WILF, JEFF, and GRANDPA in a pickup truck. JEFF has his knapsack on his lap.

WILF So what do you think Jack's gonna say about that letter? Hope he doesn't take it personally.

JEFF Dad takes everything personally.

GRANDPA I don't even know this woman. Who's this Mary Clarke Vanderheusen?

WILF Never heard of her.

GRANDPA It is none of her business what we do.

JEFF Grandpa, you can't slip four thousand hogs into a community without people noticing.

GRANDPA You been listening to Carol again?

JEFF *(reading over the letter in the paper)* This woman's worried about property values… and tourists not coming. They don't like swimming in polluted lakes.

GRANDPA Everybody's looking for doom and gloom.

WILF Look at how they predicted the end of the world at the stroke of midnight on January first. Seems to me we're still here.

GRANDPA When did farmin become town council's business?

WILF They're all happy enough to buy cheap pork. Nobody from town ever came out to my farm and said, "Hey, we know we can buy this cheaper in the city, but we want to pay you top dollar for all your hard work."

GRANDPA That'll be the day! Is that ice on the windshield?

WILF Don't worry. This truck'll drive through anything. March is comin in like a lion.

JEFF I hope the hydro doesn't go out again.

WILF Where am I dropping you off?

JEFF At the Golds'.

WILF Gina's fiancé.

JEFF Yup.

GRANDPA Nice family.

WILF She dropped out of school.

JEFF Yup.

WILF When's the wedding?

JEFF I think that's what's being decided tonight.

WILF Well, your dad's gonna be fit to be tied when he reads this.

JEFF Yup.

GRANDPA He's just gotta toughen up a bit. Wedding should take his mind off things.

WILF Weddings are good. One of these days it'll be you gettin married and settlin down.

JEFF *(pause)* Nope.

GRANDPA That ice is really coming down. The forecast was right.

WILF They can't be wrong every single time.

JEFF I hope the hydro doesn't go out again.

WILF You young kids... can't do without your TV and your computers.

JEFF Yup.

MUSICIAN & CHORUS

It can be a cold mean season,
Make you forget the reason
For living in a country locked up in snow and ice,
Crushed beneath the weight of threatening skies,
All around you the world is grey and white.

VIGNETTE THREE

GINA is at RUTH Bender's looking at quilt patterns.

RUTH No ring yet, I see.

GINA No... soon.

RUTH *(holding the pattern book so* GINA *can see)* Now this is my favourite. It's called "Trip Around the World."

GINA Mmm… it's beautiful. Looks complicated.

RUTH All of my children have one of these for when they get married.

GINA It's so nice of the ladies to do this for me.

RUTH Well your mom's been part of the institute since you were born. We like to look after the young women in the church. We couldn't let your mom down when it's her daughter's big day.

GINA Right.

RUTH *(pushing for information)* She must be thrilled.

GINA Well, she's getting used to the idea.

RUTH She's disappointed about you not finishing school, I imagine. She was so excited when you—

GINA The quilt you made for Carol was gorgeous. All the girls at her shower were so jealous.

RUTH Really? That was a beauty. Now that was the "Log Cabin." A lot of people like that one.

GINA I think I would.

RUTH But you haven't looked at the whole book.

GINA I know, but… I think I want one just like Carol's.

RUTH But not the same colours.

GINA No… different colours.

RUTH And what are you thinking of?

GINA Uhm… I… don't know… haven't really picked a colour scheme. We don't actually have a place to live yet.

RUTH That's right.

GINA Ya… so, I'll get back to you about the colours.

RUTH All right then… if you're sure. We'll want to get this started as soon as possible. The wedding is…?

GINA Summer. Early July.

RUTH *(glancing at* GINA*'s stomach)* Oh… that is soon.

GINA No, Mrs. Bender. I'm not pregnant!

RUTH Well, there wouldn't be anything wrong with it if you were! Children are the greatest gift in a woman's life.

GINA Okay… but I just turned twenty so… maybe not right away.

RUTH Old enough to get married, old enough to have kids.

GINA Oh… I never heard that before. I'll keep it in mind. Well, bye Mrs. Bender.

RUTH Call me Ruth, dear… you're going to be a "Mrs." now. I think we can be on a first-name basis.

GINA Okay… bye… Ruth.

MUSICIAN & CHORUS

Talking weather becomes a pastime,
Check the forecast every hour,
Flurries tonight or freezing rain,
Promise or threat, it's all the same, so let the storm roll in,
Just let the storm begin.

SCENE TEN

The end of March, 7:30 p.m. In the kitchen JACK*'s at the table paying bills,* JEFF *is helping* EDNA *use the computer.*

JEFF And if you need to centre something, click on this.

EDNA How will I remember all this?

JEFF You can just type for now… I can help you organize it later. You remember how to save stuff?

EDNA That I've got.

JACK If I'd known you wanted to waste time, you could've looked for the money to pay these bills.

EDNA When I get a job I'll be able to help you, so don't tell me I'm wasting time.

JACK Ya… we'll be living on easy street once you start bringing in a paycheque.

EDNA Fine, I'll keep my money for myself then.

JEFF I just never get enough of this argument… please… go on. *(goes over to a chair to read)*

EDNA We're not arguing. You're dad is just adjusting to my new approach to life.

JACK Oh… is that what this is.

EDNA I'm learning to look after myself the way everybody else around here does.

JACK Give me a break… this is all because Gina quit school. It's sour grapes, Edna… don't turn it into something heroic. *(to JEFF)* Must be a woman thing.

JEFF You mean menopause?

EDNA / JACK No!

JEFF Okay… sorry. Pretend I'm not here.

JACK *(looking out the window)* Someone's coming in the lane. *(to JEFF)* You going out?

EDNA Carol's helping me with my resumé.

JACK Resumé… oh, right. Geez… maybe I don't want to see my sister-in-law right now.

EDNA Well, I do and as far as I know it's still my house, too! Get over it, Jack. Don't be all sour grapes.

There is a knock on the door.

CAROL Hello. *(entering with a couple of books)* I come bearing doughnuts and books. Don't shoot me.

EDNA Come on in. You didn't need to do that. Coffee?

CAROL Please. Hi, guys.

JEFF *(waving from his chair)* Hi, Aunt Carol. Love the books.

CAROL Asimov? *(JEFF nods)* I thought you'd like them. Hi, Jack. Doughnut? Peace offering?

JACK mutters an ungracious hello/grunt.

Paying bills?

JACK Trying to.

CAROL That's funny. So is Mike. Is it… like… accounting night for farmers?

JACK Now, how would I know? I'm not a farmer. I'm a corporate-pawn-polluting-sold-his-soul-to-the-devil factory farmer.

CAROL I don't think you're any of those things, Jack… at least not yet.

JACK Don't start… don't… start… that with me. Obviously you can control your husband, but you have no clout with me.

EDNA This isn't getting over it, Jack… remember that Carol is family.

CAROL It's okay, Edna. Go ahead, Jack. Say what you need to say.

JACK I think I just did.

CAROL You barely got started.

JACK Jeff, get your coat. We're going for a drink.

JEFF I'm reading.

JACK Not anymore… you're drinking beer with me. Hurry up.

JEFF What's wrong with this picture… uh… "Father encourages son in lifelong addiction to beer"?

JACK Shut the book and get in the car.

CAROL I don't think you can stay mad at me, Jack.

JACK Jeff… I'll wait for you outside.

CAROL Bye, Jack.

JACK gives an ungracious goodbye grunt.

JEFF *(exiting)* Thanks a lot… another innocent bystander gets caught in the crossfire.

CAROL Sorry, Jeff.

EDNA I'm sorry, Carol. I thought he could be civil if nothing else.

CAROL Well… Gotta blame somebody… and I'm an easy target.

EDNA He's angry at Mike, too. The hog barn was Mike's idea in the first place and now he's changed his mind. Jack gets left with all the flack.

CAROL Are you upset?

EDNA Me? It's not my problem.

CAROL Mike changing his mind probably saved our marriage.

EDNA Because you won?

CAROL That's kind of extreme… but sort of, I guess.

EDNA It was just a power struggle.

CAROL No… It wasn't just a power struggle. I thought you understood. I can't not have any power in my marriage. Mike created the situation. Mike fixed it.

EDNA I still think that a couple thousand hogs is a safe investment.

CAROL And I don't. I thought you weren't upset?

EDNA I'm not.

CAROL Oh… okay then. *(beat)* I brought a couple books on job hunting… and I brought my most recent resumés.

EDNA *(looking at* CAROL*'s resumé)* It's two pages. Look at all your qualifications. I don't have anything to put on paper.

CAROL Yes, you do. We can take the things you do around the farm and put them into updated career-skills language.

EDNA How exactly is shovelling manure a career skill?

CAROL Umm… easy one… how about "nutrient management facilitator"?

EDNA Everybody around here knows me… they know I don't have any job skills.

CAROL Anyone who knows you would probably get down on their knees and beg you to work for them.

EDNA But I don't have qualifications.

CAROL You have your grade thirteen… and twenty some years work experience.

EDNA In being a wife.

CAROL And mother… and running a farm.

EDNA I don't run the farm. Jack does… with Dad's help.

CAROL Henry might be around a lot, but you're Jack's partner… I mean… you and Jack own the farm.

EDNA I'm not his business partner. He talks everything over with Dad. Dad's the one with experience, and he likes to feel useful around here.

CAROL If he wanted to run a farm, he should have kept his own.

EDNA He did… a lot longer than Mom wanted to.

CAROL Really? She didn't love the farm as much as he did?

EDNA Not… well… no, she didn't.

CAROL I always got the impression she loved the country.

EDNA She never complained, right… not to the men. And she loved my dad, believe it or not.

CAROL Oh, I can believe it. I love him, too… He's giving us the silent treatment at the moment, but Mike figures he'll get over it.

EDNA Mike let him down. I think Dad's taking it harder than Jack.

CAROL He can take it as hard as he wants to. He had no business coming between Mike and I. Mike should not have to choose between his wife and his dad.

EDNA Dad's harmless. He'd do anything for you.

CAROL It didn't feel harmless when I was looking at apartments to rent if we separated.

EDNA You're blaming Dad for that?

CAROL Partly. Your dad didn't come to us and tell us about this great hog farm business. He went to Mike and left me out of it. It's our money and our land now.

EDNA But it was Dad's farm. He gave it to Mike.

CAROL Past tense—"was Dad's farm."

EDNA You can't just cast someone out when he's not convenient.

CAROL I'm not casting him out. I'm trying to establish his place in our lives. He doesn't run Mike's life anymore.

EDNA No… Apparently you do!

CAROL Ouch. Edna… I thought you would understand.

EDNA Maybe you'll understand when you have children how it feels to be irrelevant in their lives… to be put in your place.

CAROL But parents have to be aware of limits…

EDNA What about respect? They devote their whole life to you and then you throw them away when you have enough cash to be on your own.

CAROL I want to be respected, too. I don't plan to throw anybody away.

EDNA Everybody wants respect… whether they've earned it or not. How exactly do you respect a twenty-year-old who drops out of school to get married? Am I really supposed to respect that?

CAROL Are we talking about Gina or your dad? You're so angry, Edna—

EDNA I'm not angry, I'm confused. I'm just a dumb country wife who doesn't know all the rules. I'm certainly learning a lot these days… probably good for me.

CAROL I guess you haven't been talking to Gina, then. *(no response from* EDNA*)* She's delaying the wedding.

EDNA Really?

CAROL No… Not to go back to school. She can't stand the way people are looking at her… checking out her stomach.

EDNA Because everyone thinks she must be pregnant.

CAROL Ya.

EDNA Like mother like daughter they'll say.

CAROL Oh… I didn't know that. Mike never said.

EDNA One minute you're going to the spring prom, and the next you're married with a kid. Everybody thought I was so lucky… Dad lent Jack the money to buy this farm, and he never held it against me that I got pregnant.

CAROL I would hope not.

EDNA *(beat)* So, Gina's not pregnant and not getting married.

CAROL You need to talk to her soon.

EDNA Why? So she can tell me to get out of her life and respect her decisions?

CAROL I think she's already told you that… in her own way.

EDNA What do you think her resumé is going to look like? Like mine, maybe… with nothing to show for her life… nothing to put on paper.

CAROL I don't know what to say to convince you that your life is… um… it's admirable. I do admire you so much… for your great kids… you're the pillar of the family and you're so kind about it. You are an unbelievably gifted person.

EDNA Don't, Carol… you must despise me. I am the kind of woman who obeys her husband and father. You don't admire that!

CAROL And you despise me, right… a bossy, independent woman who is completely self-centred and disrespectful to others.

EDNA You're not those things.

CAROL If we can like each other, Edna… then there must be hope for both of us!

EDNA Well… I don't despise you, that's for sure.

CAROL And I really do admire you whether you believe me or not.

EDNA *(beat)* But I still don't have a resumé.

CAROL Why don't you go through my books? I'll leave them with you.

EDNA Maybe I'll just fill in applications. I have good handwriting and I'm a good speller.

CAROL Hey… you're on the right track now. I'm on my way… I don't want to upset Jack again.

EDNA Are you still planning to have Easter at your place?

CAROL Yes… I think it's necessary.

EDNA You'll let me know what I can bring.

CAROL Oh… you can count on that. Once more, let me say… I really appreciate you. Bye.

EDNA Thanks for putting up with me and my stuffy old ways.

CAROL rolls her eyes and gives EDNA a quick hug before exiting. EDNA goes to the computer and turns it off. Looks at the papers she was working on and crumples them up.

SCENE ELEVEN

MUSICIAN & OLD BOYS

In your dreams, there's just you and some friends in the driveway
Taking shots, taking turns, taking fun where you can.
But now there's money invested and the stakes get so high
You take the good with the bad on this ride.
'Cause it might just be your ticket to big money and fame,
It might just be the best ride of your life.
You'll be king of the castle; they'll all know your name
If you're fast on your feet
At the hockey game.

The hockey moms, RUTH, and LINDA are watching a game with CAROL. It's the first weekend of April, a Sunday afternoon, raining and cold outside. The game has just ended and the their team lost.

LINDA I can't believe they lost—they were up two points…

RUTH At least Tyler scored a goal. That's his first this year.

CAROL We should try to smile in case they look up here. I think Eric's waving at you, Linda.

LINDA *(fake smile and wave)* Doesn't he look happy… the little wiener. He's just glad it's over.

RUTH *(looking for a Kleenex)* It was so close. Winning a trophy might have turned Tyler around. What's he gonna do with all his free time?

CAROL Aren't you glad it's done for another year? What about your free time?

LINDA I'd rather have the trophy.

RUTH At least I still have Teddy's games. His team's in the finals.

LINDA You're lucky. Boy, I'll miss this… it's almost better than sex.

RUTH Almost?

CAROL Well, I have appreciated the lessons in watching hockey. It's a lot more participation than I'd expected.

LINDA You'll make a great hockey mom!

RUTH Oh?

CAROL Someday… maybe. Not pregnant, Ruth!

RUTH Just don't wait too long.

CAROL One thing at a time.

LINDA I saw you and Mike at the Stanleys' buck and doe last Saturday. Looked like making a baby might not be such a chore.

CAROL We are sort of having a second honeymoon. I recommend it to anyone.

RUTH You're getting a second honeymoon and Gina doesn't even get one. She seemed upset when I talked to her… poor thing.

CAROL They're just postponing it.

RUTH But they are going to live together.

CAROL Ya…

RUTH Isn't that a fine thing. No responsibility… just play house. We even had her quilt pieced.

LINDA Just hang onto it, Ruth. I'm sure they'll get married eventually.

CAROL Or not. You never know… living together can open your eyes quite a bit.

RUTH I'm sure Mike got his eyes opened.

CAROL Oh… he did, Ruth, but he seems to have survived the shock.

LINDA Who's ready for one last shot? *(pulling out her Thermos)* Let's skip the coffee. *(they pull out their cups)*

RUTH Don't mind me, Carol. I admire you for standing up to Jack and your own husband. I don't like the idea of those hog barns at all.

CAROL Thank you.

LINDA Course, we all know that Jack Cameron is not exactly the toughest of opponents—the big softie.

RUTH He's almost too nice to coach.

LINDA Even with our constant encouragement to toughen up.

CAROL He doesn't like being in the public eye. I am just the one he can blame. I think he holds me responsible for every letter against him.

RUTH I hope he read my letter.

CAROL He reads them all.

RUTH I don't care what anybody says… the large barns are hurting the small farmers.

LINDA That's what Ray says, too.

CAROL Thanks ladies… it seems like the fight never ends, does it. What say we treat ourselves and the boys to some pizza?

LINDA The losers?

CAROL Yes! Linda… they did their best. Winning isn't everything, right?

LINDA Coming from you… that's a joke.

CAROL Hey… fighting for the environment, for equality in marriage… those are battles worth winning. This is… after all… just a game.

LINDA Bite your tongue. Have we taught you nothing?

RUTH It's never just a game.

LINDA No… We'll resume our lessons next fall. We're not finished with you.

CAROL Oh no…

RUTH Here's to young women who must be taught our ways.

LINDA Here's to the boys we love… even when they lose.

CAROL Here's to friendship, born in strange places and surviving the season.

ALL Cheers.

MUSICIAN & CHORUS

Only looking back is there a pattern where all the pieces rest and form a star,
And bits of light from days well-lived,
Gifts of touch and taste and sight,
Can shine into the darkness, light.
The past was not a better place.
Life was not so simple then.
But it seems the good will cling to us,
It seems the good will rise,
And I can wrap it around my heart and live beyond goodbyes.
Only looking back is there a pattern where all the pieces rest and form a star,
And bits of light from days well-lived,
Gifts of touch and taste and sight,
Can shine into the darkness, light.

SCENE TWELVE

A sunny but cool late afternoon on a Sunday in mid-April. EDNA *is preparing a ham dinner,* GINA*'s gathering a few things together to use in her new place.*

GINA *(unwrapping some dishes in a box)* I like these.

EDNA They were Mom's everyday set. I thought you might need them someday.

GINA I do. Thanks. I plan to get a lot of stuff at garage sales—they'll be in full swing in another month.

EDNA When do you move in?

GINA Two weeks.

EDNA That soon?

GINA They were desperate. Nobody wants to live out in the boonies if they can avoid it.

EDNA The house looks like it needs a lot of work from the road.

GINA Nothing major. Apart from a lot of shag carpet and panelling, it's quite pleasant inside.

EDNA Oil furnace.

GINA Ya. And a wood stove.

EDNA Sounds rustic.

GINA Mom, we heat with wood… and we're not exactly pioneers.

EDNA True.

GINA Do you want me to set the table?

EDNA Okay.

GINA Are they all outside admiring the calves?

EDNA Yes… and pacing out the new barn.

GINA I wish you could have talked Dad out of that.

EDNA I'm not Carol, Gina. I don't talk your dad out of anything.

GINA Dad is taking all the risks, and he's only guaranteed the price for five years.

EDNA Why are you telling me? Who listens to me anymore?

GINA Don't you care?

EDNA What do you think? Of course I care. Do you think I want another big, ugly barn in my backyard? Do you think I like having people in town point at me and write letters about my husband in the paper?

GINA You never say anything.

EDNA That would just make it worse.

GINA Well, you shouldn't just go along with something if you don't like it.

EDNA Since when? Isn't that what you're asking me to do?

GINA Oh, come on. Does everything have to come back to me?

EDNA I just don't think you're in a position to be advising me about speaking my mind.

GINA Fine. I won't. *(looking out the window)* Jeff's home.

EDNA Good. I was afraid he'd be late.

GINA You're going to miss him next year.

EDNA That's what mothers do—they miss their kids when they're gone. We'll need about six serving spoons.

GINA Are you going to miss me?

EDNA I tried to miss you, Gina, but you kept coming back.

JEFF enters.

How was the concert?

JEFF Fine. My solo went really well.

GINA *(laying out the serviettes)* All that hot air… got to be useful for something.

JEFF Two weeks, right… just two more weeks. Things are going to be so different around here. Did you congratulate Mom on her new job?

GINA New job?

JEFF Early morning shift at Tim's.

GINA You didn't tell me.

EDNA I don't start till June.

GINA I don't believe it.

EDNA It was just the right job for me, Gina—they didn't require any college or university.

GINA Thanks… got the message.

JEFF What are you gonna do, Gina? Be a kept woman and let Barry do all the work?

GINA Maybe I will apply at Tim's… if I can't get my job back at the nursing home.

EDNA You're going back to your old job?

GINA For now.

Enter JACK and GRANDPA.

JACK Smells good in here. I could eat ham five times a week.

JEFF Guess you're going into the right business then.

GRANDPA Now there's a girl causin all kinds of trouble.

GINA Hi, Grandpa.

GRANDPA First you're quittin school, then you're gettin married, then you're not… then I hear you're expecting a baby, then you're not. And now I hear you're plannin to live in sin.

GINA Grandpa. Nobody calls it that anymore.

GRANDPA Are you gonna be sharin a bed with your young man or not?

GINA Grandpa!

JEFF These modern women, Henry… what's a fella gonna do. They get so uppity nowadays.

GINA Ya… like you know anything about women. When's the last time you wrapped your lips around something besides a trumpet mouthpiece.

JACK Hey… cut that out.

JEFF We're sorry, Gina. We men… well, we get carried away sometimes.

GINA Oh, you're now officially a man? Did you pass some test?

EDNA Gina, go down to the pantry and get some pickles—bread and butter and dill.

GINA Fine. And when I come back up, can I get all the "men" in my family a drink and a snack?

JEFF Only if you really, really want to.

GINA exits with a glare at JEFF.

EDNA I don't think you should tease her about living in sin, Dad. It's better than getting married too soon.

GRANDPA I'm not teasing. I don't like it. Why buy the cow when you can get the milk for free?

EDNA She's not ready.

GRANDPA Then why is she moving in with him?

JACK Don't try to figure it out, Henry.

GRANDPA *(to JEFF)* You wouldn't live with a girl before gettin married, would you?

JEFF I'm looking forward to not living with any women for a while… nothing personal, Mom.

EDNA See if you get any cookies in the mail.

JEFF I just want a peaceful existence… studying, reading, practising.

JACK Practising what?

JEFF Trumpet.

JACK You're going to learn the science of agriculture, are you not?

JEFF I can do both.

GINA returns with pickles.

GRANDPA I still don't understand going to school to learn to farm. Makes no sense.

GINA There's a lot to learn, Grandpa.

GRANDPA Talk to your neighbour… talk to another farmer. You don't need a book.

GINA And you don't have to make the same mistakes over and over again.

EDNA Is that right, Gina?

GINA Yes, Mom.

GRANDPA Well, I know Jeff's got his plans. Enjoy the freedom while you can, I guess… get it all out of your system.

JEFF I'll see what I can do.

EDNA Dad, leave him.

GRANDPA I just want to make sure he's got the whole picture.

EDNA It's his business what he does with his life, not yours.

JACK Edna!

GRANDPA I'm just givin my opinion. I think I'm allowed.

EDNA No… not about my kids. Keep those to yourself. If I'm not allowed to tell them how to live their lives, then I don't think you should be either.

JACK Edna! What the hell is the matter with you?

GRANDPA I see. My money's fine, but I can't speak my mind.

EDNA I don't remember asking for any money from you, Dad.

JACK Henry, let's go to the barn. *(to EDNA)* Have a drink. Have a nap. I don't care. Just get a grip.

Don't take your personal problems out on your father.

EDNA They're not just my problems.

JEFF Mom, I don't mind. Grandpa means well.

GINA He's just teasing.

EDNA Well, I do mind.

GRANDPA You never said anything before. I only try to help.

JACK And I appreciate it, Henry. I wouldn't know what to do without you.

EDNA Thanks, Jack. Do you hear yourself? Do you hear what he just said, Dad? I am supposed to be the one he couldn't do without.

JACK What is the matter with you? Grow up.

EDNA Do you get everybody to do everything you want all the time? Do all our lives belong to you—Mom's, Mike's, mine, Jack's?

GRANDPA Don't you mention your mother. She'd be ashamed to hear you talk like this to me.

EDNA Yes, she would. We were never allowed to complain to you—ever! But that doesn't mean she didn't complain, Dad.

GRANDPA What did she have to complain about? No woman was better taken care of or more loved than Alice.

EDNA You never let her forget it.

GRANDPA You're just bitter, Edna.

EDNA I'm a lot like my mother, actually, Dad. Not the saint part, no, I'm not a saint. But I am like her.

GRANDPA If you were like her, you'd be content with all the good things you have here instead of making everybody miserable.

EDNA I didn't learn that lesson as well as my mother did.

GRANDPA It's not too late.

EDNA Oh, I think it is.

JACK Jeez, woman, why don't you lie down?

GINA Mom, do you want a drink? Something strong?

EDNA Wine, please.

JACK Henry and I are going for a drive. When we get back, we'll eat. No more fighting. If you're mad at me, take it out on me. If you're mad at Gina… get over it. But do not take it out on your dad. He's like a father to me, too.

EDNA I will not let him interfere with the kids.

JACK He's teasing them! Can't you tell the difference? It's harmless. *(exits)*

GINA Here's some wine.

EDNA Thanks.

JEFF You don't have to stick up for me, Mom.

EDNA He has no business telling you what you should and shouldn't do.

GINA goes to the piano and starts playing a simple grade three sort of tune.

JEFF Well, he's my grandpa. I don't mind listening. You know, I'll do what I want to do in the end.

EDNA You will?

JEFF Planning to.

EDNA And what is that?

JEFF I'll let you know when I do. That's just a great song, Gina. Do you think now is the best time for the talent show?

GINA I bet Mom doesn't know when I learned this song.

EDNA You used to play it all the time.

GINA Grade three piano book. Remember how I took lessons right up to grade eight?

EDNA You got a high-school credit for it.

GINA And when is the last time you heard me play?

JEFF Years… thank goodness.

EDNA Not very often.

GINA Jeff's right, Mom—years. I don't like the piano… I hated the lessons, hated practising.

EDNA But you were good. You played at church.

GINA I wasn't very good. And I never liked it. I took lessons because you wanted me to.

EDNA You must have enjoyed it a little. Your marks were good.

GINA Only because you wanted me to.

EDNA But what a waste… all those hours of practising.

GINA Ya.

EDNA Did you ever try to tell me you didn't like it?

GINA In about a million ways.

JEFF Remember the battles to make her come in from the barn to practise? No one was allowed to watch TV till Gina had put in forty-five minutes on the piano? We all suffered.

EDNA *(trying to absorb the full impact of* GINA*'s revelation)* My dad didn't want me to go to university. He was pleased when I got married to Jack Cameron at nineteen. His vision for my life was so limited. I didn't want to do that to you.

GINA I have my own vision.

EDNA You seem to.

GINA But you're in it. Being your daughter is part of the good picture of my future. I don't ever want to have the fight with you that you just had with Grandpa.

EDNA It wasn't a fight.

JEFF & GINA Mom!

EDNA Okay… it was an unpleasant disagreement.

JEFF You lost it, Mom.

GINA You went ballistic.

EDNA It's true. I am losing it. It's humiliating. And in front of everybody.

GINA So?

JEFF Can we at least try to have a peaceful meal? I'm starving.

GINA Always thinking of others, aren't you?

EDNA I think I might have another glass of wine first.

GINA Hello, Mom. I've never been so proud of you.

SCENE THIRTEEN

WILF, JOE, JACK, and GRANDPA are at the barber's on the Thursday afternoon before Mother's Day. It's an unusually cold May day.

WILF *(to* JOE*)* Doesn't kill you to take her out once a year.

JOE Why do you have to make reservations?

JACK You could always cook a meal yourself, Joe, then you wouldn't have to go to a restaurant.

WILF Joe's cooking would not be much of a treat for Eleanor… or anybody else for that matter. Just call the [Governor's Inn].

JOE Who makes all these rules anyway? I wouldn't care if they didn't do a damn thing for Father's Day.

WILF But they always do.

JOE I don't ask for it.

WILF For cryin out loud, get your wife out of the kitchen for one meal and stop whining. It's not gonna break the bank.

JACK I didn't know you were such a romantic, Wilf. This is a new side of you.

WILF A man can't rely on good looks alone.

JOE You don't say.

WILF Louise is a good woman—I've got no complaints, but if she doesn't get a dinner out once in a while and flowers and jewellery on special occasions, she gets ugly. That's the only word for it.

JOE Eleanor would kick my ass if I paid money for flowers when she's got half an acre of them growing all summer long. She'd rather go to the races on Saturday night and blow a few bucks on a fast horse.

JACK Edna never liked getting flowers either.

GRANDPA Alice liked chocolates—Black Magic…

WILF Alice was an excellent woman.

GRANDPA God must have needed another angel up there.

JACK Amen.

GRANDPA Do you think she was happy with me?

JACK Absolutely.

GRANDPA Edna got me to wondering if there was something I didn't notice.

JACK Edna was just upset that day. You have to ignore her, Henry.

GRANDPA Edna's a good woman.

JACK Yes she is, but even a good woman can be difficult.

WILF They get these ideas in their heads and they can make life hell when they want to. I think it's these afternoon talk shows.

JOE Eleanor's never watched TV in the afternoon in her life.

WILF How do you know? She might be watching it right now.

JOE I know Eleanor.

JACK You can live with them a long time and still not really know what's goin on in their heads.

WILF I suppose you could ask them.

JACK Ask them! That's just inviting trouble. Better to wait it out.

GRANDPA I think Alice was ready to leave the farm before I was. Do you think Edna blames me for Alice dying so soon after we moved into town?

JACK That's not your fault. Nobody in their right mind would blame you for that.

GRANDPA I would have done it differently if I'd known how little time she'd have.

WILF I say our wives are lucky to have us. I bet they're not sitting around this afternoon trying to figure out what makes us happy.

JOE No, they're probably busy makin our supper and getting a load of laundry off the line.

GRANDPA I was lucky to have Alice for forty-six years. It seems like a long time, but it wasn't really long enough.

Uncomfortable pause.

JOE Maybe I could make those reservations.

WILF I gotta go. I haven't got a card yet.

JACK *(to GRANDPA)* We're still expecting you on Sunday. I'm going to barbecue a salmon along with some steaks. Gina's bringing three kinds of dessert.

GRANDPA You spoil that wife of yours, okay.

JACK I'll do my best.

GRANDPA I thought I did my best, but maybe there would have been room for asking questions.

JACK What if you don't want to hear the answer?

GRANDPA *(pause before answering)* That was always my reason, too, Jack. *(beat)* I better be off.

JACK See you Sunday right after church.

GRANDPA nods and exits without speaking.

WILF How many years has it been since Alice passed away?

JACK Four.

JOE Never gets easier.

WILF Guess it's gonna happen to all of us sooner or later.

JOE There's always the off chance that our wives will outlive us, you know. Louise might have to find herself another husband.

WILF Wouldn't bother me. I just want her to be happy.

JACK You are a romantic, Wilf.

WILF She'll never get a better husband than me anyway.

JACK Well, you are one of a kind.

JOE Thank the lord for that!

MUSICIAN & CHORUS
He steps out on the floor,
Still dancing for two,
Though his arms are empty
His heart is so full
Of memories and pictures and souvenirs
Of his dearest partner
Through all the good years.
(chorus) So he's dancing for two
Though he's dancing alone.
Dance to the echo of all the old songs,
His love was the sweetest
His love it was strong.
So he'll dance for what was
And what's gone.
Each anniversary he counted his blessings
And hoped he could count on many years more.
After forty-six years, she was more than his wife
She was half of his heart, and all of his life.

Chorus.

When the minister turned their two lives into one
He never looked back, he liked it that way,
And after forty-six years, he still needed to see her,
The touch of her hand, and the smell of her hair.
He steps out on the floor,
Still dancing for two,
Though his arms are empty
His heart is so full
Of memories and pictures and souvenirs
Of his dearest partner
Through all the good years.

SCENE FOURTEEN

A warm and sunny Wednesday afternoon. EDNA's sitting on the easy chair listening to the news on the radio. The broadcast is focused on the Walkerton tragedy. EDNA's just listening. JACK enters, listens, clumsily makes himself a sandwich, and searches for some way to break the ice.

JACK It wasn't a hog barn—it was cattle manure that got into the well. *(silence from* EDNA*)* It was all the rain.

EDNA How could this happen?

JACK Bacteria in the water.

EDNA Jack… water! Water is sacred. It's life. You should be able to take it for granted.

JACK I guess you can't take anything for granted.

EDNA I want to do something for them. I want to help.

JACK I know.

EDNA You know what I can't get out of my head?

JACK What?

EDNA What if it had been us? Our farm? This is exactly what they said could happen because of intensive farming. They said it could get into the water supply.

JACK I suppose you've been talking to Carol.

EDNA No. I managed to think of that all by myself. Do you think I'm a complete idiot?

JACK Do you think I haven't had these thoughts, too? Couldn't you try to make me feel better for once instead of worse?

EDNA You want me to think of your feelings when the entire town of Walkerton is in a state of emergency?

JACK Well, you don't have to look at me as if I caused it!

EDNA I'm not. But I can't help looking at you as someone who could have done it. What if we had a crack in the holding tank… what if a freak storm rushed fresh manure into the lake? You're building a big bonfire in our backyard, Jack. What if you can't control it?

JACK We… we are building it, Edna. You're in this, too.

EDNA No. I'm out. I'm officially out. You're in it with my dad and the two of you can take the heat together.

JACK You're my wife.

EDNA Only when it's convenient. And I haven't felt like a wife for a long time.

JACK Fine. You want to take the high road while I make sure the bills get paid. That's great. Thanks for being there, Edna.

EDNA Now you want me. Where was I when you made these big plans? How many hours of discussion did we have over this million dollars we're borrowing?

JACK You don't trust me to make good decisions?

EDNA It has nothing to do with trust. I don't want you to make all the decisions.

JACK If you didn't like the hog-barn idea, why didn't you tell me?

EDNA It seemed to make you happy… for a while… Dad, too.

JACK You care?

EDNA I did… used to.

JACK What does that mean?

EDNA I seem to be noticing more when I'm happy or not…

JACK Are you trying to tell me that you're leaving me?

EDNA Leaving?

JACK Well it's pretty obvious you're not happy. At first, I thought it was Gina… then the crap in the papers. But it's been a long time since… since you seemed to want my company… since you brought a couple beers to the barn so we could have a few minutes to ourselves.

EDNA A long time.

JACK Ya.

EDNA You thought I might leave you and you never said anything?

JACK Nope.

EDNA Why?

JACK I didn't want to know.

EDNA But I never thought of leaving. I just thought my good life had gone bad, that my good husband had turned into…

JACK A bad husband?

EDNA My father.

JACK What?

EDNA Well, you wanted meals on the table, clean clothes, big gardens. You seemed to stop seeing a person in this kitchen.

JACK But everything I do is for the person in this kitchen—you and the kids.

EDNA I know… I guess. That's what Dad always said. That's how he justified getting his own way about everything.

JACK I don't see your dad as selfish. I don't get this big grievance you have with him lately.

EDNA He's not your dad, Jack. That makes a difference. To you, he's a wise, supportive pal. To me, he's a tyrant. He ran our lives; he did what made him happy, and he didn't really even want to know what the rest of us wanted out of our lives.

JACK Do you hate him?

EDNA No… I love him like crazy. But he's not perfect, okay. Stop idolizing him. Stop being him. If I want to get a job, I want you to sit down and ask me what kind of job I'd like. If you want to make more money, I want to spend hours talking with you about it. I want us to go on drives together and dream about what we'll do when we finally have enough cash.

JACK So, even if I build the barns… you won't leave me?

EDNA I wasn't planning on it.

JACK But you'd be happier if I didn't?

EDNA It's up to you.

JACK That's not what I asked. Do you want to be an equal partner or not?

EDNA Fine… okay. I would rather you didn't build a hog barn. I don't want one here.

JACK And you don't want Jeff to have a business to come back to?

EDNA No.

JACK I see.

EDNA Do you really think he's cut out for farming?

JACK Not in a million years.

EDNA Then why have you been pushing this?

JACK I thought it was the right thing… that maybe this was a phase. He used to be pretty damn keen about the idea.

EDNA He was five years old. He was keen on doing everything his dad did.

JACK He got over that, too.

EDNA They all do. Kids aren't supposed to idolize their parents forever.

JACK Least you and Gina seem to be back on track.

EDNA I'm making a comeback.

JACK You've done well.

EDNA It's not what I'd hoped for with my daughter. I saw us going to all these neat things together in the city. Getting cultured and eating in interesting restaurants. I didn't expect to be helping her dig up sod to plant her first "very own" garden.

JACK She's a lot like you.

EDNA I don't know about that. But at least it's nice to see the light back in her eyes. She must be doing something right.

JACK Well, I don't know if this will put the light back in your eyes, but I'm not going through with the barn… I can't do it. I've hated this whole thing. Since Mike backed out… I felt it was wrong. He let on it was his marriage, but I know that he got scared by the liability… and the hate mail.

EDNA Why didn't you get out sooner?

JACK I didn't want to let your dad down.

EDNA So now do you understand what I mean about selfishness pretending to be generosity?

JACK He's a good man. He's more of a father to me than my own dad ever was.

EDNA It's okay to love him, Jack. But we can say no, too!

JACK I know. Do you want to tell him?

EDNA Are you kidding! That's your job. But… I will be there with you if you want.

JACK Always. That will always be what I want.

SCENE FIFTEEN

JOE, WILF, and GRANDPA are at a church supper. It's a very humid evening in late July and they frequently wipe their faces with handkerchiefs and lift their hats off of their heads to cool themselves.

WILF Louise only let me take one piece of pie. I'm sure it used to be all you can eat.

GRANDPA It's still a good deal. Better than you get in a restaurant.

JOE And you don't have to tip them.

WILF Every dime counts, doesn't it!

JOE I pay attention.

WILF Did you hear what Al Hunter got for his farm?

JOE Not one dollar more than he deserved.

GRANDPA Good land. Even got some hardwood bush on it.

WILF Half a million!

JOE He earned it.

WILF My place must be worth that, eh? It's the same size.

GRANDPA And your house is almost brand new.

WILF That's right.

GRANDPA You thinking about sellin?

WILF Louise is. They all want to move to town sooner or later.

JOE Eleanor doesn't. I told her when we got married that nothing would make me happier than dyin on my tractor while I was plowing my back fifty.

WILF Who needs a Hallmark card when they've got you around?

GRANDPA You don't have any sons waitin to take it off your hands. It's different when you know you'll be losing the place to strangers.

WILF Your plans haven't worked out so well, eh Henry? The Camerons and the Webers not going into business after all?

JOE Wilf. Shut up.

GRANDPA It was Walkerton that changed everything.

JOE They couldn't wait to find some farmer to blame.

GRANDPA It wasn't his fault. He didn't do anything wrong.

WILF Jack always said the hog barns could be safe.

GRANDPA Maybe… but if one farmer can do all the right things and still have problems, Jack figured a hog barn was just inviting trouble.

JOE It was the management of the water supply where the risks were taken.

GRANDPA It was a disaster and a tragedy. Period.

JOE Now I suppose everybody and their brother are gonna be stickin their noses into my farmin business.

WILF They'll try.

GRANDPA When something like this happens, you'd be crazy not to think about what's safe and what's not.

WILF You're startin to talk like your daughter-in-law at one of the council meetings.

GRANDPA Not everything she says is irritating.

JOE She ought to start having babies and doin something productive with all her free time.

GRANDPA Oh, she's all right. She's a hard worker.

JOE Well, I work hard, too. But I don't go stickin my nose into other / people's jobs. They better keep their noses out of mine. I'm not doin anything wrong.

WILF Nobody's ever told you what to do. Relax.

JOE You never lost your farm, did ya? Never had the bastards from the bank call you into their office and ask for their money back in sixty days—money they talked you into borrowing in the first place.

WILF Oh ya.

GRANDPA I remember the auction.

JOE Took me three years to buy my own farm back. I haven't darkened the door of a bank since.

WILF And how much interest does your sock pay?

JOE We're better off now than we ever were. I don't owe a cent to anyone and that's how it's goin to stay.

WILF Well, I owe money. Louise's got expensive tastes. I'll get it all back when I sell.

JOE Don't blame Louise. She's not the only one in the family with a hole in her pocket. You're the one trades in the truck every year… get all the new bells and whistles.

WILF Got a CD player in this one. You only live once I say… and you can't take it with you.

JOE Live and learn is what I say.

GRANDPA *(wiping the sweat from his face again)* Well… all I can say to that is… it's not the heat, it's the humidity! And I think I see Louise waving at us and holding up some pie. Must mean there are seconds.

WILF What are we waiting for? Let's grab another slice before Louise changes her mind.

SCENE SIXTEEN

Labour Day Monday, 8:00 a.m., cloudy day but still warm. EDNA *is dressed up for a trip. She's putting together a care package of home-baked treats for* JEFF.

GINA *(carrying bedding, pillow, towels)* Where am I supposed to put this?

EDNA Lay them in the back of the truck. It's clean.

GINA I know. I cleaned it.

EDNA Oh ya. Thanks.

GINA What if it rains?

EDNA We have the tarp.

GINA Where are you staying tonight?

EDNA The Holiday Inn.

GINA Nice.

EDNA It's a treat.

GINA Is that Dad's way of cheering you up after saying goodbye to Jeff?

EDNA No, it's to celebrate twenty years of being married and starting our lives as a couple with grown-up children.

GINA Wow. I don't think of myself as grown up.

EDNA I do, now. And I'm getting to like the idea. *(comfortable and affectionate pause)* Now you're sure you don't want me to pick up some brochures from the university while we're there?

GINA I can always use them to get the fire going in the morning.

EDNA Good answer.

GINA Tim's is letting you have two days off in a row?

EDNA They have to be nice to me. They know I work hard when I'm there.

JACK enters from the barn still in barn clothes.

JACK All set to go?

EDNA I thought we were leaving at eight?

JACK I'm ready.

EDNA You stink.

JACK I'll be down in five minutes. *(exits upstairs and yells down)* Your dad wants a coffee.

GINA Jeff's not dressed either. *(exits to outside)*

EDNA *(yelling upstairs)* Jeff. You've got five minutes. What's not in the truck by then stays here.

Enter CAROL with a printer-sized box.

CAROL Hi. Everybody on their way?

EDNA Not yet. Thanks for feeding Dad supper tonight.

CAROL I'm going to invite him tomorrow night, too. I think you and Jack should have your first evening alone in your house.

EDNA We're staying in a hotel tonight.

CAROL You deserve a little holiday.

EDNA *(looking at the box* CAROL *is carrying)* Is that for Jeff?

CAROL It's my old printer. Mike and I have two.

JEFF enters with a huge suitcase and a duffel bag.

JEFF Hey Aunt Carol. *(seeing* EDNA*'s care package)* Mom, you know they will feed me.

EDNA Anything you don't eat, you can bring home.

JEFF Thanks.

GINA enters from outside.

CAROL This is the printer I told you about. And there's a little cheque in the box from your Uncle Mike. He says goodbye and good luck.

JEFF Thanks so much. Tell Mike goodbye for me.

GINA I'd give you something as a parting gift but you might get the wrong idea.

JEFF Parting from you is enough of a gift for me.

GINA How can you say that when I'm going upstairs to carry more of your crap to the truck? *(exits upstairs)*

JEFF Will we ever actually be nice to each other?

EDNA I certainly hope so… although… I might miss the sniping. People get more polite once they start drifting apart.

GINA *(yelling from upstairs)* Jeff! You're not taking the yearbooks. They're mine.

JEFF *(yelling back up the stairs)* I paid for them.

GINA *(still upstairs)* Did not!

EDNA Enough!

JEFF Mom, I bought one every year.

EDNA Go deal with this civilly and don't come down until it's settled. *(JEFF exits upstairs.)*

CAROL It's hard to believe they're grown up, isn't it?

EDNA Sometimes.

CAROL I must run. I have to go into the school and do my bulletin boards—they're going to be spectacular this year. *(giving* EDNA *a quick hug)* Have fun today. And remember, it's okay to be sad, too.

EDNA I will. I'll talk to you when I get home.

CAROL Bye. *(yelling back)* Bye kids.

JACK enters from upstairs.

JACK Bye, Carol.

CAROL Bye, Jack. Have a good time. *(exits)*

JACK Thanks.

EDNA That was fast. Did you shave?

JACK If you can't tell, then I don't need to.

EDNA Fine. You do look pretty good.

JACK So do you. And we're staying in a hotel tonight. No chores… no kids. *(hugs her playfully from behind)*

EDNA Jack… later. Right now take this stuff to the truck please. It's all perishable so be careful.

JACK Have you made coffee?

EDNA Oh no. I'll put it on right now.

JEFF and GINA enter.

JEFF This is it. *(goes to set it down)*

GINA Keep walking. I'm not carrying everything.

JEFF Can't I have breakfast?

EDNA We're just going to stop on the way.

EDNA pauses to watch them on their way, realizing suddenly that JEFF is leaving home.

JEFF and GINA exit as GRANDPA enters.

GRANDPA Jeff, I have something for you.

JEFF *(calls back from outside)* I'm under strict orders from my sister to keep moving.

EDNA Sorry, Dad. I just put the coffee on.

GRANDPA That's okay. No hurry. *(there's an awkwardness between them)*

EDNA Thanks for looking after the place while we're away.

GRANDPA You just go and have a nice time.

EDNA We will.

GRANDPA *(reaching for an envelope in this pocket)* I should take this out to Jeff. I want him to have a little spending money.

EDNA That's really nice of you.

GRANDPA goes to exit, but turns back.

GRANDPA Edna.

EDNA Ya?

GRANDPA Your mother…

EDNA won't look at him.

She did want to leave the farm before I did… by a few years.

EDNA Yes…

GRANDPA I wasn't ready to go. I just wasn't. But if I'd known how little time she had—

EDNA I know that, Dad. None of us knew. And Mom wanted you to be happy.

GRANDPA You and your mom… you don't speak up much. You should have said something sooner.

EDNA It was easier not to.

GRANDPA Well, it was easy to look the other way, too. I knew you wanted more education.

EDNA You did?

GRANDPA I'm not blind. If you hadn't… been… in the family way, we could've helped you out with schooling. But your mother and I didn't want you to have a baby without a husband.

EDNA You talked about me going on in school?

GRANDPA Why wouldn't we?

EDNA I don't know. I just assumed.

GRANDPA I guess we made a mistake, but it seemed like the right thing to do at the time.

EDNA No mistake was made, Dad. Look. *(draws him toward the window)* There's my family—not a mistake or a regret in sight. I don't really think I made the wrong decision.

GRANDPA Well, even if you did, you lived up to your responsibilities just like your mom. She'd be proud of you.

EDNA Thanks…

GRANDPA *(trying to lighten the mood)* I should get this cheque out to the boy. Should I bug him one more time about getting that music thing out of his system?

EDNA Oh, do! And be sure to complain about Gina living in sin.

GRANDPA Will do. *(exits)*

EDNA watches out the window for a few seconds. Then she tidies up the last cups and dishes, sets out a clean cup, cream and sugar for her dad, and wipes the counter one last time. She picks up her purse, glances back once, and exits.

MUSICIAN & CHORUS

I'm no saint
I've had my dreams,
I want the easy road and a sunny day
But like every traveller on this journey
I've learned my lesson the hard way.
So now I let love be, let love go,
Let love find its feet,
Let love rest, let love part.
I let love be the only circle I build
Around your heart.
You're no saint,
You have your dreams,
You want the easy road, a sunny day.
But like every traveller on this journey
You'll learn your lessons
The hard way.
So just let love be, let love go,
Let love find its feet,
Let love rest, let love part,
And let love be the only circle you build,
Just let love be the only circle you build,
Yeah, let love be the only circle you build around your heart.

The end.

Printed on Silva Enviro 100% post-consumer EcoLogo certified paper, processed chlorine free and manufactured using biogas energy.